Entrepreneurial Strategic Management

Entrepreneurial Strategic Management

Ken R. Blawatt

Entrepreneurial Strategic Management
Copyright © Business Expert Press, LLC, 2014.

First published in 2014 by
Business Expert Press, LLC
222 East 46th Street, New York, NY 10017
www.businessexpertpress.com

ISBN-13: 978-1-60649-866-8 (paperback)
ISBN-13: 978-1-60649-867-5 (e-book)

Business Expert Press Strategic Management Collection

Collection ISSN: 2150-9611 (print)
Collection ISSN: 2150-9646 (electronic)

Cover and interior design by Exeter Premedia Services Private Ltd., Chennai, India

First edition: 2014

10 9 8 7 6 5 4 3 2 1

Printed in the United States of America.

Abstract

Entrepreneurial Strategic Management (ESM) is a managerial book that goes beyond the verge of traditional texts on the subject. It brings to management a challenging dimension: Create an entrepreneurial organization and you will exceed in the realization of your goals and objectives. The entrepreneurial organization thrives on developing innovation, customer retention, productivity, and growth. The role of management has changed dramatically in the last decade with the joining of powerful new forces in the environment. A new social awareness and demographic shift in the workforce coupled with a shrinking of markets in a technological and global landscape demands new ways of planning, organizing, and directing organizations. ESM argues the need for implementation as the force *majeure* in fulfilling strategic plans and the engagement of the whole organization in strategic management to achieve organizational goals.

The text also introduces a new approach to understanding the economic marketplace in four quadrants or fields that each determine what strategic responses are needed to thrive in those fields and which direction the organization is to go if it is to survive and grow. It lays out the cycle of corporate products and services from profitable innovation to decline and failure and offers the executive a road map to renovate and build the organization.

Keywords

corporate culture, employee engagement, entrepreneurial employees, entrepreneurial management, entrepreneurial mindset, innovation, marconomics, organic organization, performance expectation, price-cost leadership, strategic management, value perception

Contents

Preface

The challenge in business today is to survive. The happy constancy of economic growth, during the previous few decades, created a comfortable complacency in managers who spent more time massaging past strategies that seemingly worked than worrying about change and the sharp features of a looming crisis. While there have been bumps every decade or so, on the road to higher revenues and profits, these were seen more as business cycles rather than indicators of a system starting to come apart at the seams. The global meltdown was a failure of economics as much as bad decision making. It was also due to the flawed structure of financial markets still in need of much repair. The economic system ignored the real economy, which is based on the linkage between jobs, production, and customer demand. It encouraged the giveaway of the productive soul of the nation as it farmed out the basic jobs and assumed, since these were low level functions, there would be no loss.

But along with this fundamental element of economic strength, corporate America gave away basic technologies, marketing, and organizational skills; and it is now surprised to no end that not only has it created astounding losses within the economy but also promises an intense flow of highly competitive goods and services surging out from low-cost nations in the future. Those nations will enjoy for some years to come the cost-price leadership that will take market share from established domestic companies.

Companies in North America will need to rebuild their organizations, but unlike General Motors, they will need to do so without the largesse from government bailouts. They will need to find new ways to survive in a globalized world so that perhaps one day they may grow and regain the capital value they had lost. They will need to become more creative as never before. It is the major thesis of this book that we need entrepreneurial thinking and action to do that.

There is an entrepreneurial revolution sweeping the globe and those not riding the crest will surely tumble in its wake. New technologies in IT have opened new doors of opportunities for smaller companies to reach a global community and a broader customer base. Yet even as technology opens new opportunities, other issues are adding to the dynamics of change taking place. The classical lines of authority are dissolving with the growing ability of employees to do the job on the ground better when left alone. The rise of the knowledge worker, for example, is imposing a new partnership between corporate owners and those who work for them. The notion of a wage is moving to the concept of sharing in profits, and corporations are being valued for their intellectual content not just at the executive level, but throughout the organization. There is the sense of an entrepreneurial revolution in the making.

There are any number of strategic planning tools and models you can use. There are hundreds of consultants, facilitators, coaches, and guides, who will lead you to the ultimate strategic game plan. But how can you make a choice, assuming they all serve a good purpose in some fashion or another? What model should we apply? Who or what should we turn to for guidance and information?

Unfortunately, there are few given references about creative thinking and entrepreneurial action. None bring together the plans of the organization and the members of the organization, who make it work as a creative and responsive organism. *Entrepreneurial Strategic Management* builds the argument that today's manager—faced with dynamic and continuous change, diminishing demand, and other pressures—needs a coordinated system to make strategies happen; a fully integrative management process that incorporates customers with the company, its people, and its resources, all in an entrepreneurial mode.

This is a management (rather than academic) book. It is unique and different in its treatment of how we make and apply strategic plans. It introduces readers to the concept that *executing* strategic plans is the more important role. The traditional strategy approach emphasizes the planning side; the creation of a procedural map as the primary vehicle that will reach the goals we set in place. It has been found wanting. We now know this classical approach does not usually work. Most strategies die aborning. Most plans are never fulfilled.

Instead, the text gives importance to *doing;* the actual execution of plans. Doing is what is important. It is the entrepreneurial prerogative.

Pfeffer and Sutton[1] in a *heads-up* article tell us "Corporations pay out billions of dollars each year for consultants who tell them what to do." And nothing much happens. Companies hire a number of consultants over a few years and they all come to the same conclusion. Then they tell management what they should do... but as with previous reports pointing to the same list of thing *to do*, nothing is done. We see the same disparity and frustration when governments carry out investigations, inquiries, commissions, and hearings; all of which come to a concluding list of what should be done...and most of it is never carried out. Nothing comes of it. As the authors point out, there is a *knowing-doing* gap that looms large in most organizations. Doing is more important than knowing since knowing, particularly in a shifting, moving marketplace, comes from doing and though mistakes may be made they only add to the depth of the company's ability to do better.

This text is about doing. It comes to its final wisdom in three parts. The first part asks the question: **Where Are You Now?** Where are we operating our business? What good programs are we implementing? What's happening now? That's an important question since it's difficult to go where we want to go if we don't know our starting point. The second part asks: **Where Do You Want to Go?** Here we use a mix of conventional strategic planning but wrapped up in the corporate of people in the organization and its resources. Finally, **How Will You Get There?** The text introduces the reader to a new model that is based on the customer and how he or she responds to your company. The model is a four section playing field and it has been empirically tested. It shows where your company sits on the perceptional map that customers use to judge your products and services. The map is an arrangement of four positions or playing fields that coincide with the perception of worth or value a customer holds for your company and what you are offering.

The book offers managers the opportunity to create a new essence for their organizations by fostering an entrepreneurial spirit in their people, employees, managers, and suppliers. It proposes that you follow the lead of a new brand of successful enterprises[2], who have outperformed all others for example, returning 1,026% for investors over the 10 years in 2006, compared with 122% for the S&P 500. This model encourages the release of latent power and innovativeness in their people by encouraging them to be entrepreneurial in their workplace and is a major thesis of the book.

Entrepreneurial Strategic Management

The book develops the strategic approach from a marketing standpoint. It is a fact that the creation of strategies begins with the marketing perspective and in particular the customer—company channel. Consequently, the discussion throughout the text works at the development of strategy from the marketing position and leaves the development of other factors—human resource management (HRM), manufacturing, finance, and so forth, as issues that typically follow the marketing plans. The application of the entrepreneurial approach is a treatise that is in the HRM purview. The arguments presented in the book clearly establish that this is the direction all firms must take if they are to be competitive in the future. Similarly, the application of resources with an emphasis on innovation in the organization is presented in the book, as a direction companies need to go if they are to be competitive and successful.

Ken R. Blawatt

PART 1

Where Are You Now?

CHAPTER 1

Introduction to Entrepreneurial Strategic Management

If you want something new, you have to stop doing something old
—Peter F. Drucker

The 21st century is unlike any we have experienced in the course of human history. It is a world of advanced technologies beyond anything we could have imagined a few decades earlier. The comparison between then and now is enormous. In the 1950s, the telephone and the teletype were the main rapid communication links between companies at home and around the world. The telephone was the instrument for immediate use, and if you wanted a hard copy, you used the now almost defunct teletype system: A device that recorded information on large ribbons of perforated paper, three-quarters of an inch wide, that often filled the small teletype room.

Today, communications are almost instant. Huge chunks of data including live audio and video are transmitted both instantly and inexpensively over the Internet and private local area network (LAN) systems. Timeliness is no longer a question but a requirement. And waiting three days for a hard copy is virtually unthinkable; certainly, it's unacceptable in current business practice. And along with these instant communications the rate of change in doing business continues to escalate along with the advance of innovations and new demands from the market.

There was a time if you introduced a new technology it took months for competitors and copycats to reverse engineer the technology and come out with a substitute or a knockoff. Today, in the fashion industry, for example, it is a matter of days. *A Second Life Herald*[1] article tells about a fashion rip-off that came out in 24 hours; one day the style was on a fashion runway, the next it was on the rack in unauthorized retail outlets!

But it's not just the pace of business that has changed. The scope of running an enterprise has also changed. Again if we turn back the clock a couple of decades, there was a time we could actually see the competition. They were visible and often local. We knew who they were, where they were, and as with our own company, they too were slow paced, responding "in the fullness of time" to any new threat. There was always time to respond, and in any event there was enough market to go around. Back then the demand for goods and services grew strongly over the long haul, and it was comparatively easy to maintain sales increases, even if market share stood still. Today's competitors are not just local but global too. And they are not standing around waiting for things to happen in the fullness of time.

It's a New Ball Game

We have just experienced in the last few years an era of turmoil and business disruption. If we look over the previous financial landscape, along the jagged lines of up and down cycles, it soon becomes clear that the current economic issues are likely due to three trends that grew from the extraordinary expansion that followed the 2000 financial market crash. On the one hand, there was the rush by financial managers to recoup their losses by plunging into the unrealistic and dubious pools created by fund managers playing an almost suicidal game of subprime and hedge-fund financing. The second factor was the arguably irresponsible display by governments in accepting or implementing the removal of restrictions and guidelines regarding financial activities. These uneducated (in the ways of finance) politicians bought into the schemes of the financial community. Alan Greenspan, the otherwise commendable Federal Reserve chairman, allowed if not encouraged the removal of restrictions and the United States led the way into an historical catastrophe.

But there was another factor. Much of the business fallout during and after the crisis may very well be attributed to companies who had outgrown or ignored their strategic planning. The most evident example is in the contrast between General Motors and the Ford Motor Company.

Ford Motor Company saw the changes coming. They had a strategy that carried them through the tough economic times.[2] "In this respect the company (Ford) is the best example of an American automaker dealing with the global competition and developing a strategy to survive and profit during tough times. They have excelled the other U.S. auto companies with strategic and smart marketing plans by facing the poor economic conditions and targeting customers that buy their products."

But what about survival for your company and the thousands of smaller firms in the country you ask? What can you do to keep afloat in an increasingly competitive world, let alone produce a profit? The quick answer is to focus on what has to be done and tend to your knitting. Al Reis came out with a book in 1997 that made the point, *Focus: The Future of Your Company Depends on It.*[3] America lost its focus because, like the housing market, it assumed growth would continue—a "serious strategic error," according to Reis and one that corporate America is now paying for. Managers must now return to the basics of their businesses and rebuild from the ground up; but they must do so with a new business model.

The Problem with Traditional Strategic Planning

The ability to execute a strategy is now considered more important by some authorities than the quality of the strategy plan. Kaplan and Norton,[4] in a cover story in *Fortune* magazine about prominent CEO failures, found the emphasis placed on strategy and vision in companies created a mistaken belief that the right strategy is all you need to succeed. They concluded that "in the majority of cases (70%) the real problem isn't [bad strategy]… it's bad execution." Thirty years ago it was reckoned about 10% of developed strategies were effectively prosecuted. As we proceed through the second decade of the 21st century, we still find things have not improved all that much.[5] Corporations are still struggling with ineffective strategic management. Okay, so perhaps it's all about bad execution, but what does that mean? How can the giants of industry with all those resources and skilled people fail in putting together a good strategy?

In a recent McKinsey article, Richard Rumelt wrote, "Despite the roar of voices equating strategy with ambition, leadership, vision, or planning, strategy is none of these. Rather, it is coherent action backed by an argument. And the core of the strategist's work is always the same: Discover the crucial factors in a situation and design a way to coordinate and focus actions to deal with them."[6] The argument is that managers need to uncover the crucial factors that either empower their organizations with a strong competitive advantage or to seek out those critical issues that will do that. For the most part the answer is to be found not on high but within the customer domain and the people who make up your organization. For this you need the involvement of the whole organization and the people in the company who will be the first to point to the hot button, and then to provide the coherent action to meet the new challenges as they arise.

The Linear Strategic Model

It can be opined that the failures of the past are in the details. Executives may hold positive expectations of their strategies but somehow their hopes never blossom. For decades, executives were taught that the principles of good strategic planning followed a well-received pattern. First, you laid out the well-respected template of *mission-values-vision-strategies-programs*. The overview was a mission statement that said: "This is who we are and what we are doing and why." Then you needed to know what were the strengths and weaknesses, opportunities and threats, before you could weave a strategy. Then you would set objectives and goals and then build a strategy.

The linear model (Figure 1.1) illustrates the procedure and we have all been imprinted with the use of procedure. It's almost genetic; it's in our DNA. Step 1: develop a vision; Step 2: set objectives; Step 3: create new strategies; Step 4: implement the strategy, and then watch for the results in Step 5: where one monitors and evaluates the results. Then revise the plans and start all over again. But you have to ask yourself the question— Where is the interconnect within the process? Where can one sense and feel the pulse of strategy at work throughout the organization? Where is the coherent action?

There is none. It's all linear and in larger organizations it is doubly restricted by the silo effect and shortfall in communications. Worse yet,

Step 1	Step 2	Step 3	Step 4	Step 5
Mission, vision, values	Objectives, goals	Strategies to achieve objectives	Implementation of strategy	Measure, evaluate performance

Revise strategy as change, new opportunities, threats, and technologies emerge

Figure 1.1 Strategy making and strategy executing process

the managerial prerogative is linear. Thinking is not allowed, let alone any action that might be applied to change things and avoid pitfalls.

Building a Better Business Model

So what should a new business model look like? Thompson et al.[7] point out that *building* and *executing* strategies are core management functions and "whether a company wins or loses in the marketplace is directly attributable to the calibre of a company's strategy and the proficiency with which the strategy is executed." It is not enough to design a great strategy but there must also be within the design the ability to make it happen. So we really need a flexible, dynamic model that is responsive to change, sensitive to the customer, can revise plans as it proceeds, and achieve the desired outcome: strategy calls for good entrepreneurship.[8]

The problem with our conventional view of strategic planning is that it ignores the reality of the marketplace. A study[9] of senior executives finds two issues that prevent the consummation of good strategic planning. First, the planning process is conducted annually, and secondly, it focuses on individual business units. This is out of sync with what managers actually do. The business of strategic management is incorporated in a daily activity where the manager deals with any number of intruding events even as she or he strives to implement strategic plans. The marketplace is a dynamic, moving field. So it is more convenient to go along with the usual order of business and accept the standardized procedures of the corporate culture rather than make any change.

Toyota's rash of recalls in the summer of 2010 and its loss of reputation give no little importance to the need to be constantly vigilant in applying company strategy. In an interview with John Shook,[10] Professor Takahiro Fujimoto declared that:

> Most important of all, Toyota's new position as global leader appears to have influenced leaders to lose sight of a fundamental way of thinking at the company. Toyota's thinking had always been 'seek quality, and volume will follow' (*a customer orientation*). But the looming prize of becoming the world's number one automaker led some managers to replace the company's quality first policy with a plan to achieve a volume (*an ROI approach used by GM*). The result was to chase volume and to overextend on quality—a flaw that was amplified by the multiplying effects of increasingly complex designs and rapidly increasing volumes.
>
> —Comments in parentheses by author

To offset this drift to complacency and the reluctance to adjust to a changing world, some authorities[11] have advanced their ideas about improving the linear strategic planning model using, for example, a *balanced scorecard* technique. In this procedure the strategic process begins where (a) executive leadership mobilizes change and then (b) translates the developed strategies into operating terms followed by (c) aligning the organization with the strategy. A very important, if not critical, step is then introduced, which is to (d) make strategy everyone's business and then to (e) make formulating strategy a continuous process. The last two steps are absolutely vital in the strategic process.

Implementing Strategies: It's the Execution That Counts!

Okay, planning is important. This book is about planning but it is also about making your strategic plans work. Companies need to plan. More importantly, we need to implement our plans; but not slavishly by following the strategies we developed earlier. Business conditions change and there is a need to revise the plan. It is this responsive process that becomes important. It is about implementation and having the ability in the company to accommodate to changes that surely will come into play. Perhaps an organization will need to revise its plans almost instantly without seeking approvals from those above. The firm that can build this kind of adaptive "skill" into its structure will be the winner in the big game for market share and profit.

The classical textbook approach to developing strategies has taken on what is called a "front-end-load." We are told that good strategic planning starts with a *mission statement* along with a declaration as to company's *vision* and *values*. We are instructed that with these precepts in hand we can go on to develop a great strategy. But instead we develop bad strategies. We raise a banner over the heads of our team that says this is our vision and purpose. Let us rush forward and seize the day! We call on the charisma of "inspirational leaders" to whip up enthusiasm to execute the plan. We cite the great icons such as Jack Welch, Sir Richard Branson, and Steven Jobs as examples who inspire the strategic process. But most firms don't succeed. Why? Because what we have developed with the front-end approach are bad strategies that don't work out. And most companies don't have the inspirational leadership that's needed to carry out the plans anyway. They fail in the execution.

University of California at Los Angeles (UCLA) management professor Richard Rumelt has spent some time working with seasoned corporations, both those who have hugely succeeded and those who have failed. In his new book,[12] he examines the idea of bad strategies that have "many roots, but I'll focus on two here: the inability to choose and template-style planning—filling in the blanks with vision, mission, values and strategies." So it is that, with a great deal of enthusiasm whipped up by the vision and purpose of what the company is supposed to do, the organization rushes on with an emotional commitment to "go out there and win one for the gipper!"[13] In this scenario management calls on the team to strive for what appears to be the impossible because if you have a great attitude the impossible will become the possible. Not Really.

A *Harvard Business Review* (HBR) article[14] gives us some insight as to why organizations fail in the implementation of strategies. "A brilliant strategy, blockbuster product, or breakthrough technology can put you on the competitive map, but only solid execution can keep you there. You have to be able to deliver on your intent. Unfortunately, the majority of companies aren't very good at it, by their own admission." You see, the implementation process is the result of thousands of decisions that need to be made every day by employees acting according to the information they have and their own self-interest.

The End of Management

That's the title of a challenging book.[15] It's about reversing the classical style of management. We don't live in a top-down world anymore where the guys upstairs run the show. Major corporations are falling by the wayside and many are simply missing the boat in the new age of the 21st century where change is the only constant. Mainframe computer builders did not lead the world into the personal computer (PC) era. Traditional telephone companies with their landlines were left in the lurch by digital phones, iPhones, and BlackBerries. They all lost the opportunity not because they were poor managers but because they were excellent managers who performed their tasks in the manner of successful executives for decades.

On the one hand, there is a need for a different management when it comes to creating and introducing change and innovation. The new era will not respond to traditional good management. It needs a new model where people in the organization behave more organically and more entrepreneurially and where the rules of engagement call for team behaviour and open, translucent communications. In his book *The Innovator's Dilemma*, Clayton Christensen[16] tells us that managers in traditional companies did all the 'right' things." They researched their customers, studied the business environment, carried out research and development (R&D), and invested resources into incremental innovations. But they missed out in recognizing and implementing the really radical new innovations that changed the world.

The Need for a New Strategic Management Model

Here is the nub of the problem—and the solution. It is not the plan that makes things happen. *It is the implementation.* Certainly the plan provides a direction, a goal but execution ensures you arrive there. And strategic planning must begin by analyzing the capacity of the organization to implement the strategy. We need the participation of key employees in the company who are part of the strategic process; who are provided with access to information on which they are able to carry out their responsibilities, guided by the plan boundaries. It calls for an entrepreneurial platform and behavior.

The traditional management model is a hierarchy wired together by relatively tight lines of communication, power, and resource allocation with a tendency to be cautious if not risk-averse in decision making. The old model was and still is an efficiency-focused mechanism that strives to smoothly organize resources and people to a sterile end goal—profit and return on investment. It has run its course, according to Gary Hamel,[17] and to see the future of management, in addition to our biological comparison we need to look to the Internet, open sources, open markets, and free, democratic institutions.

If you think about management in the simplest way, it does two things. One is to amplify human capability by giving people the instruments that allow them to achieve more than otherwise they could alone. Employees are an organization's greatest untapped resource. Good people who are trained and skilled in their work are willing and able to accept all responsibilities within their scope. The other management function is to aggregate human capability: How to put together the efforts of the individuals so they can do collectively what they couldn't do individually.

And successful implementation requires knowledge of the customer, the accommodation for the people in the organization, and the application of resources directed at carrying out the strategic plan and making adjustments as needed. These three factors are the most important to a company and are often the least understood or mismanaged. When the organization is able to meld these into a program of action, the results can be astounding. They are the core dimension of the book and entrepreneurial strategic management.

But the key factor in this trilogy is about the people in your organization. When they become involved entrepreneurially and when they are engaged in their work they will not only reach the goals set out but will exceed the performance levels you hope for. A study by Watson Wyatt[18] tells us that organizations who involve their employees in the strategic process outperform those who don't by 286%! According to the study, three-year total returns to shareholders (TRS) are three times higher at companies where employees understand corporate objectives and the ways in which their jobs contribute to achieving them.

Strategic Execution and Planning

The working dynamic for *Entrepreneurial Strategic Management* begins with an understanding of the company's *business environment*. Here one finds the uncontrollable variables the company normally cannot change, at least not without considerable effort. Managers need to know the effects of government and legal issues that will directly bear on the company's business. Will new environmental laws cause changes in customer demands? Will a change in government hail a new opportunity through deregulation or, in the opposite sense, new restrictions of one sort or another?

Will the dramatic shift in the economy, the debt burden, and constrained spending require a new marketing approach or product changes? Will technology threaten the company? Right now there is an emerging trend that will dramatically change the future of the IT world. It's the whole spectrum of "cloud computing." Presumably PCs will become a thing of the past and the software world will take on a whole new application. Not only will the marketplace change in the new business environment, so too will the need for change itself impose new demands.

Your Customer

The strategic planning process begins with the *customer*. It is her or his demand that sets in motion all economic activity along with the ability to pay for the products and services, of course. The reality of the marketplace is the entire relationship between the buyer and the seller, not the contrivance of an assumed line that slopes downward to the right. It is so often the case that planners will call into play the classical supply and demand curve to establish potential demand in the market. But the world of economics has been set on alert as to its shortcomings in the real world of business. Many knowledgeable people agree with David Orrell[19] that "the fundamental assumptions that form the basis of economic theory are flawed. This means that not just the mathematical models, but the actual mental models that economists have developed for the economy are completely wrong." So the new economy is one that will likely need to revert to the original model, which is the unadulterated exchange between buyer and seller. It is this emphasis that gives grounding and meaning to the customer's importance in strategic planning.

Your People

A company is a social organization; it's about people. It is not a process, an abstract model, or a machine but comprises individuals who seek fulfillment in what they do with their lives. In earlier times and even to this date some companies apply a feudal approach toward managers and employees alike, inferring they are vassals who work to feed themselves and their families. Thus, if they do not wish to starve they'd best pull their weight, put nose to grindstone, know their place, and above all not question those in authority. But successful companies look on their employees and managers as vital components in the operation who deliver the value customers look for in a service and a product. People in the organization all the way to the shop floor are a key part in making the strategy work. And they must be involved. Dallas-based Southwest Airlines continues to set new standards for productivity, affordability, profitability, and fun in an industry that isn't exactly renowned for its innovation and responsiveness. If you ask the industry insiders who made this happen, the real reason, according to CEO and chairman Kelleher, is the employees who make Southwest great.[20] He believes it's as simple as seeking out exceptional employees, treating them with respect, and giving them the latitude and encouragement necessary to do their jobs better than anyone knew possible.

Value is created for the customer in the manner by which a company carries out its marketing, its manufacturing, and its administration functions; really the whole company has a role in creating value and when this is manifest in the organization it provides value for the shareholder too. In today's dynamic, the need to produce quality goods and services by manufacturing organizations will require skilled and motivated employees; the old style method of recruitment and selection will not meet the needs of manufacturers.[21] Employees must be a part, a cellular part of the organization. They will have to be more *googley*, a term the Google organization uses to identify its employees as being entrepreneurial, scrappy, and outside-the-box thinkers.

Your Resources

A company's resources include its assets and money. How one engages this capital in combination with people and customers is the real test of good management. One management style, as with Kelleher at Southwest, leads to success and profit. The same assets employed by another management style can spell failure. The bottom line of the company's performance is expressed in its profit: That vital earning that supports investors, shareholders, employees, and continued spending to improve its offering and financial health. Even more importantly is how an enterprise renews its processes and research programs. Companies will need to constantly innovate and improve their products and services and their processes.

Finally, but more importantly, the firm needs to adopt, inculcate, assimilate, and take on an *entrepreneurial* culture. The new economy is one of change and innovation. It is a world where the dominant characteristic is uncertainty; there are no givens that will allow managers to apply old and time-tested principles. Implementation is the domain of the entrepreneurial manager with an entrepreneurial mindset. "Once entrepreneurial thinking becomes second nature, you will be able to continuously identify uncertain yet highly potential business opportunities (*or problems*) and exploit these opportunities with speed and confidence. Uncertainty becomes your ally instead of your enemy."[22]

The Entrepreneurial Strategic Management Model

There is a conventional wisdom in management that senior executives should do the planning: That since they concern themselves mostly with the big picture they can leave the details to staff and lower rank managers when it comes to implementing strategy. But that outlook is not valid if ever it was. IBM's failure to continue domination of the PC market after its spectacular rise in the early 1990s is a case in point. The company had some of the greatest planners and executive staff in the world, but they could not get the organization to act on the new strategies needed to launch a strong bid for PC market dominance. They could not cut through a bureaucratic culture that had grown to massive maturity during previous years of great success.[23] Nor could they act as swiftly as Sun and Hewlett Packard who were introducing new technologies to the market. Their operation system was mired in glories past and no one could affect the changes needed to respond to new realities in the marketplace. In 2004, they sold the PC division to Lenovo for $1.75 billion. IBM was known for its superb planning. But planning must have superb execution. Plans are nothing if they are not consummated.

Managers have struggled for decades to conjoin strategies and the implementation of those strategies. Almost 30 years ago Robert Burgelman[24] developed a process model with the hope of stimulating corporate behavior that would accomplish that. The idea was to encourage strategy fulfillment by having the whole organization behave in an organic or cellular fashion in which the implementation of strategies becomes an interlocking entrepreneurial activity of multiple participants. Unfortunately, he reduced what might have been a seminal effort to incorporate entrepreneurship within strategic management by developing instead a process model that ignored the dynamics of creativity and implementation. He struggled to make entrepreneurial behavior a part of management strategy execution but could not quite make it happen. As Shook[25] noted years later, "It's easier to act your way to a new way of thinking than to think your way to a new way of acting."

Strategy and Entrepreneurial Action

New insights by researchers[26] reveal the importance of entrepreneurship and what it offers to the fulfillment of strategic management. They summarize their findings with four observations:

1. Firms can be entrepreneurial in achieving results; they can be flexible and evolve as they deliver their goods and services but management must create the environment to enable the process.
2. The achievement of results is a pluralistic, interrelated process. It involves the entire cast of managers, customers, and others as components of the response and solution process.

3. Executives can establish an outlet for the inherent tension between creativity and efficiency by setting out boundaries (but not compartments) as with Google that provides bootleg time for technical people to be creative for the sake of creativity and not necessarily in line with objectives.
4. The comingling of entrepreneurship and strategic management can produce results that equip the firm with competitive differentiation. It is this that enables the potential to harness imaginative activity such that management can control the outcome.

The issue is to build an organization that encourages and experience these elements but it requires a very different process from what we currently have in our companies today. Managers will need to move decision making down into the lower levels of the organization and trust their fellow employees to take on greater responsibilities than before.

Integrating entrepreneurship and strategy is a dynamic duo that will ensure successful implementation. Ireland et al.[27] reaffirm the point that entrepreneurship is the process "through which individuals and teams create wealth by bringing together unique packages of resources to exploit marketplace opportunities." Moreover, entrepreneurs, ever alert to opportunities, create these goods and services to newly identified markets while managers on their part are ever alert to creating competitive advantages for the firm. Thus, there is a symbiosis of the two and their actions are complementary.[28]

Entrepreneurship in Organizations

Entrepreneurship is as much an attitude as a way of thinking; specifically it is a mindset that enables the individual to see opportunity in a sea of uncertainty and change and draft a vision of what the opportunity can do and to pursue the application with passion and vigor. We cannot think about strategy unless we also include implementation. While linear models represent a continuum of strategy events, they as much suggest these are discrete and not necessarily tied together. In fact, to successfully manage the enterprise and its operations there must be a conjoining of the two—of ideation and application as noted earlier.

Entrepreneurial strategic management aims for efficiency. It integrates strategic planning into the execution process with the expectation that more than 80% of strategic plans are put into action, which is a generous estimate for implementation. The proposed model begins by committing everyone in the strategic planning process and then allowing these stakeholders to carry out their own specific goals and objectives as part of the overall strategy.

The Dyadic Nature of the Model

What is called for is a dyadic model that melds the dynamic elements of entrepreneurship and strategy within an organization. The model needs to deliberately give emphasis to execution rather than to planning and needs to include the triad of the *customer*, the *people* in the organization, along with its *resources*. These three factors are pillars on which the company can raise itself to great and sustainable levels. All strategic action begins with the customer. It is implemented by people be they managers, employees, suppliers, and others in the community directly and indirectly, who utilize the organization's resources to effect the strategy and reach the desired goals.

Most discussions, papers, and references tend to cite firstly the *strategy* component in which the classical mission–strategy–implementation (or execution) flow is the central focus. The concept is sound. The output is usually deemed a feasible, good plan. But as Winston Churchill and other historical figures have noted, plans are nothing, but planning is everything, which we might assume includes implementation at the same time as the planning is taking place. Execution does not take place in the sheltered confines of conference rooms or airconditioned offices but in the hot, smelly, and busy environment of the workplace and a market that is filled with uncertainty and risk. It is this uncertainty that imposes the need for flexible, responsive changes to what might have been an initial idealistic strategy.

Of course, the strategy must be "translated into operating terms" and usually this takes place after the "company is aligned to the strategy," which is then assigned to functional areas where programs are developed in accordance with the strategic direction set out by management.

The marketing department will set up its sales force to carry out the selling objectives. R & D will develop new and improved products while production prepares for the assembly of supplies and equipment needed to manufacture. What is clearly implicit in the rendering is that all parties to the process are involved and are attuned to the desired outcome. But it does not work that way. There is a loosening of the strategic vision the further one gets from the executive boardroom.

Entrepreneurial strategic management is not about leadership and the rah-rah concept of stimulating attitude in the organization to win! Richard Rumelt tells us that:

> Despite the roar of voices equating strategy with ambition, leadership, vision, or planning, strategy is none of these. Rather, it is coherent action backed by an argument. And the core of the strategist's work is always the same: Discover the crucial factors in a situation and design a way to coordinate and focus actions to deal with them.

It is to that issue that entrepreneurial strategic management directs its methodology.

The design to coordinate and focus is displayed in the model in Figure 1.2 and shows the way in which the organic, entrepreneurial organization fulfills the mandate. The model proposes that the development of strategies is foremost in the concern for the *execution*

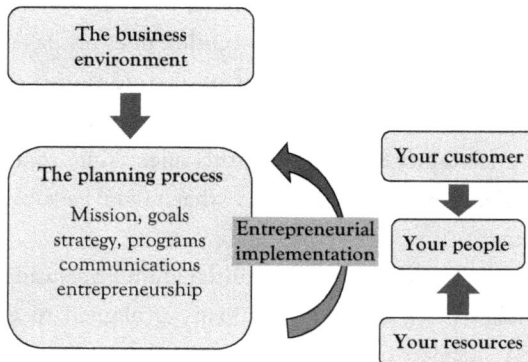

Figure 1.2 Strategic execution and planning

component and it should be foremost in the minds of planners and all key personnel in the strategic planning-implementation stream. The *entrepreneurial action* section of the model addresses the dynamics within the *customer-people-resources* (CPR) paradigm as the entrepreneurial triumvirate in the company's strategic plan. It requires the organization to have an entrepreneurial culture that is attuned to the customer in the allocation of resources as to products, services, future products and services, company response to customer issues, and so forth.

The CPR paradigm is the heart of entrepreneurial strategic planning and implementation. It is the motivational and affective dimension of planning and the drive to make the objectives happen even as it guides the innovation and adjustments to the strategy as new issues come up in the business environment. A major difficulty for new ventures is that once they have been funded they strive to follow the business plan and achieve the results projected on the initial pro forma financials. Those who are successful have found that data from customers as used in the original business plan is usually based on current needs and not those that may arise in a few months or year or two. Consequently, the strategy has to change with customer needs and failure to do so surely leads to failure.

These three elements are a company's vital organs. They are inherent to any planning and execution process. Customer's needs and preferences, indeed the customer's success, is integral to the planning organization's operations. It is the constant thematic in virtually everything the enterprise does: its research and development of innovation, its communications with, and its continuous service to the customer is paramount to its own success.

A study of Acer's success[29] illustrates how the move to an organic, entrepreneurial model helped the company grow to number two in the world. The company applied the five rules of rules of evolutionary management (REM) in developing its strategies. The concept, first introduced by James Hines,[30] posits that policies or strategic choices by companies are affected by the people in the organization who evolve policies. The REM rules declare that people are integral to the selection and determination of strategic policies. It is people who develop strategies, people who learn from the experiences, and people who can grow and contribute even more significantly to the company's success. Consequently, Acer continued to grow even through the last few years of economic turmoil and inhibited growth, with an annual rate of 16% to command 13.4% of world sales at the end of 2009.

Appendix

Testing Your Organization: Where Is It Now?

The book is about entrepreneurial strategic management. It asks the reader to consider three basic but important questions when engaged in strategic planning and execution. These are the following:

1. Where are we now?
2. Where do we want go?
3. How will we get there?

Here are eight questions you will want to answer. They will give you a picture of where your organization is now on the strategic quads of business. Do the test now, then compare where you are with where you would like to be. However, there is a caveat in this exercise. The test results are a reflection of *your perception* of the company's operation. It does not give you the customer's view. You may wish to have one or two of your close customers give you their appraisal of how they see your organization. We usually start with you or the senior executives in the firm. Our consulting procedure is to have a few of the top managers do the test and then we have two points of reference: the CEO point of view and then those of his team. In some cases, there is a diversity of views about where the organization is functioning and this serves as a point of departure in questioning the reasons for the differences and making adjustments accordingly.

The test is based on empirical work that examined how customers and people in general make their decisions to buy a product or a service. As you will learn later in the text, people make their purchase decisions based on two and only two variables—(a) what is the expectation they have as to the performance they will receive from a product or service and (b) what is their perception as to the worth of that item. These lead to the four quadrants of the strategic field and will be developed later on. The test will place you or your organization in one or more quads including

1. innovation and entrepreneurship;
2. cost-price leadership;
3. product line;
4. branding and reputation.

Each quad has differing customer perceptions and expectations. Products and services in the Innovation quad are highly innovative as a rule and command higher prices and expectations of performance. On the other hand those goods in the Cost–Price quad can be looked on as commodities in that the expectation is for items that are utilitarian and useful but without any enhancing features as to evoke any sense of value. Those goods in the Brand quad of course carry with them the enhancement of brand identification that gives the perception of value and an expectation of consistent performance. Finally, the Merchandizing quad is all about product line and brand extension, which conveys the notion of usefulness through variety, packaging, and physical options.

The ESM Test

The following questions reflect on the kind of strategy you are following at this time. It presents an approximation of the company's marketing and selling activities within your overall plan. Please answer each question on a score out of 10, or 1 to 10, in the boxes at the end of each statement. The number 10 means you highly agree with the statement. A score of 1 means you disagree. If you feel a statement does not apply to your organization, you may ignore it or place a zero in the box. Please respond as quickly as you can.

1. Our products/services are all standard and we believe they readily meet all our customer's needs. ☐ SP
2. Our marketing emphasis is to ignore competitive pricing and to concentrate on developing a strong relationship with our customers. ☐ HV
3. Our products/services are very well branded and well known in comparison to others in our industry. ☐ HR

4. Our company has modified/improved our products/ ☐ HI
services almost every year in the last five years.

5. Our primary goal is to sell a lower priced product/service ☐ LP
in the highly competitive industry we operate in.

6. We believe all employees should participate in receiving ☐ Q
a share of the company profits.

7. We offer the marketplace a full line of standard products/ ☐ HPL
services.

8. We know where our customers will be three years from ☐ C
now.

The interpretation can be found in The ESM© Strategy Test Holbrook Manufacturing Inc. at the end of Chapter 4. It gives an illustration and you can project your own company's position from it.

CHAPTER 2

Foundation for the Entrepreneurial Model

Plans are only good intentions unless they immediately degenerate into hard work.

—Peter F. Drucker

The environment of the 21st century is about innovation and change. The focus of strategic management is to adapt to change and more importantly it is about initiating change. At one time General Motors (GM) was the largest corporation in the world and it failed because it did not recognize this very simple dictum. Firstly, they did not listen to the customer, the source for much change. In 1970 U.S. auto manufacturers owned 87% of the American light trucks and car market and by 2005, their market share had fallen to 57%. They had lost almost one third of their market to foreign competitors and leading the decline was GM. In 2002 GM[1] held 32% of total market share; by 2007, it had fallen to 22%. They let things happen in a world where the old rules no longer applied and the 21st century brought on a new set of guidelines for businesses and organizations.

If there was a case of blind insensibility, it surely can be seen in the case study of GM. Perhaps it began with their denigration of Peter Drucker and his concepts on management.[2] Here we see an historical denial of change and unwillingness to accept it. One can only wonder what would have happened had GM embraced Drucker's concepts of management. What might have happened had they had been more entrepreneurial? The new economy is about entrepreneurship. Peter Drucker declared, "Because the purpose of business is to create a customer, the business enterprise has two—and only two—basic functions: marketing and innovation. Marketing and innovation produce results; all the rest are costs. Marketing is the distinguishing, unique function of the business." Here we see a robust reference to the need for entrepreneurial action in knowing one's customer, finding an opportunity, a new product, or innovative new service, and exploiting it.

Strategy in a Changing Environment

But let's take a few minutes to really understand what business is about and the role that strategy takes in directing where it goes. The business world and in fact the economy is about people: people acquiring goods and services, making decisions about goods and services, and planning their organizations and lives around goods and services. We are a consumer society in which products and services play an integral part in our business and social development. Obviously, the degree to which we let consumption direct our affairs is a personal choice and we would hope it is guided by good intentions and outcomes, but the reality is that we make an economy happen.

That being so then all economic behavior is a manifestation of human behavior. The way in which people, either acting alone to their own purpose or working in corporations and institutions as decision makers to acquire goods and services, are directly responsible for the direction of the economy. It is no coincidence that the GDP and Consumer Confidence Index (CCI) correlate almost exactly, which is to say that as the CCI improves so does consumer spending and the domestic output. As consumers gain confidence in the economy, they spend more on goods and services, which in turn expands the production system.

Governments often take their cue from economists, which likely accounts for the many ways governments screw up. Perhaps that will change with more attention being paid to the diseconomies of economics and such texts as "Economyths[3] that tells us how government gets thing wrong." To this we might add that the media are prone to report on changes in the economy by adding their own emphasis and emotions. Most often, they lend more color to events than is warranted and it would seem they encourage swings in economic activity. More than one analyst has commented that before the media paid much attention to the financial markets there were virtually few large fluctuations in market performance.

Economists maintain that an economy is the result of business and government action. In other words, if you want to improve an economy, the levers that need pushing are those that will benefit business, particularly big businesses by providing tax cuts and government spending. In his new book, *The Origin of Wealth*, Eric Beinhocker[4] proposes that business leaders are key to revolutionizing the process of wealth creation within their organization and that by working hand in hand with government they will all create economic well-being. He is wrong, of course. Institutions, governments, and Wall Street do not create wealth for the nation: only for the players themselves. Economic national wealth is created by entrepreneurs, entrepreneurial managers, and productive organizations responding to the needs of the customer.

The business environment is based on economic principles going back to Adam Smith and his contemporaries of the 18th century. Here's what Smith said:

> Man does not labour for the public interest but for his own purpose in which he intends only his own security; and by directing that industry in such a manner as its produce may be of the greatest value, he intends only his own gain, and he is in this, as in many other cases, led by an invisible hand to promote an end which was no part of his intention. Nor is it always the worse for the society that it was no part of it. By pursuing his own interest he frequently promotes that of the society more effectually than when he really intends to promote it. I have never known much good done by those who affected to trade for the public good.[5]

To which one might add government and corporations. History and latter day economists have overlooked Smith's original observation and missed the importance of the individual in creating and sustaining an economy. It is the creativity of the entrepreneurial person that produces the wealth of a nation, not big business and government.

For good or bad, economics has become the expression of the organized system. But it has wandered from the original concept. The result is a whole cadre of economists in government and business who make observations that are confusing and often misleading. The 2008 financial crisis for example was a failure of economics:[6]

> Few economists saw our current crisis coming, but this predictive failure was the least of the field's problems. More important was the profession's blindness to the very possibility of catastrophic failures in a market economy.

So it is that economics is revealed for what it is—an ineffectual tool in the business of management. It is not a useful consideration in understanding the dynamics of strategic planning. Nor is the use of economic forecasting[7] a choice since it is proven unreliable and cannot be used in developing management strategies with any degree of confidence as to outcomes. We can only refer to the discipline as a belief system that has no basis in fact. The foundation of economic thinking comprises propositions supported by assumptions and as such they form the foundation for a dogmatic belief system.

The Origin of Business

Demand is not a curvilinear glyph posted on a graph. It is people who create demand. In his development of iTunes—followed by the iPod, and then the iPhone—Steve Jobs perceived in the community an emerging market with consumer demand. In each case he grasped the opportunity, often accompanied by questioning if not scepticism by the media, and successfully launched these new products. In answering his critics, Jobs[8] would declare:

> There's an old Wayne Gretzky quote that I love. "I skate to where the puck is going to be, not where it has been." And we've always tried to do that at Apple. Since the very, very beginning. And we always will.

Jobs saw customers where no one else saw them.

The development of a strategic model must therefore begin with the customer. What do customers look for in products or services, not only now, but in the future? What are the decision criteria they bring into play?

What are the important determinants that influence them? An understanding of basic customer behavior is fundamental to understanding strategy and the development of any strategic template. Otherwise, we are caught up in the age-old problem of second guessing what people want.

Classical economists employ a demand curve to presume their understanding of the marketplace; they force-fit a number of assumptions into a procedure that is unreal and implausible. They conclude that people only buy on price or cost and so the measure of satisfaction or demand is related solely to price. At best this is a naïve consideration. At worst it has been remarkably misleading. More astonishing is that businesses and governments have accepted the premise for centuries.

People purchase goods and services for many reasons and not just price. Above all they must feel a real need to have them. The average consumer is exposed to hundreds of advertising and promotional cues each day to buy one product or another. Individuals in a large city, for example, may be hit with as many as a thousand impressions displayed in newspapers, on TV and radio, on billboards among others, but there is no rush to go out and acquire these goods. They have no need for them.

The Drivers of Market and Economic Activity

The underlying demand that powers economic activity comes from consumers, institutions, and industries that acquire goods and services to their own purpose and desires. Their motives are based on internal needs, wants, and desires that include psychological, anthropological, and social drives as well as economic considerations. Their motives are not purely cognitive in nature, which is the underlying principle that defines classical economics. People have emotions and these come into play in economic behavior. It also refutes Lord Keynes's theory about supply side economics where government action is claimed to be the key determinant for economic stimulation. What is factual is that an economy is based on people or customers satisfying their needs.

We all look to improve our state of satisfaction. Our needs might be physical in nature as in obtaining satisfaction from eating or it may be something more intangible as in receiving comments or praise for a new garment we've just bought. In the first case an individual looks to satisfy a utilitarian need where we want to gain a simple functional or practical benefit. On the other hand, the second form of need satisfaction is more personal where we look for an experiential or an emotional benefit. So we look for a range of experiences through consumption.[9]

All of the decision criteria and all of the motivations in purchasing a product or service therefore come to center on two aspects: a physical characterization that implies a promise of performance and a second aspect that addresses the perceived worth or value of the item. In the first case, the customer is concerned that the product will perform as it should. Will it fit comfortably if it is a dress? Will it shape steel if it is a manufacturing tool? At the simplest level there is the need for an item to perform a simple utility function, doing the basic job expected of it. On the other end of the scale, there is an expectation that the item has a number of features and benefits that beyond the single, parsimonious utility function. There is a range of expectations that go from a very basic expectation of performance all the way up to an expectation of many benefits that can be psychological, sociological, as well as physical.

The second aspect is an estimate of what the service or product is worth. Obviously, you have to pay something for it, but will it be a low price, which says it does not have much worth or does it have a worth more than just a perception of cost and to the buyer it takes on a higher value? Here again we have a range from low to high.

The Real Origin of Demand

So it is with the factors that tell us why people make their final judgment when it comes to making a purchase.[10] These two principal dimensions summate all the motivations that drive a person to purchase goods and service coming to rest in two variables; *the expectation* of *performance* and the *perception of worth*.[11] In the first case there is a range of expectations as to what a product or service will provide from a very basic or *utility* function to a whole hosting of *benefits*. On the other hand, the perception of what a product or service is worth ranges from a minimum *cost* level to an expectation of high *value* for the item. The final decision to purchase, of expressing economic behavior, is vested in the evaluation between these two constructs as seen in Figure 2.1. They constitute a paradigm that identifies the basis for consumer choice and is the foundation for the

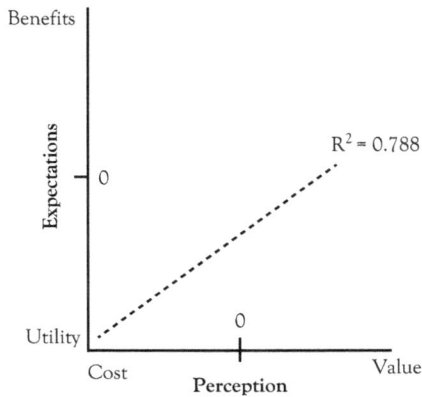

Figure 2.1 Demand behavior paradigm

behavioral economic and strategic macro-model. Empirical research[12] has established that a correlation exists between the two subsets and it sets the framework for a new brand of economic thinking called "marconomics."[13]

The argument is that low or zero expectations about a product or service offering is matched by a low determination as to worth and therefore the price one would pay for that item. A commodity such as salt, for example, would have a minimal cost associated with it. The homemaker purchases salt from the supermarket as a matter of course and with little regard, except that it is of nominal cost. However, should none be found in the home and while the utility remains the same, there is a higher value attached to the product given the urgency in needing it to cook a dinner. In this case, one is willing to pay the higher price by going to the convenience stores. This is the purview of marketing where conditions of urgency or other techniques such as the use of brand names stimulate the creation of additional value and encouraging a higher price. Associating the salt with a well-known object, calling it sea salt for example, may elicit a higher market price in which case the buyer perceives and accepts the implied additional value.

When there is the perception of a number of benefits tied to a product or service, there is also the acceptance of a higher value and price. A Mercedes Benz is essentially an automobile that is valued on reputation rather than the fact it likely costs no more to produce than a high-end consumer sedan. But the buyer has the perception of status and prestige attached to this automobile and so pays more for it.

In the same manner, innovation and new technology have the effect of commanding a higher order of benefits and consumers perceive the higher values and prices. The higher the perception of benefit, which may be psychological as well as physiological, the higher the acceptance of the perceived value, and therefore price.

Strategic Entrepreneurial Economic Model

Economic activity then is determined by market forces with the two variables of a cost-value range, and performance as defined by a utility–benefit range (Figure 2.2). These two spectrums can be aligned on two axes that would see cost and utility connected at the zero point and value and benefits orthogonal to each other and they produce four uniquely different fields, each having very different economic and strategic implications. The given is that the lines meet at a midpoint where cost becomes value and where utility becomes a benefit.

The first in the benefit–value quadrant is indicated by the *entrepreneurial quadrant*. Here we find innovation and new technology, for example, that offer a product or service that is unique and appeals to individuals who seek those norms. The buyer of innovative products and services wants to enjoy the benefits of new technology even though it is above the price that might exist for conventional, standard products. She or he perceives a value here and they are willing to accept and pay for it. This quadrant is also the early stage of the product life cycle (PLC) where

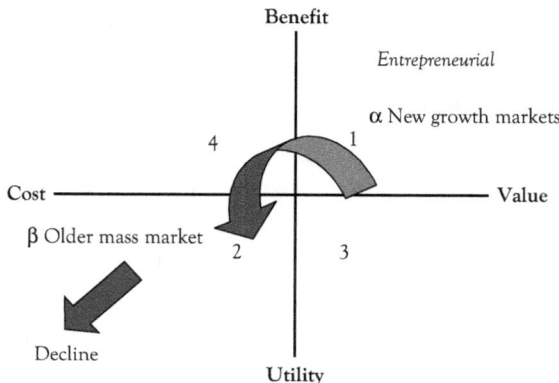

Figure 2.2 The entrepreneurial economic model

the product or service is seen to be new and different, thus not in demand by the general population but only to a narrow, small, or niche market for which the item has a particular appeal.

The need for new software is associated with the need for better performance or increased output and a higher price is justified. On the other hand, the old software is standard material and while large numbers of buyers may want the product, they do so only at a significantly lower price since all that is of value is the utility of the product. It has little to offer the buyer neither in terms of new knowledge nor innovation and thus contains lesser intrinsic value; it is purely functional.

At the onset of a new product offering, a small number of buyers will respond to the innovation. These are the niche innovators in society who quickly adopt new technology. They are the trend setters and they influence others to purchase the new offering and are characterized as "the early adopters of new technology or innovation."[14] Should the item appeal broadly to the market then in a comparatively short order it becomes well known, popular, and in demand with a resulting growth phase, which is the growth stage of the PLC. Earlier in the 20th century, the adaptation process took place over a few decades. The adoption of the telephone in the early part of the 20th century took half a century to reach maturity. More recently the adaptation to wireless technology has only taken a few years.

It is a fact of the entrepreneurial revolution now taking place that innovation is the driving force of economic growth. Will Baumol[15] clearly makes the point that it is the entrepreneur who by exploiting the new technologies, the inventions perhaps of others, sees their applicability to the marketplace and commercializes them to his profit and advantage. It is this commercialization within a free enterprise society that stimulates growth and improves an economy.

Improving on Innovation or Not

At some point, competitors become aware of the new product and they worry about the effect it may have on their own revenue. They may begin to revive their "old product" even as other companies come out with new products. In time, this places the innovator in a challenged position and he begins to reduce price or finds new ways to cut costs as the demand for his product repositions into the cost–utility sector of the marketplace (2) (Figure 2.2) where the primary advantage is price leadership and cost reduction. By this point the customer sees the product or service in a lesser performance, which again serves to lower expectations and perception of worth.

As the market perception of value for a product or service slides down the product life cycle (PLC) the firm keeps working on price or cost adjustments in an effort to stay in business. It will likely turn to offshore sourcing in a final effort to put off the final shift to decline. Eventually, there is no longer sufficient economic incentive to maintain the product, or the business and the operation contracts, closes down or is acquired. GM's problems and the elimination of 30,000 jobs in the United States is a manifestation of this stage. The subsequent move for GM is to employ offshore manufacturing to enable competitiveness in the home market. Moreover, the company has lost its brand name advantage because its products were not as well built as others like Toyota and Honda, causing the company to lose customer satisfaction and much of the loyalty it once had. In those conditions where brand loyalty still remains strong, the value is maintained and this is exhibited in the value–utility quadrant (3) (Figure 2.2) where the continued strength of the brand continues to shore up the product in the marketplace.

Here we see the role of marketing in economic activity. The strategy of the organization is to move the customer expectation upward toward the higher benefit position. Of course, the product or service must meet or exceed these expectations to remain credible. The result is an increase in the perception of value and the acceptance of a higher price for the item. It is this reality of human behavior that sets in place the basis for marconomics[16]: market-driven economics.

The Four Quads of Strategic Management

Here's where the rubber hits the pavement. The foregoing discussion is based on published papers and empirical testing. It tells us that demand, as determined by the customer (or the marketplace), is different in each of the four sectors and each responds differently to strategic effort (Figure 2.3). In the *innovation strategy quadrant*, the market is defined as a unique and very

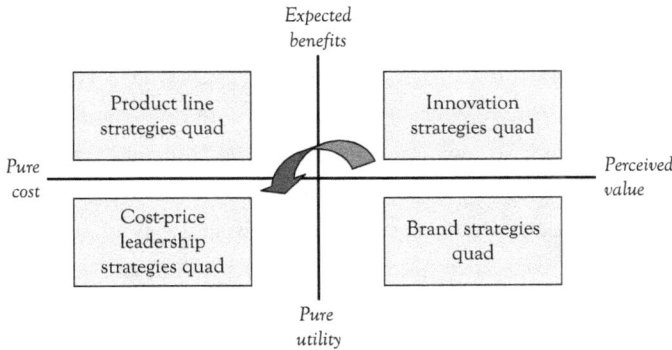

Figure 2.3 The four quads of business strategy

specific quadrant that has high expectation of performance and there is a willingness to pay whatever is asked. It may be products that are the newest in technology or an innovative service—both appealing to a smaller, innovator segment. As the product or service goes through a period of growth, it follows the profile of the PLC to maturity and then on to the saturation where we see it has achieved a position in the larger, mass-market cost-price sector. This is the Abernathy-Utterback[17] *specific stage* where process innovation and cost cutting are the essential strategic variables. So as the product or service moves in due course down to the beta sector the usual effort is to try to sustain the life cycle with one or all of three strategies.

The first is to expand the product range with a number of offerings to appeal to a broader portion of the market using *product line strategies.* Companies expand their product lines by varying the sizes or modifying features in an incremental fashion hopeful of appealing to a broader market or taking a commanding share of retail shelf space. Or they might enter into exporting to new markets that have yet to see the goods.

The second choice is to create a *brand strategy* that stabilizes product or service usage in a satisfaction-loyalty cycle. The intent is to create a strong position that will appeal in a competitive manner so customers will prefer the brand. Or they may change the product or service as they introduce new, innovative products with the same brand name. It is this constant need for innovation that marks the future for successful companies. Here we see the problem with a single product company, which has only one way to go and that is into corporate decline.

The Innovation Quad

The sector is characterized by Schumpeter's *turbulence zone* where disequilibrium is the constant force. It is also and more importantly the *entrepreneurial* zone where new opportunities and technologies are introduced and commercialized. The strategy in any case is one that employs a niche approach directed at the innovators and early majority of the adoption process or to customers in need of particular product and service solutions. The creation of new jobs and growth in the economy is dependent on the entrepreneurship that powers the system and offsets the decline taking place in the Price Leadership Quad.

The Innovation quadrant represents the dynamic sector of Innovation and Entrepreneurial Strategies. It is where technology and new concepts flourish in meeting and exceeding the needs of customers. Companies operating in this field would include Intel, Apple, Oracle, Boeing, and Magna International where Apple and Magna's strategies rest on customer cocreation and innovation.

The Cost-Price Leadership Quad

This quad is governed by economies of scale and productivity issues. Products in this sector take on the nature of a commodity where the determinant of purchase is generally on price. The low-cost leader in any market gains competitive advantage from being able to produce at the lowest cost. Factories are built and maintained, and labor is recruited and trained, to deliver the lowest possible costs of production; *cost advantage* is the focus. Costs are shaved from every element in the value chain. Products tend to be no frills. However, low cost does not always lead to low price. Producers could price at competitive parity, exploiting the benefits of a bigger margin. Some organizations, such as Toyota, are very good not only at producing high-quality automobiles at a low price, but have the brand and marketing skills that allows a premium pricing policy.

The Cost-Price Leadership quad is the battleground of titans and companies with deep pockets offering products and services that are comparatively without strong value and are generally sparse in the utility or service provided. Consequently, consumers look at price as the determining factor in the purchase. In order to meet that requirement, companies strive to increase productivity and cut expenses. The move for many consumer goods to outsourced supply from China, Thailand, and others is a direct response to that strategic requirement. Even brand name companies such as Levi Strauss, Tommy Hilfiger, the Gap, and many others have moved offshore to keep costs and prices in line. Of course, in their case it has resulted in staggering profits too.

The Managed Sector: Product Line and Brand Strategies

The strategies in the second and third quadrants and some of the fourth quadrant are used to manage the products in larger, multiproduct organizations. This provides a supply of differentiated goods and services to satisfy the needs of customers by using competitive techniques in the managed sector. It allows companies to desensitize prices and focus on innovation value that generates a comparatively higher price and a better margin. The benefits of differentiation require producers to segment markets in order to target goods and services at specific segments, generating a higher than average price. The differentiating organization will incur additional costs in creating their competitive advantage. These costs must be offset by the increase in revenue generated by sales. Costs must be recovered. There is also the chance that any differentiation could be copied by competitors. Therefore, there is always an incentive to innovate and continuously improve.

Two sectors comprise the managed economy, the cost–benefits *Product Line* Quad (3) and the *Brand* Quad (2). The Product Line Quad provides different segments in the market with variations in the product that are principally cosmetic and appeal to the combination of *packaging* aspects and lower cost. The variety of breakfast cereals, automobile variations through accessories, and merchandizing concepts are manifest in this sector. The Brand Quad provides value and enhanced pricing (profits) through branded offerings whereby the item has an intrinsic value beyond cost factors, Crest toothpaste exhibits the case where higher prices are paid to specific markets (the worriers of cavities) in the sector. High-priced vehicles such as Rolls Royce and Porsche vehicles command higher than usual margins because of the identification attached to the product.

Corporate managers may apply one or both of the techniques in an effort to sustain the PLC through an extended saturation stage of the PLC. The battle of brands as in beer and cola drinks is a sustained saturation stage powered by advertising and marketing applications. It should also be noted that brands and product line goods can be improved through incremental innovation where changes are introduced to stimulate application and sustain the life of the product. Tide laundry detergent has been modified or changed dozens of times to accommodate new washing machine designs, fabric texture, and colors.

Corporations have created brand identification of such strength that customers perceive higher value in the offering than what might otherwise be the case. A firm in a community might have a solid reputation for good service, and people deal with them in the knowledge they are receiving value for their money. The Coca-Cola Corporation has created such high equity in its brand name that it is valued at $79.2 billion (Interbrand, 2013) and is first among brands worldwide. Executives recognize that all products are subject to PLC action and eventually decline in the view of customers. Thus, building a brand image extends the life cycle and improvements and innovations recycle the brand, keeping it on top of share of mind cognition.

The third quad, calling for Product Line Strategies, applies the principles of broadening the product offering in a variety of configurations to appeal to more segments or to occupy shelf space. When combined with brand strategies the merchandizing strategy can enjoy a long life. But, it also eventually requires rebirth and some of the range may need to be eventually discontinued.

Cycles in the Economy

The American economy can be looked on as the cumulative effect of the oscillating effect of technology. New technologies become the compensating activity (born from the technologies of the Information Age, biology, electronics, medicine, and of nanotechnology, to name a few) that come into the market and overcome the losses of declining industries. The resulting new, innovative companies redefine the economy and create a new class of labor, the knowledge worker.

Larger enterprises, particularly those with commodity type products, are able to globalize their reach and become even larger, at least for a period of time. The expansion of soft drink, fast-food chains, and other consumer goods is a mark of the effort to extend the life of products about to reach their mortality. Unless innovation is applied to these items, thus increasing their value, they will in time decline.

What transpires then is a continuous process of innovation and improvement to products and services in response to competitive pressures and market demand. New firms or divisions in existing firms create new products to meet demand; they progress through a life cycle to a point of maturity. They may be recycled for a time but eventually they die. It is this continuous change to products and services in response to market demand that power the growth of the economy based on new venture formation. But larger enterprises have a difficult time adapting to change and some are unable to thrive except through market extension and incremental innovation, or buyouts and acquisitions. The real creativity is existent within smaller firms and individuals and there is a growing realization that, since the end of World War II, small entrepreneurial firms have been responsible for most of the innovation in the American economy.

Developing strategies depends on where you want to go or where you have been. Often both are called into play. The goals and objectives put in motion the forward thrust of the company's plans to win market share through, for example, the introduction of innovative new products and services in which case the attack will draw on the deployment of sales force and promotional programs. The past is also an indicator of success in that if the company has in place a winning strategy the edge will be to improve on it. Or it may not have been a good strategy and now there are changes to be made.

The Impact on Your Business?

What we have is a framework against which you can examine your business strategy. The four quads tell us what the customer is looking for. Now the question is: What are you offering? What are your strategies? How will they be carried out? As Michael Fullan declared, "Good ideas with no ideas on how to implement them are wasted ideas,"[18] so too with strategies, they must be applied and revised in the application to be effective. Many organizations fail in the execution of their plans and depending on your source as little 10% and as much as 30% succeed in translating strategic plans into action. It is at this point that companies, your company, must be entrepreneurial in applying the strategic plans laid out in the planning process.

Entrepreneurial implementation is needed to overcome four issues that impede the execution process.[19] First managers must overcome the culture of the organization, if not change it. You cannot assume other managers in the company will share the new vision, so to speak and persuasion is needed up and down the chain of command to reach the new position. Secondly, the structure and the decision-making process are related. A silo structure precludes any hope of quickly reaching the desired goals, if they are to be reached at all. The entrepreneurial approach demands a singularity of action from all levels and functions in the company to the purpose of the company's desired position. Companies are often encouraged to engage a matrix approach to structure a project and perhaps even the attainment of strategic goals. It may temporarily prove encouraging but often the structure runs out of steam because of interdepartmental issues or it becomes simply a tiresome procedure.

Thirdly, entrepreneurial action assures success in capturing the strategic ends as with a quarterback and a charged up football team. The common theme is the strategy and it must be ingested, assimilated, and translated into action in an entrepreneurial creative fashion by all members of the team. A fourth aspect is the importance of engaging the entire organization in the strategic undertaking. People make things happen and people are creative. In today's new environment of innovation and change, there is the emergence of knowledge workers across the organization who are better equipped than management to implement many of the details inherent in strategic plans.

Implementing strategies through action plans and programs requires the intervention by entrepreneurial people in changing organizational procedures to facilitate the desired end goals. Bureaucratic administrators in a structured organization cannot do that and the end goals become lost dreams. Entrepreneurial people on the other hand are able to convert strategic objectives into operating plans because they are able (or are permitted) to select from alternatives and make decisions on the ground, hopefully consistent with the same strategic outcome in mind.

The Need for Controls

Implementation demands feedback and feedback demands controls. You don't know if a strategy is working if there is no measure of its effects and how well the programs have worked to produce the desired results. Controls take the form of setting standards against which the outcomes can be measured, analyzed, and corrected or modified. In the entrepreneurial firm controls take on a heuristic role that allows management to learn from the past and regroup to the future. When Jeff Bezos founded Amazon.com in 1995, his strategy was to deliver a book-selling model unlike the conventional book stores of the time. But when he found he was not going to be as profitable as he had hoped, he added to the model by including sales of CDs, videos, and other items. He modified his strategy. The income statement and balance sheet told him he had to change; that selling books alone did not cut it and so profitability was assured when additional items were put on the website.

Controls are usually budget and financial reports of one form or another. They can include market research feedback as to changed awareness levels in the case of advertising or it can be measured in the increase in customers, acquisition of larger territories, or improved productivity. Feedback should also include a flow of intelligence back from the environment as to governmental, economic, demographic, and technological (PEST) changes taking place. Many companies subscribe to media clipping services that scan news items in print, online, in radio, television, and so on with information that might impact on the company's strategy. One of the larger agencies is The International Association of Broadcast Monitors (IABM), a worldwide trade association made up of news retrieval services that record, monitor, and archive broadcast news sources including television, radio, and Internet. It acts as a clearinghouse or forum for discussion on topics of collective concerns and acts as a united voice for the news monitoring industry.

A very important and growing function is that of monitoring customer satisfaction. In the last few years managers have come to realize that it is far easier to keep old customers than it is to gain new ones and there has been a rush of papers, conferences, and texts on the subject. It is a thesis of this text that a linchpin of building a strong entrepreneurial strategy is to include customer satisfaction and measurement of that expression as a part of the control and replanning activity.

Summary

The chapter develops the basis for the entrepreneurial strategic management model. It is an empirically proven principle that identifies the purchase activity as an economic activity for all human transactions. It develops the *performance expectation–value perception* correlate, which explains the buying process. It transcends the assumed demand curve used by economists to explain economic activity. It disproves the validity of that artifice and instead tells us that marketing and innovation are the drivers of economic activity.

The paradigm leads to the creation of a new way to look at economic or market functions in the construct of a four-quadrant playing field. Each of these is unique. Each requires a differing strategic approach if one is to succeed in that market space. The emphasis in the analysis is on the marketing side. This is where all strategic analysis begins. It leads to the allocation of resources in operations, manufacturing, finance, administration, and HRM. Resource allocation is developed in Chapter 9.

Organizations and your company too need to build an entrepreneurially responsive organization to implement the plans you make. In effect, you will determine where your organization is today—is it in the good quad or bad quad. Then you will set out the objectives and goals you wish to attain by moving toward a more positive quad or strengthening your position in the quad you find yourself in. Then you will go down into the organization and develop the strategies you will need to achieve those goals by involving literally everyone in the operation: managers, supervisors, shipping clerks, and machine operators. With their inputs in hand you will develop the company's strategy and then return components of the strategy to your key people for execution. They will implement it because they are stakeholders—they are empowered through the process to achieve the objectives they themselves have had a hand in crafting. Chapter 10 develops the process that begins the creation of your entrepreneurial organization.

PART 2

Where Do You Want to Go?

CHAPTER 3

Business Conditions

The Way Ahead

It is not the strongest of the species that survive, nor the most intelligent, but the one that is most responsive to change.
—Charles Darwin

Now that we understand the foundation of the *Entrepreneurial Strategic Management* model, let's look at what is ahead. Creating a strategy is hard work. You will need to muster all your resources to deal with business conditions that are constantly shifting in an environment of technological, political, social, and economic change. It will take a concentrated focus to deal with those business conditions that are going to impact on your business. Will the dynamics of new cultural, social, and demographic shifts bring on new opportunities or threats to your market? And what new innovations will come along to assist you in gaining market share, or losing it if you don't respond?

The combined effect of these major issues and changes in your markets on both the global and local fronts will demand a new dynamic within the company if you hope to thrive. Then there is the growing need to not only know you customers but also to retain them for life. Indeed, all strategic planning begins with the customer who is truly the source for the company's purpose and profit.

What Lies Ahead

The future is never easy to predict. Most forecasts are inaccurate and changes can be imposed from any part of the globe. It is probable there will not be much improvement in the world economy until after 2015.

The European Union is problematic with some parties calling for dissolution of the union. Asian exports to North America have dropped. On the other hand, domestic expansion in China and India seems promising as they experience a surge in the growth of their newly emerging middle class. North America remains locked in a stagnant economy with higher than usual unemployment. Has the decrease of the middle class sucked out the potential for growth or renewal of the economy? Some believe that is so and are talking about protectionism as a means of repatriating the economy. After all, goes the argument, at one time the United States consumed over 95% of its production. It was virtually self-sustaining and growth came from exporting goods and services abroad.

A more realistic avenue will see entrepreneurship blossom as new technologies develop and are introduced into the global community. At the same time, there is the realization that outsourcing is not as attractive as it was when energy costs and transportation costs were lower. Should oil prices rise so will the urge to produce more at home. A Deloitte article shows the trend is reversing. "Six percent of U.S. manufacturing firms in the northeast moved outsourced jobs back to the States last year.[1] And it will continue to reverse. U.S. policy makers know manufacturing is critical to long-term economic prosperity." To that observation we can add the latest study from the Boston Consulting Group[2]: "We estimate that the United States is poised to add around $100 billion in manufacturing output in this decade through higher exports and the return of production work from China in a range of industries that have historically experienced offshore outsourcing. This added production could create 600,000 to 1 million direct factory jobs and 2 million to 3 million jobs in total putting a significant dent in the U.S. unemployment rate and trade deficit."

Large Corporations Fail

The business economy is a paradigm[3] in four sectors as we discussed in Chapter 2. There is an Innovative sector comprised of entrepreneurship with new, emerging products and markets. This playing field thrives on introducing innovation. It is the region of new tech and high-performance companies whose managers carefully target their markets and strive to establish a close bond with the customer. It is the realm of Proctor & Gamble, Google, and 3M who have mastered the strategy of positioning their goods to this sector. The next two sectors are what can be seen as *managed* quads. They comprise the growing and competitive companies whose cachet is a mix of (a) brands and (b) product lines and bundled merchandise. There is a nominal amount of innovation in the strategic mix for these groups. They choose to ride on their brand equity and ability to accessorize their product offerings until they are spurred to reinnovate and move their strategies back toward the alpha sector. We'll discuss this strategy in more detail in later chapters.

The fourth sector is a *declining* sector. It is a demanding place to be. It shows little creativity except in the ability to offer low-priced products and services. It is the realm of mass production and economies of scale but it also gives answer to the question: Why is it that General Motors and others to come, as with the airlines and a number of industry giants have had and continue to have a hard time of it? The answer is that many larger companies have been reluctant to adapt innovatively to the markets they serve, compounded by a failure to truly understand the changes taking place in those markets. For example, the BlackBerry was once high in the market with its executive version of the smartphone. But, the company ignored the market, and the needs were responded to by Samsung and Apple, causing BlackBerry's share of the market to fall dramatically.

Large corporations have a shortage of the elements needed in the new economy to survive and succeed. Initiative, flexibility, creativity, and entrepreneurial leadership do not long survive in a stifling corporate culture. Consequently, these handicapped organizations find themselves poised on the cusp of a declining life cycle with nowhere to go. One has but to compare the Fortune 500 list of today with that of, say, 1990 to realize the extent of corporate decline. Alvin Toffler, the well-regarded futurist, once observed that within any one decade as many as a quarter and more of these corporations will not be found on the list. Late in 2008 GM and Chrysler were in discussion about a possible merger still looking to old, tired strategies to survive.

And there's even more bad news for the big guys. Based on studies of the S&P 500, Fortune 500, and Forbes 100, it's likely that only about a third of today's major corporations will survive as significant businesses over the next 25 years.[4] To this we can add research from Kaplan and Foster[5] who tell us the average life span of a major corporation isn't very long; most will not reach their 40th anniversary. If current trends hold, only one-quarter of today's S&P 500 companies will be part of the index by 2020 and the other three quarters probably don't even exist yet. Who says they are too big to fail?

Six New Dimensions of the 21st Century Environment

The new economy is characterized by intense and rapid change. Company business models need new information and a new understanding of these changes and what they mean to the business. When we see the profound effects that globalization, new technologies, market shifts, and the extraordinary dynamics of the changing workforce has on industry and commerce, we can only realize there is a very challenging vista ahead. It has produced an atmosphere of continuous revolution that really supersedes anything we have seen in the past. The introduction of the telephone and all the new services it provided to businesses and organizations is as nothing compared to the impact of the PC and Internet. The telephone took over 50 years to come to maturity in providing services to the world. The Internet has taken less than 20 years and has done so to three times the population. Forty years ago, Alvin Toffler[6] said "Change is not merely necessary to life—it is life."

A major issue is that the new century is powered by a new demography pushing the demand for goods and services toward new segments of the market. Not only that but the expectation is for growth in the North American population of only 27% by 2050. This hardly compares with the booming 76% increase in the previous half century and it foretells of smaller increased markets but with more competition in those markets. New populations of immigrants, legal and otherwise, will stimulate the demand for goods and services. The maturing rush of baby boomers will add their liquidity to the flow of cash in the system from 2010 and onwards. The population is getting older and, by some measure, perhaps better and wiser in seeking out quality goods rather than the cheapest available. The decrease in the youthful population with a commensurate retention of older citizens will move the demographic profile from that of a pyramid to a rectangular shape. The new mix will see a demand for value in services and goods: quality versus quantity.

A positive issue, one hardly mentioned in the press, is the dramatic emergence of smaller, entrepreneurial companies that are being created by what is referred to as *involuntary entrepreneurship*, when older people are let go or laid off. Tens of thousands of new ventures are being formed in this upheaval where individuals are either starting their own companies or they become contractors providing their specialized skills to the marketplace. Downsizing, layoffs, and outright firings, according to Capital Match Point,[7] who note they "have created thousands of small businesses and a huge market for skilled, freelance labor, all with the information technology world at their fingertips, waiting for the next clever idea, perhaps in the very industries they have recently, but not so voluntarily, left. We see it every day, gaining more steam and frankly, the pace and breadth of innovation is stunning. The crisis may have turned our economy into fragmented arenas, but the actions of bright, well equipped entrepreneurs may render the big box companies irrelevant in the not too distant future."

To this can be added a recent Bloomberg Blink video[8] that shows how people are creating new enterprises that will have enormous impact on the way we obtain automobiles, consume food, and create new products. But while there is a promise of growth, that growth will be different. Businesses will face considerable challenges in the future centering on the need for faster reallocation of resource. If there is one word that will describe the new economy, it's speed, or specifically, the faster reallocation and rationalization of human, financial, and physical resources. Competitors will force pressures on their industries to act quickly with improved outputs in productivity, quality, and value. If anything, the by-word in business in the future will be value, value, value. And company operations will need to build on the growing importance of intangible assets; *intellectual property, marketing communications, and communal goodwill*. These issues will require that managers become knowledgeable in and master six areas:

1. The global environment—cycles and structure
2. The changing marketplace—in particular the customer
3. Innovation—the need for constant renewal and product improvement
4. The Internet and Digital Age—to enhance business strategies

5. Productivity—in people and processes
6. A knowledge-based workforce—both the future and strength of a
   company

The Global Environment: Cycles and Structure

The financial effects of the American "meltdown" were felt by most countries but some were impacted more than others because of trade relations
and associated infrastructures. The common issue in these cases is the
American dollar; Asia, the Middle East, and most developed nations hold
large chunks of U.S. currency in reserve or debt instruments as collateral. Any changes in the dollar will have consequences to their financial
institutions and so on.

Notwithstanding the ongoing dilemma, Carolyn Corbin[9] points to
a number of structural trends that will have an impact on business conditions in this century and there are two factors that you will need to
appreciate for your business. The first is cyclical. We are most aware of
cyclical change. It's the boom and bust situation. For almost two decades
proceeding from the bust of 1987 and Black Monday to the high stakes
period of the 2007 to 2008 housing boom and the escalation of energy
costs, we ran through a business cycle that some economists were able
to predict, or at least thought they could. Then there is the well-known
Kondratieff cycle of economic activity that spans 60 years in a continuous
rhythm, going from peak to peak; from 1870, 1929, to the present there
has been an expected nadir of economic activity that is followed by
increased growth and prosperity. We are about to enter the sixth wave of
new and dynamic growth.

If structural change is the first emerging trend, the second is that
changes are taking place at an increasing rate of speed. Ray Kurzweil[10] is
an inventor, an entrepreneur, an author, and a futurist. Ray is the creator
of the first reading machines for the blind, speech recognition technology,
and many other innovations that help shape the future. He is one of the
most innovative creators of our time. He pictures the rate of change taking place in the IT world as stages of humankind's development. It took
tens of thousands of years for human-directed technology to advance.
The stone tools used by humankind spanned thousands of years and the

wheel, a more recent invention has been evident for only a few thousand years. In the last millennium a paradigm shift has taken place within only a few hundred years.

In the last century, the paradigm has accelerated and today with the World Wide Web it is measured in only a few years' time. Kurzweil notes that "the first computers were built with screwdrivers and were designed with pencil and paper, and today we use computers to create computers. A computer-aided design (CAD) operator will sit down and specify a few high-level parameters, and 12 different layers of automated designs will be done automatically.... And because of the explosive power of exponential growth, the 21st century will be equivalent to 20,000 years of progress at today's rate of progress."

Competition

The new drama of changing industry conditions is even more pervasive in the competition that businesses will face in the next few decades. Kirk Tyson, author[11] of a recent book on the subject, tells us the business world is changing with breakneck speed and only those companies that adapt to change will continue to exist. He coins the phrase "Evolve or Dissolve" as the new business mantra. He stresses the importance of creating a company intelligence system that continuously acquires information and upgraded data on one's competitors in a *Competitive Knowledge Base*. Obviously, as the business environment emerges in an incessant, regenerative process where new products, services, and technologies are the norm one needs keep a sharp eye on the competition. We will need to keep abreast of all the changes in our markets and in the environment too.

Emerging Economies

The emerging economies of Brazil, Russia, India, and China and now South Africa (the BRICS nations) will have an effect on all business activities in the years to come. India and China will doubtlessly compete for the world resources to fuel their growing middle classes, which may raise inflationary pressures. But even so these nations will more likely pay attention to the needs of their own domestic markets than they will in competing for other global markets, except through the multinational corporations who will use lowcost labor to supply their own product needs. Levi Strauss, the auto makers, and electronics producers, will continue for a few years to support their beta sector companies until they decline and fade from the world scene, or innovate and return home.

The miracle of China and its creative evolution into a free enterprise economy is now turning toward improving the state of its own rural people. They are moving to elevate the well-being of the nation to equate what has occurred with the 20% who live in the rich cities of the nation. If anything, there may be increased export opportunities to these countries for innovative and aggressive SMEs. Here we see in India and China huge markets that account for 40% of the world's population and a quarter of its GDP starting to rise on the business horizon with the promise of new opportunities but also the challenge of competing for global resources. In the years ahead, the global economic growth is expected to go from 3.6% to 3% after 2017. However, the emerging economies will continue at 5% to 6% and then slow to 3.3% after 2017.[12]

The Changing Marketplace

The integration of Canadian-U.S. business relations will continue to provide a continental market with a combined population of 313 million souls as we entered the 21st century, growing to 462 million by 2050. This compares with European markets where they expect to see population declines even as South America and Asia realize a considerable expansion of numbers. The North American market will continue to grow and expand but more modestly than it did in the past. When we compare what happened in the previous 50 years with future population growth, we see a dramatic difference and this will have a definite impact on the way we do business. From the 1950s to the present, the North American population more than doubled and grew at an average rate just under 2% per annum. These were the boom years as the population expanded with increased family production and waves of new immigrants (Table 3.1).

However, the years ahead will not be so dramatic and in fact markets will grow at about one quarter the rate of the last century. *The new market*

Table 3.1 North America population by age groups, 1950–2050

Age/Year	1950	1975	2000	2025	2050
Number (In thousands, rounded)					
Total	166,000	239,100	313,000	387,300	461,700
Percent in age group					
0–19	33.9	35.0	28.5	26.3	26.0
20–64	57.9	54.5	59.0	55.5	53.4
65+	8.1	10.5	12.4	18.2	20.6

The Changing Demographic Profile of the United States, May 2006, Laura B. Shrestha, Domestic Social Policy Division, CRS, Library of Congress. Canadian data has been added-in.

place will be an older market place. What is significant about the over-55 older population is they are active, healthier, and wealthier. This group comprises a third of the consumer market, control 70% of the net worth of all households, represents $1.2 trillion in annual income, and will inherit more than $11 trillion in the next two decades.

Consumers will be looking for a new genre, a new way of living. According to Faith Popcorn, (www.faithpopcorn.com) eminent U.S. trend expert, "Life after 2000 is going to be primarily focused on living and being rather than buying and having." There is a growing spirituality in people and a need for more durable and quality goods and services. Many are becoming sensitive to the environment with the likelihood of moving to a green lifestyle, which would include electric vehicles, less waste production from packaging, better foods, and durable products. A surprising result is that many seniors remain in the family home, choosing not to downsize or move into retirement communities. In many cases, they have gone on to build their dream home for their retiring years.

Innovation in the Market

The new economy will demand continuous innovation and improvements to products and services. But not just cosmetic improvements! Not more shiny *incremental* innovation. For decades, the American auto industry, for example, gave the consumer a continuous supply of what might be termed smarmy cosmetic changes. The most serious disrespect to sensible choice was the development of fins over the rear wheel wells of the Plymouth, Chrysler, and Cadillac line from 1957 into the 1960s. Since that time we have seen a plethora of interesting to trivial options ranging from power seat adjustments, motor size, GPS finder, to cup holders, and seat warmers. These may have created a sense of difference to buyers, but they were really not all that innovative. In the same industry, the internal combustion engine remained almost unchanged for 40 years, again modified weakly to give a sense of change without really changing much. It wasn't until fuel injection, a feature used in Europe for a couple of decades, was introduced to North American markets that we saw a serious effort to provide innovation.

Innovation in Two Varieties and Why We Do It

Innovation comes in many forms and processes but we can identify two important sectors that clearly are different and imply different market impacts. Firstly there is incremental innovation, a quasi step above or beyond some conventional level and then there is radical innovation that upsets the status quo and possibly advances a whole new industry. Much of the commercial activity during the last quarter of the 20th century was all about incremental innovation, about changes that built on the established tableau. Managers simply made cosmetic changes to existing services and products. But eventually, this approach ran out of steam and those still applying this technique literally found themselves standing still, which allowed their competitors the opportunity to enlarge market share as they came out with truly innovative products or procedures, or both— radical innovations. Toyota's quality and efficient methods for example gave it the edge over General Motors.

The need for change and new product offerings is an inherent aspect of social and human existence. Factually, we do not need many of the things we buy. What is the sense in buying, say a Pet Rock? What does it serve that could not be satisfied with any old rock off the beach? Indeed, many socially conscious people deplore the consumer commercialization that seemingly pushes sensible people into insensible purchasing. Dr. Michael Solomon, professor of marketing at St Joseph's University,[13] explains that people don't buy things because of what they do; they buy things because of what they mean. "Our choices of products and services, whether food, furniture, or fax machines, reflect a pattern of consumption that jointly defines a lifestyle," he explains; as in the saying, "You are what you eat (or drive or wear)." And this will continue to drive demand in the years to come.

The Internet and the Digital Age

In his book about the new digital economy, Kevin Kelly[14] makes a very bold statement. "The new economy deals in wispy entities such as information, relationships, copyright, entertainment, securities, and derivatives. The U.S. economy is already demassifying, drifting toward these intangibles. The creations most in demand from the United States (those exported) lost 50% of their physical weight per dollar of value in only 6 years. The disembodied world of computers, entertainment, and telecommunications is now an industry larger than any of the old giants of yore, such as construction, food products, or automobile manufacturing. This new information-based sector already occupies 15% of the total U.S. economy."

The Internet and the Web are more and more becoming the focus of business activities and functions in this century. In 1998, there were 102 million people accessing the Internet worldwide, up from 57 million and an increase of almost 100% in just a year and a half. As of March 2012, there were over 2.3 billion users, a sixfold increase in 9 years with one in three people on earth with access to the Internet.[15] The growth in the Asian market is huge with China making giant gains, followed by India. Over one quarter of the people on the Internet use English followed by Chinese and together they make up half the users on the "Net."

To this, we can add the global trends according to the Budde Group,[16] the largest telecommunications research site on the Internet, who advises us that there are billions of mobile and online Internet users around the world who are creating huge opportunities for the development of e-commerce and m-commerce (mobile e-commerce). This movement will expand the Internet to international proportions and open up even more opportunities. Budde sees all of this opening up government activities—e-government, e-health, e-education, social media, and e-science as becoming important elements of a digital economy.

The Wireless World of Tomorrow

The introduction of wireless technology is greatly expanding all e-commerce capability. David Mock,[17] author of the *Qualcomm Equation*, reflected on what wireless communications looked like back in 1985. In those days, it was a cumbersome system with a three-pound brick mobile "phone" and at least 30 pounds of equipment in a car trunk. Today one's communications take place through a small earpiece with a wired connection to a cellular clipped to the belt. Mock suggests in the future that "wireless technology will ensure everything is accessible immediately upon payment for service or transmission of identity. It will speed your way into work, VIP parking areas or any other areas restricted on the basis of identity. Hopefully, it will also do something to improve long lines at government offices and the airport, though I'm not holding my breath."

This opening up of the Internet as a free-ranging business facility will see great advances in three areas. It is expected that online advertising will grow by 10% to 20% annually. We'll see new methods for payment that will replace credit cards and we'll continue to see growth if not a large shift in social media markets, all of which will encourage more direct services in mobile or m-commerce and m-payments.

Adaption of Social Media

An important characteristic shared by both social media and industrial media is the growing capability of reaching small to large audiences. A blog post as with a television show, for example, will be able to communicate with intimate or huge numbers of people. What gives the social media even more importance is the fact we can reach millions of people with little cost and if we want to be creative in what we present we can do this with easily obtained programs and again at little cost. And it can be done quickly and with nominal effort. A great example of the power of social media was the Obama campaign for the U.S. Presidency in 2008.

The Internet has created a number of social networks that are organized into six forms.[18] These are

1. collaborative projects (e.g., Wikipedia);
2. blogs and microblogs (e.g., Twitter);

3. content communities (e.g., YouTube);
4. social networking sites (e.g., Facebook);
5. virtual game worlds (e.g., World of Warcraft); and
6. virtual social worlds (e.g., Second Life).

In addition, there is the application of blogs, picture-sharing, blogs, wall postings, e-mail, instant messaging, music-sharing, crowdsourcing, and voice over IP, to name a few. Most companies employ the social networks to help their marketing efforts.[19] Already a majority of U.S. companies use social networks—66% have a Facebook page, 51% have a Twitter account, and 44% have a LinkedIn page—but only 16% say their social marketing efforts are fully integrated across the organization.

Productivity

The 21st century will usher in one of the most productive periods for commercial output in the annals of world history, bar none. The implementation of new technologies, the overlay of IT systems, and the new demands of the marketplace will compel entrepreneurs and managers of all stripes to create new ways, better ways of supplying customers with products and services. The push to improve productivity goes hand in hand with the push for innovation and the transforming of goods to meet the new and changing needs of customers who themselves are under the gun to improve output and deal with competitive forces. Technology and innovation is the fountainhead that provides the increases in productivity that a nation needs if it is to be competitive. A recent study by Jorgenson et al.[20] reveals that innovation accounted for most of the growth of U.S. agricultural output with only a minor role for information technology.

There is an imminent need for productive output in both the manufacturing and services sectors. Global success and local capability demands a competitive edge if your company is to succeed against global competitors. The Chief Economist of World Economic Forum[21] made the observation that, "The United States is technologically pre-eminent among nations in the world, both in terms of research prowess and its ability to commercialize innovations." The amount of technological capability that a country has in its productive system is a *fundamental building block* in the ability to trade and do business. Your company will only be able to maintain position by innovating and introducing productive process improvements. An interesting note is that smaller firms seem more capable in this than larger corporations.

The increase of productivity takes place in two areas. The first is in the use and application of information technology as in the Internet, software applications, and such. The second is in the innovation and new technologies applied to the process-production system. Most companies have improved their productivity just by being active on the Web. What is exciting is the new vista the Internet provides for small and medium-sized businesses to compete in a global market.[22]

It is in the second area that we find a more dynamic, fragmented, and compatible production system referred to as agile manufacturing. What makes it unique is the ability to link the physical side of production with software- and IT-driven systems. The result is a highly flexible and efficient manufacturing system that is competitive with large economies of scale operations. Agile manufacturing is a new "innovative alliance between suppliers, customers and manufacturing systems in pursuit of values... and ... unique concepts of technology enabled agility."[23] The combination of solid supply chain management (SCM) and customer relations management (CRM) breaks the dependency on scale and economies of scale. It enables lower costs and the opportunity to relocate production closer to the customer. It is a new direction for manufacturing.

Applying Technology to Increase Productivity

MIT[24] reminds us of an old proverb that states "You can't cross a chasm in two steps." The Internet and the new advances in information technology along with a rising competition demands that we adopt new ways of doing our work in one step. It will not be successful if we try to make the changes incrementally. We really need to create total new ways of enfolding the digital systems into our organizations. If we do, the resulting gains can be substantial. Hallmark, for instance, used to develop their card in a sequential process. They revised their thinking and applied a more entrepreneurial approach using cross-functional teams and were able to save new product introduction time on one card by 75%.

Recent studies in agile[25] and lean manufacturing clearly point to the opportunities available to companies to be competitive and satisfy customer demand. In an effort to compete on price margins during the 1990s, Levi Strauss closed most of their production units in the United States and sourced their jeans and other wares from Asia. Had they applied the latest in technology, computer-assisted sewing operations, and strategic policies, it is likely they could have avoided the decline and even expanded operations with new productive innovations.

Of course, we need to mention the potential impact that 3D printing will have on business. Authorities now claim it will revolutionize manufacturing. It will be possible to produce goods without the need for huge factories and assembly lines. A few employees working on 3D printers that can apply concrete, steel, as well as plastics to produce houses, auto parts, and prosthetic devices using programmed computers will have no need for huge buildings and workforces. This technological innovation will allow localized production and customized designs to meet consumer needs. "Customized, no-ship manufacturing will one day be as common as desktop printing[26]. When that happens, and factories without factory floors are the norm, it will be hard to imagine how companies and consumers once lived without 3D printing."

A Knowledge-based Workforce

Along with everything else, the managerial environment is changing and continues to change. The combination of new pressures from globalization, information technology, socioeconomic change, and emerging geopolitical forces in Asia is forcing a whole new evolution that will affect every manager on the globe. But what will be even more dramatic is the pressure that many are now beginning to experience is the change of attitudes, availability, and retentive ability of firms in selecting, training, and keeping a stable workforce. Smaller firms in particular will begin to realize as perhaps more important than everything else the need to develop a positive work team.

Work Is an Attitude

Today's workers are generally happy with their jobs but they are moving up the Maslow[27] hierarchy. They now hold a different view of themselves and are beginning to seek more fulfillment, internal satisfaction, and connectedness on the job. The same might be said of management who, while closer to self-actualization on the Maslow scale, are looking for more involvement and control over their role in the workplace.

Carolyn Corbin tells us that the idea of a set workplace with its regular paycheck was historically a rather new idea when it was introduced in the industrial revolution back in the early 19th century. Before that time, most of the First Wave agricultural society did not have the security of a regular paycheck. The Second Wave Industrial Revolution changed that. We are now in the Third Wave's knowledge or information age. Just as the industrial model altered where and how people performed work, this new structure is changing and modifying "the content, place, manner of compensation, and tasks performed when people are considered to be working."

All this change is happening as the world moves to create a society where people's social value will be based on performance. This new rating system will challenge most accepted concepts such as university tenure and organizational seniority and union power. Such concepts will go the way of the dinosaur within the next 25 years."[28]

The Emerging Workforce

The job descriptions of the old days spelled out—often in rigid detail the steps a worker had to follow in the discharge of his or her duties. It was demeaning and often constrictive, so much so that it actually inhibited the worker from doing a good job. Today the knowledge worker has a different job description from that proscribed for the manual worker on a production line. Drucker set out a number of important dimensions for the knowledge-worker job and the potential that there is to improve productivity:

- Knowledge workers have to manage themselves and have autonomy.
- Continuing innovation has to be part of the work, the task, and the responsibility of knowledge workers.
- Knowledge workers must be treated as "assets" rather than as "costs." They must prefer to work for the organization, over all other opportunities.

- Knowledge work requires continuous learning and continuous teaching by knowledge workers.

The managerial environment in the new century has changed dramatically and will continue to change. The combination of pressures from globalization, information technology, socioeconomic change, and emerging geopolitical forces in Asia is forcing a workforce evolution with profound effect on all managers.

A recent study[29] finds that American workers are losing faith in the American Dream. More than half of those surveyed believe it no longer is attainable and almost half as many more declare that it was more attainable 8 years ago. Most of them, 77% blame the political system for their concern, citing health care, retirement, and fuel price concerns. However, people in smaller firms are happier with their jobs. Just over 41% expressed satisfaction compared to 28% for those in larger firms. The finding is pretty well consistent with sociological observations that smaller firms allow more participation and feeling of involvement.

At the heart of their discontent is the realization that things have not really improved that much in the last 20 years. They see a greater discrepancy in the system where senior executives are no longer held in esteem, but are viewed with a mixture of resentment and dislike. Executive income has increased a hundredfold[30] compared to a bare tripling of the common income.

The Aging Workforce

But discontent is not the only issue managers must address in crafting their strategies. The "aging boomer" brings another dimension to decision making. Twenty percent of the workforce will be 65 years and older by 2026 compared to 12% in 2001. By 2011 over 40% will fall into the 45 years to 64 years category, against 29% in that group for 1991. The workforce is aging and this will affect human resources management in demands for flexibility and motivation.

The AARP[31] points out that in 1910 only 13% of the population was over 50 years of age. Today twice as many fall into that category increasing to over 35% by 2020.

The need to revamp the workforce has been evident for over a decade. An earlier study of workforce deployment in 1992 concluded that executives are going to need a more open and innovative approach to the hiring, firing, and managing process. Towers Perrin[32] concludes that, "Human Resources management is in the throes of a radical transformation where HR policies will have to be responsive to market conditions and global business conditions. They will need to be closely linked to strategic business plans conceived and implemented jointly by line and HR managers and focused on quality, customer service, productivity, employee involvement, team work and workforce flexibility."

In the next decade the U.S. Bureau of Labor Statistics predicts there will be 151 million jobs in the economy but only 141 million people in the workforce to fill them. Prime age employees, those between 25 and 54 years will be in short supply, projected to fall from 19 million coming into the 21st century to 11 million over the subsequent two decades. At the same time the number of college graduates will remain static at 29% of all 30-year-olds. The new workforce will be very much different from those of the past. There will be a shortage of the traditional worker. Moreover, employees will be more demanding and expect more from their employers.

What Does All This Mean for Businesses Today?

The new environment presents a great challenge to you and your company. First the environment, market size, the shape of the market and global forces are all posing new opportunities and barriers to company success. Your target markets are no longer standing still but are being stimulated, shifted, and repositioned by an exceptionally active business environment. On top of that there is the pressing need to make changes, to innovate. A paper by Robert Cooper[33] raises the point that the need for product innovation is critical in any company today. He tells us that product life cycles have shrunk by 400% across a broad array of product categories in the last 50 years. The cause for this is the globalization of markets, technological advances, and everchanging customer needs and product innovation, causing companies to make innovation the principle strategy for the enterprise. In the United States, new products now account for about 50% of companies' revenues from sales and 40% of their profits. "The *Fortune* list of the Most Admired Companies are the most innovative firms in America: Pfizer, 3M, Intel, General Electric, Johnson & Johnson, Procter & Gamble, and others."

The way ahead will be characterized by a number of issues that managers will need to account for as they build their strategies. Firstly, the economy is going to improve but more slowly than would be desired. Within the decade we should see the rebirth, strong growth, and the return of good profitability of earlier decades but it will take time to overcome the debt burdens and to accommodate to energy concerns and the push to sustainability.

Secondly, the rise of new technologies will spur growth and new jobs. In the last chapter of the book, we will discuss the new wave coming that will likely create a powerful new economic boom. This will act as a fuel for entrepreneurship in companies as well as individuals as they rush to commercialize the new advances. Recently, for example, scientists were able to extract light[34] from thin air! Imagine the profound effect of this innovation! However, this will create a new demand for workers with skills and positive work ethic. The old style authoritarian management won't work with these people.

Thirdly, the population shift to an aging demographic, but one with money, that will demand a new quality of life. Populations will not increase so much as once they did. In fact, some nations are experiencing decline. So there will be increased competition for a relatively static pool of disposable income. There have been a number of papers and books written on the theme "innovate or die," a theme that carries with it an even more important direction for the future. Your company must also adopt that theme.

Productivity will be a necessary goal for all firms and organizations. Innovation will assist with improving efficiencies and output. The use of information technology to seek that end as well as the improvement of operations through flexible, lean, and agile production work flow will be a requisite for success and sustainability. Then there is the use of systematic approaches to running a business with such devices as enterprise resource planning (ERP) that can only enhance the company efficiency and survival.

But the key to all this will be the company workforce, its employees, or to put it into a more engaging term, the company team. People are the single most important asset of any organization. They are the fountainhead of productivity and innovation, but more importantly of the ability to successfully implement strategy. All companies large and small will need to form a new relationship with their workforce in which there is mutual respect and trust, so much so that they become creative and entrepreneurial in their positions, which can only add to the company's success.

CHAPTER 4

The Ever Changing Customer and Strategic Planning

The purpose of business is to create and keep a customer.
—Peter F. Drucker

Customers have come a long way from being told to take-it-or-leave-it by mid-20th century sellers to where they are now included as partners in a "customer–supplier" relationship. Part of the change can be explained by the unprecedented rise in the standard of living, but more importantly it is due the profound effect of the Information Age and all its dazzling infrastructure. We have seen a literal explosion of information in the public domain that has enabled customers to be more knowledgeable about their options than at any other time in civilized history.

Not only has the marketing effort moved from a mass approach to a "one-on-one" configuration that directly targets individuals but the process of collecting information about customers has become more intense. We used to send people into the field armed with questionnaires and surveys designed to give us the kind of information we believed we needed for strategic plans. That has changed. We now want customers to share their vision with us as to what is important and what might be desired in future. They have become cocreators and companies like Apple are active in developing new generations of goods and services by working with the consumer in a cocreation activity.

The Evolving Customer

Early in the 1900s there wasn't much advertising other than handbills and store front signs that displayed limited and sometimes erroneous information. In time the world became more complex with a great rise in the number of advertisements reaching people through the live media of radio, television, and now the vast assembly of data available from the Internet. In the early days too, there was not much consideration given to the rights of the customer or consumer. It was not until the production era that governments began to take action to protect the buyer with the creation of the Federal Trade Commission (FTC) in the United States in 1914, and the Department of Corporate and Consumer Affairs in Canada.

The 1950s saw the emergence of the marketing concept where customers were asked about their needs, wants, and desires and the resulting feedback was incorporated to some extent in the products and brands developed in the period. It was also a time when some companies began alignment to the needs of employees and the development of a more agreeable managerial style, one that was a bit more participative. Over these years marketing also became more complex and management learned that it too must change (Table 4.1). In the current period, a "social era," buyers have become *prosumers*, a term first coined by Alvin Toffler in his book *The Third Wave*, meaning they are both producers and consumers. The implication is they are as knowledgeable about products, if not more so, than those who produce them. In the future, consumers will play a major role by influencing suppliers to produce goods and services that are not only good for the buyer but also of benefit to the community and the world; an environmentally conscious market that will strive for sustainability in all aspects.

Table 4.1 Comparison of customer influence on commerce

	19th Century	1900s–1950s	1950s–1990s	1990s–2020s	2020+
Customer orientation	None	Production era	Marketing era	Social era	Sustainability
Customer influence	Take what You get	Take it or leave it	What would you like?	Let's agree to our needs	And agree what's best for society
Corporate style	Feudal	Authoritarian	Participative	Entrepreneurial	Free rein
Commercial drivers	High enterprise capitalism	Demand push and price	Customer feedback	Customer—IT union	Customer democracy

Strategy Begins With the Customer

Any successful business is about, for, and directed by the needs, wants, and desires of the customer. Peter Drucker,[1] in his seminal 1954 book *The Practice of Management*, posed three classic business questions: What is our business? Who is our customer? What does our customer consider valuable? More than half a century ago the concept of the customer was set in place as the key aspect of an enterprise. If one wants to see the consequence of ignoring that precept look no further than the Kodak Company. This once mighty enterprise has fallen by the wayside. Why? Because it ignored the customer who wanted an instant pictorial memory. What is so sad is that Kodak had a digital camera technology that they did not bother to develop.

Well, the customer is on the move. Not only do we need to know what they want today but we must ask where will she or he be in 3 years, 5 years, more? Look hard… That's where you want to be! Strategy does not begin with an analysis of the company and its resources; at least not until you have clear image in your mind of where your customer is and what you must do to stay with him or her. And customers move! They don't stand still!

Your Strategy Is to Keep the Customer Happy— Whatever It Takes

Good managers know that planning is important and necessary. The planning process begins with the customer. Strategic planning begins by looking at where your customer will be in 1, 2, or 3 years and then determining what you must do to be with her or him: What you must do to retain and expand your dealings with your customer.

Sam Walton, founder of Walmart stores, made a key observation about that:

> The folks on the front lines—the ones who actually talk to the customer—are the only ones who really know what's going on out there. There is only one boss. The customer. And he can fire everybody in the company from the chairman on down, simply by spending his money somewhere else.

Who Is the Customer?

Your customer is your primary asset. A business exists and thrives as an expression of its customers. Creating and maintaining the relationship between a business and its buyers, clients, clientele, patrons, regulars, and consumers is the company's foremost function. The old adage the customer is king or queen is not obsolete. It is alive and is the reference point from which all strategic planning starts. Peter Drucker[2] is very clear on the worth of a customer and what she or he represents to the enterprise. He says, "It is the customer who determines what a business is. What the customer thinks he is buying, what he considers value, is decisive—it determines what a business is, what it produces, and whether it will prosper."

So as to the customer two issues are of importance. The first is that the business is defined by the customer. When we have a clear picture of our customers, when we understand their concerns, needs, and problems we can then adjust products and services to help them in their lives or in their business and help them as partners to be successful. By conforming our goods to their needs we do indeed define our business.

The second issue is the idea of providing value. The marketing function creates value in what we offer to our customers. The marketing function, which is part of the customer franchise, defines the company and its purpose, again reinforcing the idea of the dyadic relationship between customers and the company.

Defining Customer Behavior

How do customers buy things? What are the motives, the processes that move her or him to purchase one product or another? The human being is a kaleidoscope of thoughts, emotions, and desires that both assist and hinder the shopping process. We usually follow a procedure, a number of stages that conclude with a purchase, a decision-making process if you will. It begins with the perception of a need, a desire to acquire a product or service. Whatever the enticement the fact is nothing happens until a need is expressed and rationalized by a prospective customer.

We are bombarded in our daily lives by hundreds of stimuli to buy one thing or another yet we do not respond as the advertiser might wish we would. People in a large city are exposed to as many as a thousand impressions each day in newspapers, billboards, rapid transit signage, radio, and TV as well as social media to buy or do something. But they do not act. In fact they ignore all of the advertisements they are exposed to and do not really "see" any of them. Not until they realize a need do they respond.

So until we start to feel an inclination to get a new coat we remain as a *latent customer* and are not inclined to participate in any economic behavior since there is no compelling reason to do so. We may wonder about a new car and banter with others about a Caribbean holiday or even a trip into space, that now being an expensive option,[3] but there is no activity to consummate the wish. But when the decision is made to proceed on a quest for the desired or needed object we become *potential customers*.

The purchasing process provides some insight into the status of customers and their sensitivity to strategic marketing overtures. The qualification is that customers have already been categorized as to segments and targets. The qualifying dimensions of one's customers will already have taken effect where the buyers' needs have been matched to fit with products and services offered by the company. The potential customers might be identified on the basis of lifestyle, demographics, occupation, or in the case of business-to-business (B2B) as to industry type, size, and so on. The following taxonomy sets out the targets in terms of propensity to react in the near future to strategic inputs. Table 4.2 points out the readiness of customers at different stages in the buying process to purchase a product. There are five classifications and each has an expected outcome to marketing effort. It serves to guide the manager to a specific target frame or to establish the nature of the communication one would need to devise in reaching those buyers.

The second type is the customer who is in the process of a purchase even though it may have a variable end-time for completion. This customer can be "sold," as it were with an appropriate selling strategy—one that hurries along the decision process by assisting with comparisons and supportive inducements such as money-back guarantees. The third classification is the customer who has purchased a product perhaps recently or at least within reasonable time period and is a *satisfied customer*. There is no guarantee that she or he will automatically return to the company and purchase again. What is required is the development of a database of these buyers so they may be reminded from time to time of the company's offerings. B2B companies use newsletters effectively in this effort with good results.

Table 4.2 Customer target strategies

Classification	Characteristics	Strategic approach	Segmentation and target
1. Latent customer	Not active. May buy in future; Perhaps are buying elsewhere	Primary stimulation, stress need empathy, product solutions	Broad target market based on segmental analysis and general needs identification.
2. Potential customer	Decision to buy. Will source many suppliers, outlets	Persuasion stimulation, stress need satisfaction, positioning	Specific target market and timely emphasis on identified needs, and desires
3. Satisfied customer	Has positively purchased from the company. May not return	Reinforcement, resolve potential problems, apply CRM, objective is to make loyal	Compiled list of established customers in database
4. Loyal customer	Purchases company goods at all times. Makes referrals	Heavy CRM application, rewards programs; objective is to keep the customer	Specifically referenced in database
5. Past customers	May be unhappy past customer or loyal to competitor	As with latent customers	Same as latent customers plus data base frame

The fourth type is the *loyal customer*, the repeat buyer who has established a relationship with the company, perhaps has strongly identified with the brand in the case of a product or service or the reputation of the outlet. Loyalty programs such as air miles campaign and cash back bonuses for shoppers is the inducement strategy to encourage continued spending. These individuals hold a special place in the company's database and are treated differently.

Past customers are a fifth classification and are the most difficult to persuade to the company's offerings. In most cases it is wiser to leave these alone until such time as there is an opportunity to rebuild their attitudes toward the company.

Creating Customer Value: Your Value Proposition

Until the latter part of the 20th century, most organizations were content with developing business strategies on finding a need and filling it.

Marketing plans were created on a theme matching customer's needs and the marketing mix was applied to entice them to respond. Unfortunately, many companies still operate in that fashion.

But today Drucker's comments echo more strongly than ever. "What the customer thinks he is buying, what he considers value, is decisive—it determines what a business is, what it produces, and whether it will prosper. And what the customer buys and considers value is never a product. It is always utility, that is, what a product or service does for him." So we see that customers only pay for what is of use to them and in the process gives them a sense of value received.

Keeping the Customer

As we enter the second decade of the 21st century there are two issues that command the business environment. The first is that customers, as never before, have taken an interest in quality and value as precursors to the buying process. The idea of value consciousness was always a part of marketing behavior but with the financial crisis, the now heavy burden of indebtedness and a slow recovery, it is now a more challenging task to sell goods and services.

The second factor is the increasing role of innovation and technology. Much of the innovation, however, is not product related, although that does remain a prime consideration at all times. What has come to pass is a change in the manner in which customers are held in regard. They are no longer plums to be picked, to infer an old maxim, but rather they have become prizes to be won; customers have become valuable for both their immediate need of satisfaction and also for the long term. Consequently, marketers now realize they must change how they use innovation and new technology in their long-term marketing approach that includes customer retention. This newer direction now places heavy emphasis on customer relations; the process of creating a value proposition between buyer and seller along with a program of retention management.

Customer Engagement: The New Marketing[4]

The major barrier to engagement is organizational rather than conceptual. The growing number of touch points where customers interact with the selling companies means that marketing can't do what's needed all on its own. Managers must collaborate intensively to adapt the entire organization to the way customers behave and, in the process, redefine the traditional marketing organization. Everyone in the organization is, in effect a salesperson. If companies don't make the transition, they run the risk of being overtaken by competitors who have mastered the new era of engagement.

The application of customer relations management (CRM) was originally applied to the conventional marketing milieu of personal, direct to customer sales, and communications whereby[5] "Customer Relationship Management is the establishment, development, maintenance, and optimization of long-term mutually valuable relationships between consumers and organizations."

Customer relations management begins with holding on to existing customers. The recent economic crisis, and its aftermath, has prompted managers to reassess their customer base and to commit more time and effort to customer satisfaction programs than was previously the case. What customers are looking for first and foremost is good and reliable service. They look for service that

- Shows them that you care;
- Appreciates and values their business; and
- Treats them as an individual, not a member.

And they expect the service to prevail regardless of where and when they interact with your company. For example, computer-assisted telephone reception where a mechanical voice asks you to select what you wish to discuss and moves you through a hierarchy of questions does little to assure a customer you care about their business.

Retaining Customers for a Lifetime

The new mantra in business is about retaining customers for a lifetime or customer lifetime value (CLV). We no longer look at the customer as a one-time participant in a purchasing exercise but rather as a partner who has at his or her command a string of purchases that total many thousands, if not millions of dollars in the period we expect to retain them. It has become a primary goal in strategic planning. Now, in order to do this, to know whether our customers are satisfied with us we need to build into our strategic plans a continuous flow of feedback information.

Sociological studies tell us that a very satisfied customer will tell one or two others, whereas a dissatisfied customer will convey the information to 5 to 10 others. Here we see the challenge; we cannot allow customers to be very dissatisfied and become "terrorists" to our business. So while the unhappy customers can also make managers unhappy, the real focus should be on retention since we can make the most real gain in profit when our customers become evangelists and generate many referrals.

What differentiates between customers who defect and those who become evangelists? Xerox showed that the overwhelming reason for defection was not price or product problems, it was how the customer felt they had been treated. How we treat customers—not our products, services and pricing—can be a powerful catalyst to a customer becoming highly satisfied, an evangelist, and leading us to the increase in profit we seek.

Customer retention has become a major theme for successful companies from East to West and globally. We know that customers leave us for one reason or another; some move away, some pass on, but most leave because of a company's insensitivity. The attrition rate is expressed as turnover and is normally taken to be about 10% annually. In fact this might be low. And the costs for the acquisition of new customers far outweigh the costs of keeping the old ones. The Council on Financial Competition, Washington, DC, suggests a potential loss of more than 17% profit each year if you don't focus on customer retention. A recent article[6] records the following snippets of retention and loss information:

Companies are losing customers at a staggering rate, without really hearing from most of them.

- "Each year the average company loses 10 to 15% of its customer base"—*Bain & Company*
- "84% of customers who leave, do so because of poor service"—*Forum Corp*
- "A typical business only hears from 4% of its dissatisfied customers; the other 96% leave, 91% for good."—Jim Barnes, *Secrets of CRM*

- Between 60% and 80% of defecting customers describe them-selves "as very satisfied" just before they leave—*Business Week, October 2006.*
- It costs between 5 and 10x more to attract a new customer than to keep an existing one—*The Council on Financial Competition.*
- 70% of the reason customers leave a company has nothing to do with the product—*Forum Corporation.*

Every business should make customer retention a goal. Bain & Company shows that in the services sector a 10% profit position from a short-term customer relationship can grow to over fivefold to at least 50% if the customer stays with the firm for 7 years. If you're looking for increased profits, focusing solely on sales isn't the answer.

Creating Strategies

A strategy is a roadmap as to how we will achieve a selected objective. It spells out the steps we must take to accomplish a goal or objective. It sets out the deployment of resources needed to reach or exceed our goals and binds your employee team to its purpose. But it's a dynamic roadmap that shows the new changes and events and arise along the way and that's why whole team needs to be involved in the implementation of strategy. Conditions change and new tactics need to be engaged in a timely and appropriate fashion.

What Are Objectives?

The objectives an organization aims for sets the mode for implementation and monitoring in the progress toward achieving them. Here are a number of key types that businesses use:

- Marketing: the objective may be to grow by some percentage in market share, sales volume, by territory, product, customer, and so on.
- Innovation: where management seeks to introduce one to three new products each year. The innovation may be incremental or it may be a radical innovation.

- Employee: the objective is to improve the caliber, morale, intelligence, and quality of one's workforce, managers included.
- Customer: one of the key objectives should be the satisfaction of one's customers in terms of loyalty, growth, retention, and so forth.
- Assets: the company may want to increase its wealth through brand recognition, patents, expansion
- Shareholders: the company may want to gain approval from its shareholders and thus improve the equity, ROI, and dividends by a certain amount.

Strategies are then devised to reach the objectives employing the people and resources the organization has at its disposal or it is able to acquire from external sources.

Strategic Planning: The Marketplace

Strategic planning takes you to your customer and offers him or her something of value to their needs. Excellent strategic planning assures you of a customer by providing something of value no one else has at that time. The implication in the first instance is that you know what your customers need. The second issue is that you know how to provide value to enhance your product or service and thirdly you know your competition and what they bring to the marketplace. Good strategic planning begins with

1. clear knowledge of your customer's needs;
2. the ability to innovate and bring value in your offering to the customer;
3. knowledge of the abilities of your competition and their competencies;
4. confidence in your team, your workforce, sharing your mission, purpose, and vision that will enable them to make it happen.

We begin the discussion with a brief introduction to what might be referred to as the four playing fields that differentiate the marketplace

Table 4.3 The four fields of strategic management

Playing field	Characteristic	Performance expectations	Perception of worth	Strategy
Entrepreneurial Innovation	Radical innovation, new products, entrepreneurial thinking	Multiple Benefits	Value in excess of cost	Constant Innovation
Price Leadership	Varying degrees of pure price Competition	Bare utility, Commodity	Best price Only	Merger, Acquisition or Reinvention
Product Line	Multiproduct line (MPC) Incremental innovation	Benefits tied to Option available	Best deal Possible	Innovation, Branding
Brand	Brand & Reputation	Brand satisfaction	Brand value	Incremental Innovation, MPC, Branding

(Table 4.3). A detailed discussion follows in Chapters 5 to 8. Strategy begins with a complete and comprehensive understanding of the marketplace, which is established in the four broad playing fields. Each playing field is defined by the customer's evaluation as to (a) their expectations of performance from the product or service that is offered and (b) the perception of its worth or value.[7] The result of this analysis is a four-quadrant portrayal of strategic behavior based on customer perceptions and expectations. Each of the fields is a position that is generally sustainable, albeit with some variance in the scope of profit margins and market position.

The Innovation–Entrepreneurial field is the most profitable and offers the strongest strategic position to be in. Its strategic thrust is toward constant innovation and renewal. The Price Leadership field is the seriously competitive and most dangerous realm to occupy. You do not want to occupy this field as a strategy unless you have deep pockets, access to a huge market, and are able to cut costs beyond and better than anyone else in the industry. Failure here will lead almost certainly to decline, failure, and bankruptcy. The Product Line field is one that relies on product line proliferation to expand market position and usurp shelf space. It is usually accompanied by strong brand equity. Finally, the Brand field is characterized by strong brand image even as it is populated by products with varying degrees of performance expectations.

It will be developed later that companies have a number of options in the economy. They may remain in a field and strengthen their position for each product:

1. They may vary strategies for each product.
2. They may elect to move toward a new position in the playing field, and
3. They may engage, at some cost in all of the fields.

However, before we get into the details of that, we will need some discussion about the technical details that are a part of strategic planning.

Strategic Planning: The Content Component

Figure 4.1[8] gives us a linear guideline as to the topics we need to address in developing a strategic plan. At the outset, you need to have a clear vision of what your company or organization does and what is its purpose:

1. Defining the business

Typically the mission statement is a broad banner that keeps everyone focused on what it is the company does and perhaps even why it

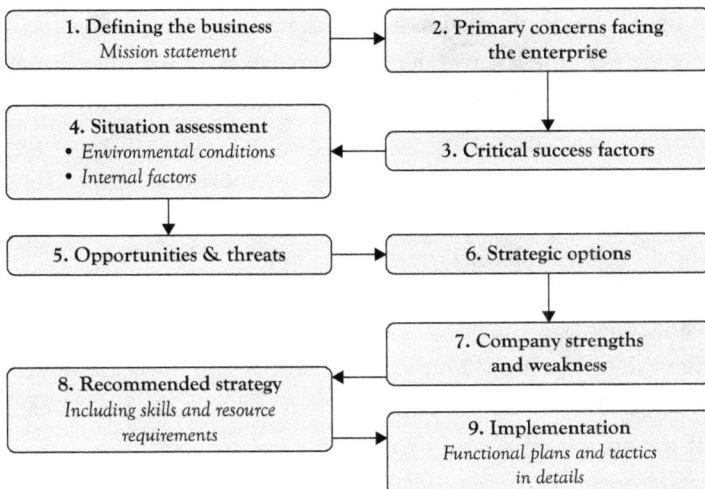

Figure 4.1 The strategic planning content process

does so. It embodies the purpose and the commitment the organization has toward the customer, the enterprise, and its important components in fulfilling its mandate. Many mission statements favor one purpose or another. Sometimes, it is a technology that is offered to better humankind. Sometimes, it is a direction to earn profit for the investors. In reality the mission statement should balance all elements as to purpose with some indication of priorities. The desirable statement would include the following:

1. The customer and the product and service engaged to provide value
2. The employees who will fulfill that principle mandate
3. The community that provides the social system encouraging the enterprise
4. The shareholders and investors

Here are two good examples:

- 3M Company is technically oriented: *To solve unsolved problems innovatively,* and
- Disney's is more inclusive: *To make people happy,* which could include employees, shareholders as well as the community.

A special notice is required as to the fourth item in the focus on shareholders. In the last two decades there has been too much emphasis on the bottom line. Long-term profitability and return on investment is important but unfortunately CEOs have been whipped by economics and money market managers to "hurry-up" short-term gains. That has caused no little harm to the national economy. A *Forbes* magazine article[9] tells us about the foolishness of that position:

The Copernican Revolution in managerial economics is a paradigm shift from the 20th century view that customers are subservient to the stationary 'center of the universe'—the value chain of the organization—to the view that the organization is one of many organizations revolving around the customer. The organization survives and thrives only so long as it is agile enough to meet the customer's shifting needs and desires. The future of the firm depends on how much value is being added. The job of the manager is, not to maximize short-term profits, but rather to continuously add value to customers with a reasonable level of profit.

2. Primary concerns

The initial concerns facing the organization or company are determined by examining the environmental factors that may have a bearing on the enterprise as seen in Chapter 3. In most cases companies focus on one or some of the following:

1. Market needs: shifts and customer satisfaction
2. Product mix: and product removal
3. Technology and innovation
4. Production and operations: processes and people
5. Distribution: global markets
6. Sources of supply: suppliers, outsourcing

An important issue is to recognize that growth may no longer be certain. In the new economy survival or at least sustainability becomes more meaningful. Al Reis[10] makes the point that too many companies look for ways to increase business. He argues it is "better to look for ways to increase the share of business you are already in rather than constantly looking over your shoulder for new fields to conquer. That way you also increase your power. Ocean Spray has 78% of the U.S. cranberry market. That's power." His point is that a firm should focus on doing what it does best.

3. Critical success factors

What are those items and events that must go well if the company is to succeed? They are the critical success factors (CSFs). With some organizations it is the weather that must be accommodating and provide enough snow to encourage skiing at ski resorts and lodges. But while this example is one that management cannot control, the organization can develop CSFs they can do something about. Oddly enough successful entrepreneurs and businesses often apply them without knowing they are doing so. These could include patent application, production targets, sales volumes to be achieved, cost reduction efforts, improving the employee pool, and so on.

A study of Dell Computer's success, at least up to the year 2000, itemizes three key factors that contributed to their success: (1) providing superior customer service, (2) achieving high velocity on inventory (speed), and (3) focusing on customer experience and the direct model itself, which gave Dell intimate knowledge of customer needs and supplier capabilities. "The study learned how Dell leverages these factors by giving value to customers while decreasing costs for the company."[11]

4. Situation Assessment

The situation assessment requires research and analysis of the external environmental factors that impact on the company. It weighs in on governmental and legal implications of the company's business. For example, the governmental commitment or lack thereof to meet Kyoto Protocol standards will have an effect sooner or later as will the carbon tax game[12] now being played across the continent. Demographic shifts and the increase in immigration changes buyer profiles and offers new opportunities for consumer goods and services. The United States is undergoing a dramatic shift in demographics. Today, Hispanics represent the largest middle class group in the United States, and over 88% have a household income of $50,000; there are 43 million customers with a Spanish heritage looking for personalized products and brands.

5. Opportunities and threats

The environmental scan is an examination of the external business conditions that are influenced by governments and legal issues, by social and demographic shift, by new technologies, and by the economy itself. Threats or opportunities will come from external sources in the business environment. Given the new economy and with structural changes taking place there may be opportunities or threats from shrinking or expanding segments in the market including growth patterns and maturity.

Of course, there is always the competition that is ever present and capable of creating new threats or opportunities through aggressive behaviour or new strategies, better customer relations, market position, and so on. Then there are new technologies that will cause fundamental changes in products, and processes.

6. Strategic options

There are numerous strategic options an organization can exercise toward reaching its goals. Growth is still a large concern, but in some instances it is likely a firm would be well disposed to retain a sustainable position in the market with modest growth, at least enough to assure profitability. The growing trend in the consumer market toward doing more with less may have an impact on some firms and require a lesser increase than would have been accepted in previous time.

A low-cost strategy requires the capability to reduce costs as with Southwest Airlines and Walmart. On the other hand, Intel and 3M apply a strong innovation emphasis to their strategies, thus maintaining growth and market position.

7. Company strengths and weaknesses

Company strengths and weaknesses can encourage or limit your ability to respond to the market or develop new opportunities. This is the first part of the SWOT anagram many companies find useful in gauging their ability to implement strategies. Strengths, weaknesses, opportunities, and threats compose an analytical framework that assesses the company's ability to perform and succeed. But an organization's strengths can also be its weakness; the key is to know the difference and build on the strengths. An example would be NFL quarterback Matt Hasselbeck of the Seattle Seahawks. Since becoming the starter in 2003, he led Seattle to five playoff appearances and a Super Bowl appearance as well as being selected three times for the Pro Bowl. Matt's strengths are his great short-mid range accuracy and release. He is also known for his on-field leadership; he can literally win a game on his own. His weakness is long-ball accuracy and fumbles. Recognizing this, the coach favors short downfield strategies and he avoids situations that might lead to fumbles.

So it is in business. Managers need to appraise their strengths and weaknesses honestly and coolly and then develop their strategies accordingly.

8. Recommended strategy

Having established a company's mission and purpose, having reviewed its position in the business environment, and after examining the various strategic options available, management must select the strategy they will use to gain their objectives. If it is the company's objective to increase sales, there needs to be a determination as to how this will occur. What options are to be examined and a selection made? Will it be by expanding the market territory? Will it be by creating new products? Will it be through increasing the sales force performance?

9. Implementation

It is easier to plan strategies for your company than it is to execute them. It requires a transfer of responsibility from those doing the planning downward through the company. In the entrepreneurial company usually the planners are also those who will implement the selected strategies. In the last chapter, we will discuss the melding of the plan with the execution using the entrepreneurial model that orchestrates the company's operation from customer to resources.

Implementation requires the dissemination of the mission and objectives throughout the company. Figure 4.2 illustrates a typical

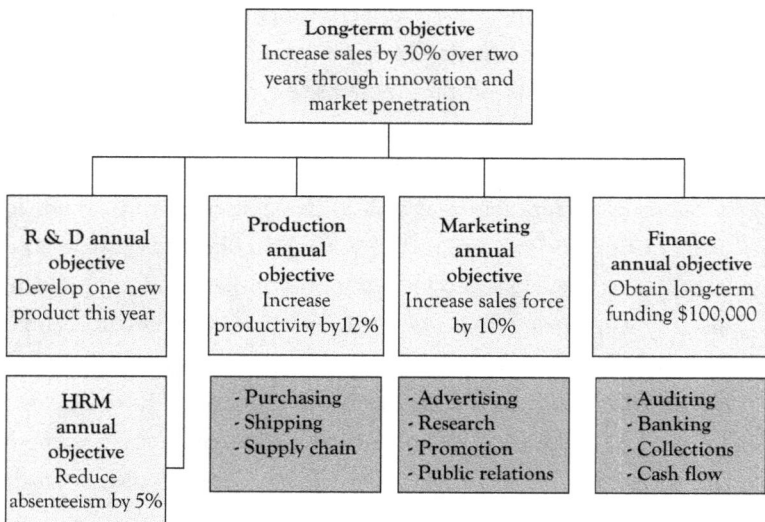

Figure 4.2 Long-term company strategic plan

portrayal of the involvement of functional departments in the strategy execution process. The broader company objectives are parcelled out to each functional area and to divisions if these are part of the company structure. Each of the departments develop the objectives and strategy that fit their particular role in the organization. The company may have a long-term objective of increasing sale by 30% over 2 years (this could be one of three or more objectives) to increase sales and profitability, even as the company remains competitive.

In turn, each functional area will carry its load. R&D will need to develop a new product for the market, sales will need to increase the force by 12% even as the production department improves its productivity. In turn, these units will draft their own plans and programs to fulfill their responsibilities.

One of the pressing areas is that of developing the important manpower and leadership skills for the company. Leading executives[13] understand that "the greatest strategies in the world will have little effect on a company unless the right people are chosen to execute these strategies." They spend an inordinate amount of time searching for the best talent in their organizations to build the teams to execute their strategies.

Summary

The planning stage of the strategic management process must be created with allowance for entrepreneurial execution, which is to say there is flexibility and accommodation for change that invariably will have an effect on the strategy mix. The chapter introduced the reader to the content side of strategic planning. Chapter 10 will dwell on the context of implementing the strategic plan.

The development of strategic plans for the company requires as much information as possible from the field, from suppliers, salesforce as well as published secondary data and market research. It is very useful for a company to have a good market or business intelligence network that will feed information back to the enterprise. The formal planning process is important. It forces management to appraise their performance and to look forward to the future and anticipate the changes that will take place. Then new plans can be drawn up for implementation. But plans are nothing unless executed expeditiously and in a timely fashion.

Laurie Maddalena[14] makes the observation that execution of strategies is the greatest unaddressed issue in business today. The absence of execution is the biggest obstacle to success and often the greatest contributor to derailment of leaders.

> Leadership is not just about creating great visions, strategies, and plans. In my work with executives, I find the most successful leaders are those who hold themselves accountable as well as their employees. Leaders are not successful if they cannot execute the strategy. It's like taking the time to plan a great vacation and then not taking the vacation. If you don't go on the vacation, the planning was just wasted effort. Many organizations spend significant time strategizing and planning, and very little time emphasizing execution.

Case Study: Holbrook Manufacturing Inc.

Building an Innovation Strategy

We will explore some of the implications for marketing and strategic planning that arise from the new model by looking at the results taken from a small manufacturer of household products. The company has been in business for 15 years. Its operations are located in a 5,000-square foot factory producing wood products for the kitchen, knife holders, spice shelves, condiment containers, wall decorations, and such. The designs were originally created by the founder and have not changed significantly in the last decade. The company sells direct to small retailers and some chains through three manufacturers' sales reps in regions within 500 miles of the plant.

The plant employs 12 people and sales in the last 3 years have leveled off at just under $3 million annually. The president and founder is concerned that with increasing costs from suppliers, wages, and overhead they will need to develop a new strategy if they are to survive. A major worry is the flood of low-priced product made from plastic and some wood coming in from Asia. The president filled out his questionnaire, Item A and the results were transferred to the work sheet grid, Item B.

Executives at the Holbrook Company also filled in the questionnaire. The ideal situation is to record the averaged value from the top managers in the firm. However, another process is to record each manager separately and to post all of these on the grid. It serves the purpose of determining how closely (or not) the company's managers are in agreement with each other as to their mission and purpose.

In practice and as a consultant, the ultimate test is to administer the eight questions to a few of the company's major customers or clients. This will provide a more realistic position for the firm's competitive position.

When we examine the results from the questionnaire there is little doubt that this manufacturer is in trouble. The company is a low-value producer. They offer a range of standard products to a broad market base that perceives price as the main determinant for purchasing (9LC). They do almost no R&D or innovation (4HI) and we would expect they have little or no reserve capital for innovation to quickly deal with a new competitor or inroads from global competitors. Worse yet, they do not know their customers and have no idea where they will be in the future (low 2C), all of which indicates the company is ripe for acquisition at a bargain price or it will fail within the next few years. They do seem to have a good reputation in the industry (8HR) that may provide some favor in the market, but that will likely be offset if the company is producing lower quality goods, which is often the case with low equity in the labor force. They apparently have a low regard for their employees (2EQ), which indicates lower worker motivation and commitment to the company's success.

However, let's assume the management comes to its senses, perhaps prodded by a seminar in Entrepreneurial Strategic Management that convinces the owner of a need to change his ways. He has two challenges: one short term and the other long term. In the near future, he needs to maintain a competitive position in pricing, which means he must reduce costs as much as possible. The ideal method is to improve productivity by elevating his relationship with employees and evoking their commitment to quality and output.

Possibly he will need to begin an immediate training program to educate and engage his workers, tied in with an appropriate incentive plan. Bringing in flex time and removing time clocks is a potential direction he might assume. On the sales front he will likely need to upgrade his marketing and communications skills to augment his good reputation. This area will need analysis and attention so he can capitalize on his reputation. He should embark on an image campaign to boost customer cognition of the company and its quality output. There is an immediate need to acquire feedback regarding the level of customer satisfaction.

The long-term strategy must address the shortfall in R&D and innovation. The management must immediately align itself with an innovations network within the industry that will open the door to new products and processes. A unique, new product might act as a market entry point where he might take up a niche strategy and hopefully expand sales as the company brings on new products or services even as the older product lines diminish and die out. Above all, management needs to build an effective marketing strategy beginning with a feedback and intelligence network that will supply much needed information as to future needs and developments in the industry.

What follows is a point form outline for one course of action the CEO might pursue.

Short-Term Strategies

Manufacturing: Innovation Methodology

1. Improve productivity through employee training and stakeholder buy-in
2. Provide incentive package to accompany the new standards and procedures
3. Improve processes, possibly by applying lean or agile manufacturing techniques
4. Introduce entrepreneurial concepts in the managing and communications process.

Marketing: Initiate CRM Program

1. Include customer satisfaction measurement
2. Commence marketing intelligence and networking system (MIS)
3. Develop customer profiles and market potential evaluation
4. Initiate social media presence; Facebook, Twitter, Skype, LinkedIn, and so forth.
5. Establish and improve e-commerce aspects, website, and so forth.

Management: Innovation in Systems

1. Commence enterprise resource planning (ERP) or other management improvement systems, or both.
2. Develop strategic planning model for the company

Financial: Secure Cash Flow

1. Build a credible business plan for the turnaround
2. Meet with banker to arrange long-term financing
3. Determine if there are governmental programs to assist in R&D

Long-Term Strategies

Manufacturing

1. Integrated ERP program
2. Developed lean and agile manufacturing procedures
3. Developed supply chain management (SCM) system tied to ERP
4. Augmented entrepreneurial program
5. Profit sharing or incentive program
6. Continuous training programs

Marketing

1. Fully developed MIS system
2. Fully integrated CRM
3. Fully augmented customer satisfaction procedures
4. Fully augmented internal marketing program
5. Automated sales force
6. Fully developed e-commerce, website
7. Rolling forecast, tied to MIS and CRM—strategy adjustments

Innovation

1. Product innovation center for analysis of data and so forth.
2. Shared innovation network through government and trade associations
3. R&D department; internal, shared, or licensed
4. Budget of 2% of sales

Management

1. Ongoing strategic planning process
2. Improved process systems; cloud management

A Challenging Note

The foregoing analysis assumes the questions have been answered in a reasonably accurate fashion and that they closely reflect what the customer thinks about the company and its products. A truly comprehensive analysis and development of strategic plans should include the answers of a few of the company's customers. If they are close to the answers provided by the company manager then it shows there is a self-awareness of the company's performance in the marketplace. If there is a large difference the company needs to take immediate action to improve their position guided by the customer's perception.

The ESM© Strategy Test[15] Holbrook Manufacturing Inc. (Item A)

The following questions reflect on the kind of strategy your company is following at this time. It presents an approximation of the company's marketing and selling activities within your overall plan. Please answer each question on a score out of 10, or 1 to 10 in the boxes at the end of each statement. The number 10 means you highly agree with the statement. A score of 1 means you disagree and 3 you are neutral. If you feel a statement does not apply to your organization you may ignore it or place a zero in the box. Please respond as quickly as you can.

To what degree do you agree with or disagree with the following statements?

1. Our products/services are all standard and don't need much change. We believe they readily meet all of our customer's needs.   [8] SP

2. Our marketing emphasis is to ignore competitive pricing and to concentrate on the development of a strong relationship with our customers.*   [5] HV

3. Our products/services are very well branded or well known, or both, in comparison to the brands and reputation of others in our industry.* `8` HR

4. Our company has modified/improved our products/ services almost every year in the last 5 years.* `4` HI

5. Our primary goal is to sell a lower priced product/service in the highly competitive industry in which we operate. `9` LC

6. We believe all employees should participate in, or receive a share of, or both, company profits.* `2` EQ

7. We offer the marketplace a full line of standard products/ services. `7` HPL

8. We know where our customers will be 3 years from now.* `2` C

The Analysis—Item B

Each question has a value from 1 to 10 that is entered into the appropriate boxes. The following analysis (Figure 4.3) is taken from a small manufacturing company producing aluminum products for the consumer market. Judging from the answers provided by the CEO the company does not have a promising future and any serious competition will bring about its decline.

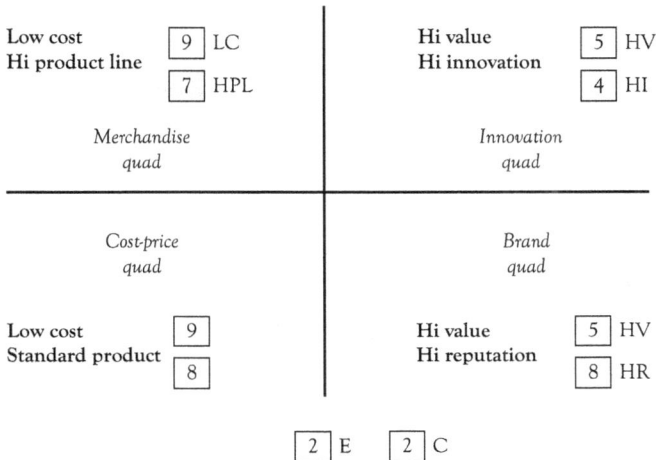

Low cost Hi product line	`9` LC `7` HPL	Hi value Hi innovation	`5` HV `4` HI

Merchandise quad   Innovation quad

Cost-price quad   Brand quad

Low cost Standard product	`9` `8`	Hi value Hi reputation	`5` HV `8` HR

`2` E   `2` C

Figure 4.3 Quadrant analysis of strategic questions

Brief Definition of Quadrants

Innovation and Entrepreneurship Quad

HV: High Value associated with the perception of many benefits that the product or service will provide to the buyer.

HI: High Innovation indicates the expectation the product is unique and answers particular needs very well. Appeals to a small but very supportive niche when first introduced as a new item. Also indicates reinvented or improved products and services that may have good or strong brand appeal and serve shifting needs and trends.

Brand Quad

HV: High value, products and services tend to higher price range in the market, supported by the brand or reputation value of the company and its goods and services. The benefit expectation is realized through the brand image and not necessarily the benefits that might be provided.

HR: High Reputation or Brand recognition. The value that is associated with the brand comes from the brand image itself and encourages loyalty and repeat sales.

Product Line Quad

HPL: High Product line, large list of merchandise products; a size for everyone approach, often associated with large inventories.

LC: Low Cost, pressure to cut costs, to outsource or to consider, but not necessarily develop innovative technologies to increase productivity.

Price Leadership Quad

LC: Low Cost products, economies of scale or outsourcing to drive cost down. Squeeze the value chain to cut the cost. Improve process costs using technology as an offset to going offshore

SP: Standard Product, little innovation

CHAPTER 5

Creating Strategies in the Innovation Quad

Innovation is the specific instrument of entrepreneurship... the act that endows resources with a new capacity to create wealth.

—Peter F. Drucker

The highest level of customer involvement occurs when the desire for benefits from a product or service is matched by a perception of value beyond price. The desire for the latest technology in IT performance, for example, is matched by a willingness to pay whatever is asked for the product. In 1983 I paid $2,200 for an Apple IIe PC with 32K RAM, two external drives; one for the OS the other for file storage and both carried a 1.44 MB disk. That was it! The printer cost another $2,100. It was an NEC mechanical printer, essentially a typewriter hooked up to the PC. That represents about $9,000 in current dollars where today the most basic PC with printer can be had for less than $700.

Why was I willing to pay so much at that time? What motivation was there that encouraged me to put hand in pocket and withdraw thousands of dollars for a relatively unknown product? First I believed I needed it for my consulting practice. Secondly, I had the money. Thirdly, it was the only game in town. If I wanted a PC to print out data I was working with, well the Apple IIe was it! And I was not the only one who held to that belief. Nearly two million people had the same need and perception of value and purchased the Apple PC in that year alone at a price equivalent to almost 13 times the cost of a vastly superior product today.

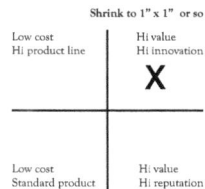

This is the quadrant of innovation and new technologies and entre-preneurial ways of doing things. Our business is better served if we can constantly occupy this field of customer expectations and perceptions. In fact it is the only guarantee for survival that an organization con-stantly reinvents itself and its offerings. Innovation and technological change are a growing activity in the marketplace; indeed it is mar-ket-driven.[1] More than 30% of manufacturing revenue is attributed to new and improved products and studies show that R&D is on the rise across developed countries. Rosabeth Kanter[2] from Harvard tells us that:

> Now, more than ever, management is a balancing act—the jug-gling of contradictions to try to get the best of attractive but opposing alternatives. Order is a temporary illusion, strategy a moving target. Leaders cannot impose authority on a world of constant motion; they can only hope to steer some of that action toward productive ends.

The leading companies today are those who constantly create new ideas, new knowledge, and they thrive on building new products and services. Not only does this strategy create more revenue but it gives you a competitive edge where your culture- and innovation-driven business model is difficult to duplicate.

The Innovation Quad

The quad ranges from an expectation of some benefit to multiple ben-efits as to product or service *performance* and varies from a higher cost to a sense of value beyond cost in terms of the *worth*. In most cases it is at the beginning of the growth stage of the product lifecycle, which tells us we are appealing to a small group of customers at the top end of the quad or have products that range down to the lower level where we are approaching maturity and appealing to a broader market. The repetitive success of various new models of the iPhone can be explained in a recycling of position where each new innovation builds on the prior technology. This creates a sense of newness and customer desire to have the latest model that continues to hold the price level and profitability too.

The strategy is to add technological innovation that is a higher order of incremental innovation, not really anything radical in fact. Of course, the social trend has a lot to do with the growth of the new product to say nothing of the strong stimulation that comes from strong media campaign that raises expectations of performance and keeps the item at the high end of the quad (Figure 5.1).

Companies such as Salesforce, Google, Apple, and others[3] continuously create new innovations and major modifications to their products. What the automobile attempted to do with the introduction of model changes each year to stimulate purchase activity, the innovative companies break new ground in technology and embed that into their offerings. Microsoft did that for decades moving from Windows 1.0 in 1985 to Windows 2.0 in 1990 on to Windows XP and Windows 8. Of course, the older versions continued to be available and they generally followed the product life cycle (PLC) curve to decline.

Why Do Companies Avoid Innovation?

Few corporations last beyond 40 years of age.[4] The corporation isn't a sturdy species. In an article entitled "Innovation's Terrible Toll," the

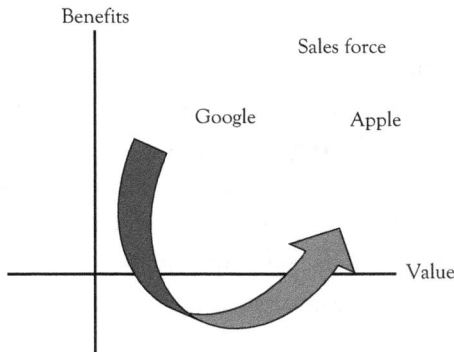

Figure 5.1 Innovation quad

Wall Street Journal tells us that only a tiny fraction reach the age of 40. Using Kodak as an example we see that managers stay with what they know and do not expand beyond that. Kodak had the digital camera in 1975 but did not know what to do with it. Working under the cover of Chapter 11 bankruptcy the company has sold off most of its assets as part of a strategy to finance the building of its commercial imaging business of providing printing and packaging services for industry and commerce.

Why do large and evidently successful companies fail? Why do long-time establishments cease to exist? Quite simply they forget or are unable to keep up with the times; they lose the entrepreneurial ability they once had. General Motors' executives were successful managers! They were doing things right! Administratively, that is. But there are two market drivers that literally impel us toward innovating; the need for newness and competitive pressures. These force us to change if we are to stay ahead or to remain competitive. Those companies that retain the entrepreneurial mindset are able to build on change and succeed.

Why We Need Innovation

A company is a living organism swimming in a sea of competitive entities. What sets one organism above all other is the ability to be innovative, to respond more quickly to change, and to evolve more rapidly than others. For the organism to survive, it must be innovative. But while companies also need to survive they must go beyond survival; they must perform in such a way as to sustain their organization and make a contribution to the social system that in turn nurtures them. They must create wealth. They must add to the economy of the region they inhabit. Innovation and the entrepreneurial ability to exploit it is a growing part of the business fabric. But the pressure to indulge in the process is more than environmentally driven. There are purely business reasons to pursue innovation as an instrument of your strategy. The following points give impetus to our quest for more innovation.[5] Companies need to:

1. Identify and pursue new opportunities

The entrepreneurial organization builds on change. It encourages innovation that creates new opportunities. The bureaucratic organization cannot be innovative. Its nature does not encourage the creative process. And it is the creative ability that is needed to see opportunity in the marketplace—from customers, new technologies, and even the competition. Joseph Schumpeter pointed out that entrepreneurs are ever alert to new opportunities. Peter Drucker observed that, "Innovation is the specific instrument of entrepreneurship... the act that endows resources with a new capacity to create wealth." Steve Jobs saw opportunities and pursued them, thus expanding Apple's wealth.

2. Increase revenues

When the enterprise earns more its profits rise. We earn more revenue when we introduce new marketing innovations with new products and services. Some organizations look to cost cutting as a solution to a need for increased profits. That is counterproductive. Obviously, an organization must be lean as well as innovative and entrepreneurial. The intelligent answer is to constantly be entrepreneurial and ever innovative in the business.

3. Maintain a competitive advantage

Keeping ahead through being innovative is the most direct way to take the competitive lead. By taking the lead you stay in advance of your competitors. It can be in product or service improvements. It can be through process improvements that increase profits or allow price cuts if needed and it can be organizationally that makes you more effective. Here are some examples of disruptive and successful innovative changes:

- Michelin captured the U.S. tire market when it introduced radials.
- Citibank made its competitors look old-fashioned when it introduced ATMs.
- Sony grabbed the music market with the introduction of the compact disc.

- The Japanese gained advantage over the Swiss with digital watches.
- Text processors in PCs made obsolete Smith Corona's product, the Typewriter.

The Drive for Newness and Innovation

A product, service, retail store, institution, and virtually any item or facility ultimately reaches a saturation point and then a decline stage as it completes its life cycle. We are all familiar with products that began a commercial life at a peak of promise and usefulness and then diminished in worth and application until they disappeared from sight. In a slower life time in the early 20th century a product could retain its position for years. Furniture was built to last a life time. Clothing, toys, books, and even automobiles were passed down from one family member to another. Things were built to last. Retail stores and hard goods were almost institutions. But the pace of life has quickened and goods and services now come and go so quickly there is a sense of planned obsolescence.

In 2008, the Apple iPod reached sales of over 50 million units. In 2011, sales were down to 45 million units and will likely top out just above 30 million units for 2012. The product life cycle for the iPod has had a 10-year run. Other products including smartphones and pads of one type or another are replacing this audio device (Figure 5.2).

The Pace Is Increasing

Why is the pace speeding up? Why do we look for new things, new ways to do things? On the one hand, there is a human desire to improve one's state of satisfaction. We constantly look for new methods to make our

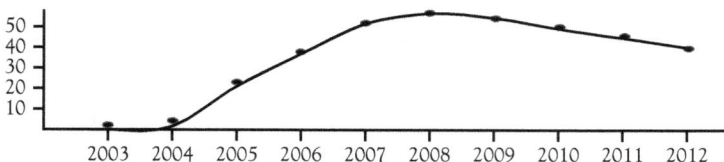

Figure 5.2 Apple iPod sales, $billions

lives more pleasant, our work more efficient. We want to make life easier for ourselves and our families. Perhaps it is a genetic issue, some motivation devolved from a primordial emotion that drives us to survive. On a sociological note it can likely be attributed to behavior that is intrinsic to one's own self-preservation. We all seek the avoidance of pain, both physical and emotional. So if we consider the Maslow hierarchy we are driven to seek out food and shelter, social acceptance, status, and so on. All of this motivates us to acquire whatever we feel is necessary to overcome our fears and so we buy things that give us the edge in survival and overcoming our concerns about those fears. Fear causes the organism to seek safety. Self-preservation may also be involved as the coping mechanism one needs to prevent emotional trauma.

There is also a more profound view of our rush to new things and change. Scientists[6] make the observation we are internally driven toward a convergence where technology and the human being come together. They suggest it is this goal that moves us onward to a singularity in which technological change becomes so rapid and so profound that our bodies and brains will merge with our machines. In his book, *The Singularity Is Near*, Kurzweil portrays what life will be like after this event—a human–machine civilization where our experiences shift from real reality to virtual reality and where our intelligence becomes nonbiological and trillions of times more powerful than unaided human intelligence. In practical terms, this means that human aging and pollution will be reversed, world hunger will be solved, and our bodies and environment transformed by nanotechnology to overcome the limitations of biology, including death." We will be able to create virtually any physical product just from information, resulting in radical wealth creation.

Whatever the drive, it seems safe to say that there will always be a motivation to bring new things: technology, processes to the market, and we will just as readily select those things we believe we need as consumers and customers. And as Rogers[7] points out we accept new technologies and processes in a diffusion process "by which an innovation is communicated through certain channels over time among the members of a social system. The diffusion of innovations involves both mass media and interpersonal communication channels. That is, by sharing communication channels such as interpersonal communication or mass communication people can get information of an innovation and perceive its innovation as useful." So as we gain access to more information through the Internet and social media we will adapt even more rapidly, hence change will come on us ever more quickly. Our customers will look for new things more expectantly and there will be a mounting pressure to keep pace, if not lead change itself.

Then there is the reality of our competitors. They are relentless. They are global, ever-pressing, and present. It is not an option to ignore the competition and so as businesspeople there is little choice but to respond and perhaps to do more than respond but take the lead in coming up with new advances and innovation to beat out the competition; the need to innovate or die. Studies by the Organization of Economic Co-operation and Development (OECD) countries show that innovation and R&D accounts for 30% of annual manufacturing sales. In effect the innovative edge increases the revenue stream for companies very significantly. It provides the competitive position to which other companies must strive to catch up.

The Innovation Blueprint

The new millennium is about innovation and new technologies. Sam Kogan, president, chief operating officer, GEN3 Partners, Inc.[8] makes the point that managers must view innovation as a blueprint rather than a brainstorm. It is a fact that long-lasting success requires a process of innovation that is inherent in the business and pursued consistently and vigorously. Moreover, it needs to be a part of the whole companies, not just management and consultants. We need to be innovative just to survive in a global marketplace where emerging economies have great advantages in labor cost and domestic process innovation as well as product innovation.

Secondly, technologies and new concepts are no longer protected by national boundaries. They can leapfrog over oceans in no time over the Internet and mobile communications. They can spread rapidly around the world and while a company with a new product may make a one-time splash, it won't be long everyone else will have adopted it.

A third point is that brands aren't as powerful as they used to be. How a customer is engaged with or experiences a product or service is now more important than brand name as the basis for a purchasing decision. People are able to appreciate a sense of value as they share a product experience with millions of others over the Internet: on Facebook, Twitter, and YouTube for example. So they choose products that will give them that higher sense of value whether well-known brands or not. Brands can give an advantage for a short period of time or perhaps longer in a domestic market. Yet even here we need to improve on the brand, making it an "all-new" Zippo with whitener! So relying on the brand name must be augmented by innovation.

Types of Innovation

In 2006, the OECD carried out a comprehensive study[9] of innovation in firms across 20 countries. The study characterized innovation as an operational activity in four areas: product, marketing, process, and organizational. Each of these is independent, although there can be a synergism between product and marketing innovations and processes that can have an effect of organizational innovation.

Product innovation—the improvement of a product or service to meet or exceed customer expectations. The innovation may be incremental in which case it is a minor perhaps even a cosmetic change toward better service, styling, or sociological favor. It may be radical or disruptive in that it challenges conventional usage or offers a great improvement over current practice.

Marketing innovation—refers to changes in delivering the product or service. It would include packaging, delivery methods, changes to presentation in retail service, e-commerce variations, and so on. There may be variations introduced to market communications and sales presentations.

Process innovation—addresses the development of production methods, processes, and flows. It can include significant changes in methods, equipment, and software to enhance the output from the operation.

Organizational innovation—the implementation of new organizational methods or techniques with the view of improving the effectiveness of the organization in reaching its goals. It can include strategic variations and processes.

Your organization can be innovative across a wide spectrum. The primary focus is the customer and what she or he needs to sustain and help them grow. Here is the major role for R&D and the expenditure of funds for research and the creation of new products and services.

Innovation as a Process

There is something of a philosophical thread to the concept of innovation. It is really an act of creativity much like that of an artist or musician. People create things but in the final analysis what we see is a conjoining of material, concepts, and things from the past that have coalesced into a new thing. The great works of art are really simple things from memory that have been orchestrated into a wonderfully agreeable presentation from which we derive some unique pleasure or usage. Arthur Koestler, a journalist, author, and Nobel nominee developed an insightful view of creativity as something that came from the world around us and not from within, driven by some spiritual pressure. In his book *The Act of Creation*, Koestler wrote:

> The creative act is not an act of creation in the sense of the Old Testament. It does not create something out of nothing; it uncovers, selects, re-shuffles, combines, synthesizes already existing facts, ideas, faculties, skills. The more familiar the parts, the more striking the new whole.[10]

What we see is that the creative act is not a mystical activity but is really quite logical and is formed in the mind of the observant individual who sees something new, an opportunity if you will in items and events from the past. For example, the Sony Walkman that burst into the youth market with a tremendous success in the 1980s is what Koestler would have referred to as a "pattern" formed from electronic components that included the idea from the original nonrecording playback cassette tape and headphones. But the miniaturization of electronic components started with the first transistor radios that originated in the mid-1950s. The Philips company used that technology to bring out the compact cassette in 1963, which was joined with the headphones that had been around for a century. Sony was simply the first organization to form the pattern of the Walkman, from components that already existed.

James Burke[11] coproduced the acclaimed 10-part documentary series *Connections* (1978), which was first telecast on the BBC and then on PBS channels in the United States. The series was an historical presentation about invention and discovery and the tie-in to history in a web-like association. It suggests that technical creativity emerges from a web or an interconnected system of social knowledge, people, and events—an ephemeral soup of knowledge and then along comes one individual who suddenly sees a pattern or a concept. It's an entrepreneurial *eureka* as with Steve Jobs when he looked at the Xerox Alto in 1974, and had a vision of personal computers for the world. Burke was also aware that "the ease with which information can be spread is critical to the rate at which change occurs." The more and the faster information spreads, the faster innovation happens. Burke says, "Every time there is an improvement in the technology with which ideas and people come together, major change ensues."

By combining the observations from Koestler and Burke we can see that innovation is a process, that it's an entrepreneurial event. It requires an individual with the mental ability to gaze upon a pattern or a flow of information and see within this mental matrix an opportunity perhaps based on a new invention or an innovation. Steve Jobs's perception of the iPod was derived from his iTunes project, the MP3 player, and earphones (ear pods). Before that he saw the Xerox desktop monitor, mouse, and graphic displays in a miniaturized and personal computer arrangement.

Of course, there are thoroughly scientific inventions that are born as a result of trial and error and perhaps the occasional eureka moment. Yet the commercialization of these requires an observer who sees the opportunity in the invention and how it might fit into a pattern of usage. The organization that will succeed is one that cultivates the entrepreneurial spirit in all its managers and employees too. Better yet they are able to open up the front end of the process to recognizing opportunities from those areas where innovation abounds—with the customer, the company, or its organization. The search process to innovation might follow five steps:

- *Step 1*: Set out the boundary for entrepreneurial involvement in the four sectors: product, process, market, and organization. Where do you want the innovation to focus? Is it in customer service? In product development? What innovations will beat the competition? What processes can we improve that will allow competitive pricing or better yet, improved profitability? Where do you want your team to place their attention as to improving and bettering the status quo?

- *Step 2*: Have everyone collect information on their area of focus. Define this information in terms of the problem as seen by each in the group. What answers does the information bring to the focus?
- *Step 3*: Share the information, questions, and ideas freely within the group. Establish a network through a closed Facebook, e-mail, or other media for the flow of ideas and questions.
- *Step 4*: Compile all the answers and refine as to how things might be different, done better, or improved. Circulate and repeat.
- *Step 5*: Implement potential solutions and reward the group.

As we can see the second step is more demanding and analytical than the other steps. It's all about describing—in detail—exactly what happens currently in the focus of attention and where it might arrive at a solution. Of course, nothing in the process should be regarded in a negative aspect. All inputs must be considered as positive and perhaps applicable. There is no room for negativity in the process of stimulating, sharing, analyzing, and solving issues and concerns.

Innovation and Research

Your intelligence system is your link to what customers want and need as well as your pipeline into the business community and the changing tide of business conditions. Part of that feedback network is the market research you engage in to understand customer needs. Your sales organization and others in the upstream and downstream side of your supply chain management system are also provisioners for your intelligence network. You need a constant flow of information to identify changes taking place.

The Lesson of Change

It is the entrepreneurial person or organization that implements change through innovation. Entrepreneurs are those who see an opportunity and exploit it, thus they bring change to the market and to society. So too must an organization be entrepreneurial if it is to manage innovation and improve on the company's strategic outcome. A survey[12] of the most successful and innovative companies in North America found that more than 70% of respondents listed innovation as one of their company's top three priorities in 2006. The chief proponent in most companies in pushing for innovation is the CEO while individuals who carried the title of Vice President of Innovation was identified as the company innovator by only 3% of all respondents. Obviously, as soon as a creative person is given a corporate title he or she assumes the position, but not the expectation.

Proctor & Gamble has been a leading innovative enterprise for over a century. Recently, it has moved its in-house R&D toward a more open sourcing direction for new ideas and products. In the past there has not been much success in promoting the more dramatic, radical innovation into products and processes. There is always a tendency to avoid risk and settle for incremental innovation. The realization of this fact has likely encouraged companies like P&G to move toward an open-source innovation strategy that reaches out to the collective brains of the world. They make it a goal that 50% of the company's new products come from outside P&G's labs. The new management style could not be built into their existing organization so they "had to tear apart and restitch much of its research organization. It created new job classifications, such as 70 worldwide 'technology entrepreneurs,' or TEs, who act as scouts, looking for the latest breakthroughs from places such as university labs."

The lesson is clear. Successful companies invest in the development of innovation. It is a priority in their strategic planning and where they cannot spur on their managerial team to be innovative they tap the world for opportunities they can acquire, license, or emulate to keep the organization in a constant innovative state. If they cannot stimulate entrepreneurial action with existing managers, they imbue entrepreneurial individuals with the resources and responsibilities to do just that.

Open Innovation[13]

Most of the dynamic and leading companies know that to thrive they must innovate. Larger firms in particular are moving to open innovation: the practice of being "open" to ideas—whether they surface internally or externally—that fit within the company's strategy. As we discussed earlier, large firms tend to be bureaucratic and limited in the ability to create new things. So they spread their antennae across the globe, looking for those technological and scientific discoveries that will supplement, if not lead in the rebirth of their products, services, and companies. They may engage in "outside-in" innovation where the company's R&D facility works with collaborators in other institutions (perhaps universities) and companies to develop the new concept to the commercialization phase. On the other hand, they can take an "inside-out" approach where they license or sell their intellectual property to other when the concept does not fit into the company business.

Not all companies will need to consider open innovation neither will they have the wherewithal to look for such opportunities. Smaller firms might take advantage of licensing opportunities that are offered by other companies from other countries, for example. The difficulty is in having the time and inclination to scour through the various agencies that might have the technologies posted. But if the firm is not active in R&D and does not have an innovations program, it might be wise to begin networking and conducting a search for technologies that would help improve your product line. There are companies on the Internet who offer services in this area. One such company is Idea Connection[14] in Vancouver, Canada, that offers services in technology scouting, idea generation, and access to research through their connection to over 80,000 associates.[15]

Open innovation is now widely accepted, particularly by smaller firms who look for growth and increase in marketshare. There is a large acceptance of the approach and as your search will determine there are many companies on the Internet who are willing to assist in your search for improved innovation.

Investment in Innovation

How good is your innovation strategy? Are you performing at a solid level? The OECD study found that on average a typical firm spent

1% to 5% (0.7% to 4.8%) of revenues on innovation. Canadian SMEs were the highest with 6.3%. The degree of innovativeness in these firms actually correlated with the investment and showed that higher inputs were rewarded with better performance and levels of success.

The implication is very clear. Invest in R&D and innovation or perish. Magna International invests a minimum of 1% of revenue. But the really innovative firms are well above that which suggests firms need to allocate at least 2.5% in highly competitive and volatile markets.

Apple's niche strategy worked well when it first introduced its new products to the market. Their niche was in some way a conventional exercise where the company looked for the innovators who were using MP3 players, or mobile phones and laptops and so they introduced the iPod, the iPhone, and iPad. But these targeted markets were also a digital community of users who cut across demographic boundaries and even socioeconomic strata. They were a specific behavioral group who latched on to the innovations as they came out. The iPod enjoyed a seven-year PLC.

Innovation Strategies

Innovation can be illustrated in a comparative table[16] that sets out the different features of these two important innovation descriptors (Table 5.1). Companies favoring their operations in an existing market will be more disposed to making cosmetic changes hoping their customers will be satisfied with the offering of presumed innovation. The example of adding racing stripes to a standard automobile with the expectation this will render it as a sport model. Companies will also push into new markets with slightly modified features hoping to extend the product life cycle,

Table 5.1 Innovation strategies

	Innovation	
	Incremental	Radical
Existing markets	Competitive, cost reductions	High risk competitive strategy
New markets	Low risk, many competitors	High risk high profits

which would include efforts to develop export markets where customers may be seeing the product for the first time.

However, when the firm comes up with a new tech product, one of a radical form, the potential for profit becomes significant, particularly if the item breaks into the early adopter segment. The Apple iPod was in some respects both an incremental and a radical innovation. It was essentially an extension of the MP3 technology first introduced in Korea in the late 1990s. It was then produced in the United States as the "Rio Diamond PMP 300." In 2001, the first iPod was released into the market. It had a 5-GB hard drive with a $400 price tag and by 2007, Apple had sold 100 million iPods. To this date it is still the most popular MP3 player brand in the world.

New Perspective on Innovation

Businesses and governments too look to innovation as a eureka moment. The idea is to have a couple of brilliant techies in an R&D department and wait for the new ideas to flow. For too long we've viewed innovation as a creative process that leaps from the minds of imaginative people like Albert Einstein or Steve Jobs. That model may work in some areas but for most companies who don't have a Steve Jobs clone working for them, we need something more concrete. We need something that can be a part of the ongoing operation something reliable that can be applied to our products, services, and processes.

Here are four steps companies can take to achieve consistent and dependable innovation:

1. *Create a culture for innovation starting at the top.* One of the proven methods is to develop someone to be an innovation champion—a person with the authority and respect to overcome resistance and encourage others in the company to think in a new way. Steve Jobs filled that role admirably, and so do hundreds of leaders in small and medium-sized companies who have a new product idea or modification that can be applied to customers.

2. *Reform administratively bound managers.* These folks are often the greatest obstacle to innovation. They're busy doing their jobs, so they

don't have time to manage or even consider the adoption of a new innovative mindset. They are more inclined to avoid risk since it could lead to errors and dismissal. So most are guided by a CYA mentality. What is needed then is the assurance that people will not be penalized for trying to be creative, particularly by the administrator. Coming up with new and innovative ways to do things is part of an attitude. It requires training and must become part of the culture of the organization. At the same time we need to put in place the proper incentives for managers to take on innovative behaviors. Penalizing people does not produce results.

3. *Adopt innovation in every department across the company.* Innovation shouldn't be geared solely for the business end, the marketing end, or the technical end. Innovation in the 21st century is a process that must involve the whole company. Everyone should be part of the process of keeping an open attitude and outlook tuned to innovating and change-making.

4. *Start "basic training" in innovation.* Choose one or a group of employees to receive professional innovation training and serve as evangelists. These people can become centers of innovation excellence that together form a self-sustaining innovation process across the company. Another technique is to incept boot-leg time for key people to come up with new concepts and innovative thinking.

Your company needs to think about innovation as a part of its ongoing business. It will lead to success and will improve customer relations considerably if you are constantly innovative and responsive to customer needs. Companies such as Google, 3M, Proctor & Gamble, Alcoa, and Intel have built innovation into their organizations. They know the old ways are no longer acceptable. Indeed that road can only lead to failure. Again as Kiernan noted, *Innovate or die!*

Innovate and Stay One Step Ahead

When developing a business, you can never stop thinking about innovation. For many business owners this is an intimidating notion—that the status quo, especially when the business is thriving, just isn't good enough. There are many examples of once successful businesses that no longer exist because they didn't believe they were vulnerable, and therefore refused to innovate. The BlackBerry is a case in point. In the early part of the first decade it held over 50% of the smartphone market. In 2013 its share fell to 2%.

Now, innovation isn't just about the product. In fact there are a number of unique opportunities to offer an innovative prospect to your customers. Here are a few ideas that grew or improved successful companies:

- *Technology*: It is unique that the gambling industry has used the Internet to create hundreds of enterprises and dozens of new millionaires in the process. We can also point to the porno industry and the application of Internet to another of mans' hidden desires.
- *Service delivery*: Why do we spend triple and more to a couriers like FedEx rather than use the good old post office? Reliable service!
- *Marketing*: When American Airlines first introduced a Frequent Flyer Program, it had a tremendous impact on revenues and revolutionized the airline industry.
- *Product packaging*: Dutch Boy developed a paint can with a spout that doesn't make a mess when you pour. The paint itself is the same. Their sales increased.
- *Customer service strategies*: Enterprise Rental Car "will pick you up." Their customer service strategy has made them unique and increased their market share.
- *Guarantees*: Great companies stand behind what they do. The Asian automakers continue to push the standard for quality, and this is reflected in their warranty policies. The Big Three American automakers continue losing market share to the Asian manufacturers.
- *Business processes*: Walmart is legendary for their logistics expertise. It's what makes them dominant, even though they carry the same products as other mass merchandise retailers.

Setting the Direction for Innovation and Entrepreneurial Strategies

Now that we know the importance of innovation and the need to constantly improve your products, services, and company too, we can seek out that can be applied to maintain your position in this quadrant. The innovation quadrant or quad is characterized by two business variables: innovation and entrepreneurship. Innovation prompts the creation of growth strategies through new product categories, services, or business models that reinvent the company and its managerial dynamic. In this manner, it should deliver significant new value to customers and benefit to the enterprise as well. But it will require an entrepreneurial approach and the combination of nontraditional, creative approaches with conventional strategy development models.

The innovation quad is also where new firms are born through the commercialization of new technologies that are introduced to new markets as start-up new venture, institution, and NGOs as well as within existing firms. It is the market where customers are inclined to perceive value, rather than cost for expected benefits beyond simple utility need satisfaction. As we see in the progression of products through a life cycle the customer tires of an old product or is forced to look to newer products and services to assist their own operations in keeping up with or exceeding competitive pressures.

The important issue is for you to embrace innovation and change. You will need to create a culture of innovation in the organization. Moreover, you will need to continuously reinforce the role of your team as they assimilate the culture and encourage their achievements equally well as their mistakes. Secondly, you must encourage the freedom of being entrepreneurial within the bounds of their area of responsibility. Above all, your mentorship as a manager demands that your style is one of transparency and equality.

CHAPTER 6

Product Line Strategies

The aim of marketing is to know and understand the customer so well the product or service fits him and sells itself.

—Peter Drucker

The two quadrants of product line and branding strategies are referred to as the managed sectors. The rationale for these quads is they serve as a kind of holding zone for products on their way to the cost-price leadership quadrant and then on to decline.

Shrink to 1" x 1" or so	
Low cost Hi product line **X**	Hi value Hi innovation
Low cost Standard product	Hi value Hi reputation

What marketers do in this area is apply a variety of practices to products and services to retain them, or to manage them in a kind of controlling pattern that can last for years. Coca-Cola, Budweiser beer, Tide soap, and Sylvania light bulbs are among the hundreds of managed consumer products that ride on this marketing strategy platform. They are held there as favored brands and can be altered as to packaging, size, and container type to remain in the consumer buying pattern for an extended period of time.

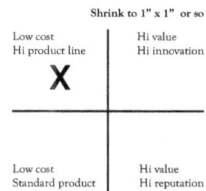

The Product Line Quad

Investopedia[1] tells us that when a company produces a group of related products for a particular market it is engaging in a product line strategy. For example, a cosmetic company's makeup product line might include foundation, concealer, powder, blush, eyeliner, eye shadow, mascara, and lipstick products that are all closely related. The same company might also offer more than one product line. The cosmetic company might have a special product line geared toward teenagers and another line geared

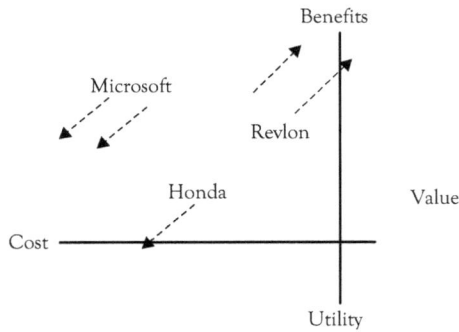

Figure 6.1 The product line quad

toward women older than 60, in addition to its regular product line that can be used by women of any age.

If your company occupies the product line quadrant (Figure 6.1), it encourages the strategy that offers the appearance of more benefits by presenting the product or service in a variety of forms that will increase the perception of value and allow a better position in the market. The strategy calls for making modest physical changes to the product directly and also to introduce complementary products that will encourage an expectation of broader substance to the main product itself. Some companies will bracket a main line product with slightly better features and promote the idea of quality in the item which allows a comparison of expectations. Thus, the buyer can move up or down (sell up or sell down) in fostering a quicker buying decision.

Another technique is to offer trial usage. A good part of customer perception is in the eye of the beholder and the idea of value is a subjective mindset that evolves with experience and exposure. Individuals will be more inclined to accept and use a product after they have tried it once, perhaps more often. This is a method used by earlier marketers who would mail out samples of modified products. Not only were they able to test for acceptance levels of the "new" item but it usually led to continued usage; having "owned" the item or as behavioral economist will tell you, because of the endowment effect they will keep on buying the product.

We should clarify the reference of product line strategies in contrast to product strategies. A company's product mix is the full range of products offered by the firm. A product line is a group of products that can be located within the product mix that are closely related, either because they function in a similar manner, are sold to the same customer groups, are marketed through the same types of outlets, or fall within given price ranges. It is often the case that responsibility for a given product line resides with a product-line manager who is responsible for the line, which means the full range of decisions from sourcing material for the product, its costing, and fit with customers.

Again, over time the product acceptance will decrease in terms of offering an expectation of higher benefit. Customers get tired of the same-old-same-old offering if it is not modified in some way as to encourage increased benefit. Automobiles are an example of this process and the example of General Motors gives emphasis on what not to do. The company was founded with a mission to satisfy the customer. When Henry Ford sold cars in "any color you wanted as long as it was black," General Motors responded to customer needs and offered a variety of colors and styles. Bur as the years progressed they took ownership of knowing what America wanted and built cars according to their idea about the needs of the car buyer.

Drucker tells us there are two kinds of changes in the market: (a) evolutionary change, which can be met with incremental changes and product line adjustment, and (b) a profound change in the market as occurred at the turn of the century and in the auto industry that were ignored by GM. Industry blogger Bob MacDonald[2] makes the point: "As changes for the industry emerged, the American auto makers continued to blithely barrel down the same highway they had been following for years and all that the management of GM did to respond was to seek round after round of cost cutting, restructuring and reorganization. Thousands of employees were laid off and management itself experienced more turnover than a pancake house. All to no avail. What the management of GM failed to recognize was that the change was not about costs and structure, but more fundamentally about product."

Sooner or later you will need to reassess your product line and remove those items no longer serving your customer no matter what "changes" you might attempt to make that you think will spice it up and generate more sales.

Product Strategies

Product strategies begin with the well-know Ansoff Grid (Table 6.1) that identifies a mix of product and market situations. Many corporations were reluctant to take any risk in the marketplace and they remained in the penetration strategies sector. The auto industry shied away from making large-scale changes and only introduced fuel injection systems decades after the Europeans had it in response to Japanese carmakers. After all, there was one sure way to jeopardize your year-end bonus and that was to come out with a new product that failed or enter a new market that did not reach its expected targets. It was far easier to put fins on the car and endure the mild ridicule rather than absorb the loss of face from failing to convince America of the need for seat belts and fail, as Ford and Chrysler did in 1956 to no avail. The history of corporate failure can be directly linked to the effort by executives to play it safe and remain in the risk-averse "product line" strategy of the penetration sector.

Penetration Strategies

Companies within an existing market will change the configuration of the product in a market penetration strategy where they will adjust the labeling or the package size and create a variety of product or brand lines. Packaging is the marketing activity of designing and producing containers to hold a product. It gives a special place in the advertising function because it is the first thing customers usually see and handle when purchasing a product. It is credited with building consumer affluence and standard of living because it allowed, if not encouraged, the world of self-service and product safety.

Marketers favor the use of packaging since it helps build company and brand image and leads to instant brand recognition. It encourages the

Table 6.1 Ansoff product grid

	Existing products	**New products**
Existing markets	Market penetration	Product development
New markets	Market development	Diversification

perception of product innovation and is used to target different segments. The typical objectives in packaging include:

- Using it to build brand identification
- Introducing important product information and specifications in product labeling
- Providing suitable packaging that enable transportation and the protection of goods
- Safety provisions, particularly in pharmaceuticals and other related products

Packaging is a form of incremental innovation that creates a perception of product or service change. Gillette, for example, began its shaving product with a single blade. As an innovation they introduced two blades, giving birth to Trac II and followed with the three-bladed Mach III. The Apple iPod is another popular example. The original unit came in plain white and enabled you to store and play your MP3 music collection only. Since then a number of incremental improvements have been added, such as different colors, and features such as storing your family photographs and even your video collection.

A second part of penetration strategy is to attach a higher level of value to the product or service through branding that item. Products from Apple and Gillette take on an identity that creates in the mind of the buyer a perception of value that enhances the desirability, and of course the price is higher too. Tide soap has retained its identity for almost two-thirds of a century even though the product itself has been upgraded tremendously along the way. The Tide soap that washed the rougher fabrics of the 1950s would not do well with the synthetic fabrics today. But the success of the brand is in the fact it does the job and does it well. It does give a brighter wash and that satisfaction is what retains its customers year after year after year. The lesson here is the need to deliver satisfaction, better yet to exceed satisfaction.

Market Development Strategies

Exporting is the simplest form of market extension and one that offers a company an easy route to rapid growth. On the other hand, it can also challenge the company's resources to such an extent it may cause hardship and failure in the effort. One study found that smaller exporters did not do very well extending their markets abroad. They lasted less than two years in exporting products with higher levels of failure being experienced by small firms over larger companies.[3] There are numerous obstacles to setting up a foreign operation that goes beyond language issues and cultural variations. The larger consumer goods companies as with Coca-Cola, McDonalds, Gillette, Apple, and others relied heavily on their brand acceptance that was, in some measure, preintroduced to the world through Hollywood movies, TV, and printed media. So when they entered those markets their products were generally accepted and gained market momentum quite easily.

Smaller and relatively unknown firms need to establish a strategic alliance with local companies to succeed. For example, Barbadian exporters of Solar Hot Water Heaters link up with local contractors in other countries in the Caribbean who are already in the business of instaling plumbing fixtures in those markets. Thus, the exporter needs only to work with one or two firms in a market, training them and supporting their domestic advertising efforts to penetrate the markets. Not having the need to make a direct investment in the country they can concentrate on providing stimulating support programs to their alliance contractors that will encourage sales growth.

Product Development Strategies

Large companies do not fare well in creating new products, particularly those that are radical or even disruptive. The caveat, however, is the role of a senior, creative champion who can literally force the organization to accept a new innovation. The literature generally supports the view that smaller firms are more innovative than larger corporations.[4] There is also evidence that the older the management in older firms, the more likely they are inclined to following a course of incremental innovation. The major deterrent to new product development is the risk factor. Senior executives get little reward for successful innovation in contrast to the risk associated with failure. Spending a lot of money on something that does not work in a large corporation is usually detrimental to one's career unless the culture is favorable to accepting risk as a precondition for successful innovation.

Companies that want to move out of the stagnating product line quad need to encourage an entrepreneurial development model. Many will promote the idea of a new product champion. We define a product champion as a unique individual in the organization, perhaps someone who would be quite entrepreneurial outside the organization. He or she is an entrepreneurial individual who[5]

- recognizes a new technology or market opportunity as having significant potential;
- adopts the project as his or her own;
- commits personally to the project;
- generates support from other people in the organization; and
- advocates vigorously for the project.

3M's approach to creativity, along with the use of "bootleg" time, which they copied from Hewlett Packard, gives employees a substantial bonus for products that are successfully introduced to the market. The company has engendered a culture in which employees know it is better to take a risk than do nothing. At the same time managers are encouraged to foster the intrapreneurial spirit and keep it going along with the regular business of the organization. There is, of course, the view that it is difficult to maintain this duality of creative work alongside usual work and that there should be a separation between the two. Some companies establish a separate innovative division within the firm and look to it to come up with innovative new products. Presumably this dividing of work effort makes sense but it likely depends on management style. 3M's program works well and may be the model that should be encouraged.[6]

A second issue is that larger corporations are inclined to co-opt the creative functions of a new innovative operation with bureaucratic procedure, centralization of control, and such. The surest way to kill creativity, goes one observation, is the presence of a conference room.

According to Bruce Herschensohn, of Pepperdine University's School of Public Policy, "Creativity always dies a quick death in rooms that house conference tables." Groups of people cannot be creative. The diversity of roles and hierarchy literally demand mediocre behavior, which is anathema to creativity. Thus, we see that the smaller, entrepreneurial organizations are best able to drive innovation and new product development. While it is true that large corporations spend more money on R&D than smaller firms, their output is far less when it comes to radical innovation.

Product Line Merchandizing

The company's product line is a group of items that are closely related because they perform a similar function, are sold to the same customer groups, are marketed through the same channels, or fall within given price ranges. The textbook strategies for product line action include the following.

Line stretching: This entails increasing the number of items in an existing product range (made up of similar products) that have additional or different or seemingly new features and perhaps lower pricing. When a company has a well-established brand it can use line stretching to expand the overall product line and help increase its share of market without taking the risk of trying to come up with a new product. However, the approach still has some risk since the competition may respond or the price difference may not be enough to encourage customers to accept the cheaper version.

Up-market and down-market stretch: The approach is to modify and price the product to appeal to a specially selected segment that is willing to pay more for a product, or one that expects a lower price. In the first case you are entering the high end of a market to improve growth and higher margins and on the other hand making adjustments to the product to appeal to a lower value perception.

Two-way stretch: Companies in a mid-position will enter both the high- and the low-end markets. These approaches can help the company to establish some market dominance over the competition.

For example, the Titan Watch company from India started as mid-level watch. It then introduced *Sonata* as a low-end brand then brought out the *Edge* and the *Xylus* to capture the high end. An interesting observation is that a high-end model of a low-end brand is preferred over a low-end model of a high-end brand.

Line modernization: Product lines need to change with the times and can be done piecemeal or all at once. If you do it piecemeal it allows a company to gauge the effect of change on consumers, but it also allows competitors to copy and pose greater challenge. The company may choose between featuring their most selling items and promoting their weak items from time to time. For this, they need to identify the less productive items and weed them out. For example, the Unilever Company found that only 400 of its 1600 products yielded over 90% of company's profits.

Line filling entails adding to the product line by introducing more items in the current inventory.

Titan Company Limited is the world's fifth largest watch company. It was formed as a joint venture between the Tata Group and the Tamil Nadu Industrial Development Corporation. It designs and manufactures a wide array of accessory products including watches, jewellery, and precision engineering components. It exports watches to nearly 40 countries around the world. Here is a list of the company's product lines in the watch line as it caters to a variety of different end-users. Note the variation of product values as the product targets very specific groups with what is essentially wrist watch.

Titan Edge—a product of innovative technology, the world's slimmest watch with a thickness of 3.5 mm. Its size is complemented by its sense of elegance and simplicity. The ultraslim design is achieved by a unique combination of style and technology. Moreover, the Titan Edge has more than 18 spinoffs in different materials such as stainless steel and gold.

Titan Fastrack—exemplary design and innovation, the high-selling brand was created by incorporating exemplary design and innovation appealing to the fashionable youth.

Titan Regalia—exclusively for men and it is available in both gold and silver. It is big, and suited to the large wrist.

Titan Raga Diva—exclusively for women, it symbolizes all that is feminine with the Isisa, Selene, Kiara, and Freya as some of the watches found in this collection.

Titan Bandhan—a set of two or a pair, the majestic Bandhan collection is meant for a couple and meant to cement the bond between a man and a woman.

Titan Nebula—a fantastic piece cast in solid 18-karat gold and other precious stones, the heavily jeweled timepieces are available for both men and women, worth its weight in gold.

Titan Heritage—the luxurious brands under this collection are inspired by the great Indian cultural and spiritual heritage such as the Sun God and the Taj Mahal.

Titan Orion—*embodies* masculinity for the 21st century man, with Alpha, Leo Aries, Centaur, Delphin as star brands making up this constellation.

Titan Octane—a multifunctional chronographs under the Octane stable made to guarantee best performance for every sportsman.

Titan WWF—themed watches for the nature lovers, the Rhino, Turtle, Dolphin, Whale, and Red Panda, are elegantly designed watches in the campaign for the protection of the endangered species.

Titan Sonata—favorite with the working class, a well-respected brand, affordably priced but maintaining the very high quality of the Titan brand.

Titan Zoop—an elegant and sophisticated watch for your child in a wide variety.

What we see in the Titan array is a modification to the watch that aligns the main product and directs value to specific targets in the consumer market. The value in the timepiece is as much in its decorative presentation as its function of telling the time. Thus, we see a cosmetic application, an incremental innovation you might say that draws the customer's attention to the extrinsic rather than the intrinsic value of the watch. And it works well.

Expanding Product or Brand Position

Another example of developing an expanding strategy to grab shelf dominance is the case of the product line for Little Remedies®, a nonprescription line of medicines and other wellness products for infants and children 12 years old and younger. One of the more important benefits of having a wide product line like that for Little Remedies® is it enables both consumers and retailers to simplify their buying decisions. For example, if a family has a good experience with its four-year-old's sore throat with Little Remedies® Honey Pops the family might consider its Little Remedies® Decongestant Nose Drops if the child's cold causes a stuffed nose.

Little Remedies® product line.

A particular benefit that accrues to Little Remedies® is that the company can obtain distribution in retail chains like Babies "R" Us and Walmart because its extensive product line enables these chains to contract with a single supplier and avoid having to deal with several different suppliers, often an expensive and time-consuming process.

The strategy combines the use of incremental innovation in making formula adjustments to the cold remedy that will provide relief to different symptoms of the same malady virus to different segments within the children's cold-relief market. The company can now combine its advertising message within one presentation to the mass market with an emotional appeal that will stir the maternal desire to give assistance to children and it offers increased revenue through multiple purchases as well.

Product Line Pricing

Product line pricing strategy comes into play as a competitive factor because the line or extended variation of the same product allows the firm to make price adjustments based on the different perceptions of these various packages. First, the management must deal with the line as a whole when it comes to pricing. Products are normally not introduced in a full line; they are brought out one at a time so the analysis of each product variation has to include keeping track of the product life cycle (PLC) for each of these. Managers need to keep in mind how interrelated the products might be when deciding on the removal or reduction of a product from the line as a whole, as well as the timing of a replacement product and how all the products in the line continue to work together.

You will establish your pricing strategy by reviewing the entire line, its profitability on an individual and collective basis, and then realigning the prices to meet with or exceed what the competition is doing. However, we should always remember that price changes are easiest to deal with by the competition. It becomes target and we really need to have some value affixed to the products if we want to keep a competitive advantage. At this point, we can bring into play the lost leader tactic for some of the items (or SKUs in retailing) when we can stress value in other items being carried to which the customer may then bend his or her attention and purchase. We are told[8] that another way to look at product line pricing is to analyze the importance of one or more products to the whole line. For example, for a car dealership, the car model is the product, and the accessories, extended warranties, service package, color, sunroof, and other options are the rest of the line items. Those line items would be rather meaningless, for the most part, without the car as the primary product.

We also need to bring into play a strong promotional campaign to support the pricing strategy, which, if we have good brand equity, will give some impetus to the strategy. In this we will need to highlight the features and likely the differences between items in the line to differentiate the value proposition we are setting in to play. The buyer clearly needs to appreciate the pricing and value differences between the products and within the line.

Product Positioning

Your product has a position in the mind's-eye of your customer. Ever since Trout and Ries[9] introduced the concept, marketers have used it to build their product strategies. In most cases, the campaign revolves around a central attribute or product feature. In the auto industry, Lexus and BMW command a leading position in the up-market segment where Lexus is noted for its *comfort* status and BMW weighs in for its *performance*. Both brands give heavy emphasis to these in their advertising and promotional efforts. Recently, Lexus decided to increase its marketshare by going after a portion of the BMW market with its IS-F high-performance model. This move launched the successful growth for the company and despite a drop over the 2008 period, the company has gained a solid sales reputation in the BMW market.

The fast food market offers a similar example of developing a product identification that links to customer satisfaction. McDonalds has developed its offering as being a *fun* food since it appeals to children with its fantasy campaigns. In contrast to this Subway promotes a *healthy* image. In both these examples we see the association of the product features with a brand activity that develops strategies from both the product line and the brand quad.

Improving Service

As with the cost-price leadership quad the competitive advantage in the product line quad is greatly enhanced with service. Paraphrasing an old real estate statement the new mantra in customer relations is service, service, service! There is a critical need to engage the customer, to make him or her "partner" in the business, and to always provide excellent satisfaction through quality service as bundled in the delivery of quality products and services. Here is what one important source[10] has to say about customer service "When two marketers are competing for the same customer's business, all other things being equal, the marketer with the greatest scope of information about that particular customer—the marketer with the most extensive and intimate relationship with that customer—will be the more efficient competitor." The ability to give service to your customer begins with knowing her or his needs and crafting your products and services, along with the entire communication process to incorporate those needs, wants, and desires.

When your company occupies the realm of price-cost sensitivity, the leading instrument you have is to engage and keep the customer through service. We know that people don't necessarily buy products or services; they also buy relationships. The purchasing activity is a human undertaking. It is based on how well one person deals with any other. If you ask a company purchasing agent or a consumer why they leave one supplier or another, the number one reason is based on how they were treated." Smart companies understand the value of their current customer base, and recognizing what they need to do in order to keep them. By focusing on the customers, the smart companies are really broadening their customer base by increased referrals."[11]

So service and continued solid relationship management is what carries the day in the product line quadrant.

Service through Technology

The growing importance of technology is evident in how much we rely on the Internet with mobile devices and all the apps associated with them. We now chat about droids, droid apps, a whole hosting of software anagrams from ERPs to SCMs. Then there is a whole host of a 10,000-plus word jargon list[12] of technical terms we use, ranging from 32-bit IP address, BitTorrent, browser hijacker to Mac OS X Lion, macro instruction, macro virus, and Y2K and zphone. It is really astounding that in the course of only a decade and a half we have literally created a new branch of the English language devoted to the Information Age technology.

But more than language itself the technology in a way more profound than any other technology in our time has created a new way of life, living, handling transactions, and human relationships. It is remarkably a new and profoundly different world. It also gives us new ways to deal with and serve our customers. We can now easily respond to and connect with customers by using a cloud computing service, for example, coupled with software programs that allow us to interact with customers via several channels simultaneously, such as e-mail, call centers, Twitter, and

Facebook, with an application that operates entirely in a web browser. Not only do small businesses and medium-sized businesses have access to world-class technology that they've never had access to before but they are able to use the tools that the big companies are using to our own advantage.

Customer Relationship Management

A major challenge for small businesses today is in optimizing customer satisfaction and developing customer relationship management.[13] It has become the in-thing to do; consultants stress it, colleges are teaching it, and customers ask for it as a means to retaining customers. Even so, it seems that the customer satisfaction rating has dropped in nearly every sector of the economy according to the American Customer Satisfaction Index compiled by the University of Michigan. What's happening? Why has this seemingly important management tool not done the job?

When adopting what appears to be a unique new methodology we often forget about the basics and try to make a template of the innovation so we can easily apply it, in this case to our customers. What we really need is to keep in mind are the four basics of the program: a comprehensive strategy, motivating the team, effective use of relationship skills, and the engagement of feedback and adjustment.

Set a well defined customer strategy: We want to continue the happy experience the customer enjoyed by using our product in the first place. We begin with a fully integrated understanding of our mission and purpose and what we expect to achieve. Customer service has to be an integral part of our communications effort and that we are not merely going through an exercise that will pass in time. Customer relationship management is an important, ongoing part of any strategy and everyone in the organization needs to incorporate the concept. And it has to be a consistent effort. We cannot call for an improved customer service function as a priority on the one hand and then see management incept tough cost-cutting measures that hinder the service we want to administer to our customers.

Motivating your team: It begins with training. Properly trained people are properly motivated people who understand what is needed and how to carry it off. While it is evident we have people who are technically and functionally able to carry out their jobs, we also need people who have the correct attitude in providing customer satisfaction. Here is a quote from a famous spiritual author, Edwin H. Friedman:

> The colossal misunderstanding of our time is the assumption that insight will work with people who are unmotivated to change. Communication does not depend on syntax, or eloquence, or rhetoric, or articulation but on the emotional context in which the message is being heard. People can only hear you when they are moving toward you, and they are not likely to when your words are pursuing them. Even the choice of words lose cachet when they are used to overpower. Attitudes are the real figures of speech.

When we recruit people for customer relations jobs we tend to hire on the basis of their expertise or technical competence and knowledge and overlook their interpersonal skills. But the right attitude is far more important. As Friedman tells us, it is the real language of communication. We know that having the right attitude can strongly impact the client satisfaction levels. You have got to have a good attitude, it is important because we can train people to do the job, but we can't always give them the attitude.

Customer relationship skills: Your people need to be trained and motivated to carry out the customer relations services for the company. But since they are exposed to a variety of demand and sometimes aggressive customers, they will need to be retrained or at least "buffed" up from time to time and submitted to attitude reaffirmation. The technical and functional elements of the job are important, but these take a backseat to positive, helpful, and entrepreneurial dynamics in dealing with the customer. Research has shown that a quick and sensitive response to a customer issue can alleviate and turn a bad situation into a positive opportunity to reinforce the product or service worth and value.

Monitor and adjust: You need to know how things are going. Sales reports and customer service reports—and complaints too!—are an important flow of information back to the company about how well you are doing. Customers get ignored or things slip through the cracks and they get agitated. It is very important that you know about all these and are able to take remedial steps immediately. The ability to implement and effective "recovery" is a very important differentiator in building customer loyalty.

Improving Price Competition with Cost Reduction

The product line quadrant is in the cost-price domain where the perception of value, along with the PLC has moved toward the cost rather than value side of customer acuity. To remain competitive at this level the company has to reduce its costs as much as possible. Whatever economies of scale there are must be improved to stay competitive. The need is to introduce technology and other control mechanisms that will reduce labor, materials, and money or otherwise improve productivity.

The use of software to improve on systems management offers a sustainable method for cutting costs. One such program is the ERP system SMEs. The use of the technique was found to be most positive for companies, based on a survey by Aberdeen Group.[14] Companies in the survey found there were savings that could be passed on in price reductions that included manufacturing cost reductions as well as savings in inventory, administration, and timeliness.

Business Benefits Derived from ERP

Reduction in operating costs	21%
Reduction in administrative costs	19%
Reduction in inventory	17%
Improvement in schedule compliance	16%
Improvement in complete and on-time shipping	17%

Improvements in supply chain management can also have an effect on cost reduction where suppliers are able to effect savings of their own that can be passed on.

Process Cost Savings

We discussed the use of methods to improve on operations costs, which can be applied to manufacturing, administration, and most any other process or procedure within the organization. It really is the application of analytical methods to the activities people undertake to make, produce, ship, store, or process products and services. The primary standard is lean manufacturing or the techniques used to assess how the process might be improved and costs cut back, without the loss of quality of course.

The Outsourcing Calamity

One of the difficulties with the American economy has been the loss of jobs due to outsourcing. Many companies, particularly those in the cost-price quad rushed to relocate their manufacturing to Asian sources. In the short term it no doubt helped these organizations to improve the bottom line, perhaps their very survival. But this is and has been a temporary solution. What was really called for was the application of good old-fashioned American entrepreneurship and innovation to the cost problems by bringing in technology to reduce costs and keep jobs at home.

Companies moved off-shoring to cut labor cost because countries such as China and Thailand had daily wages much below labor costs back home. But now there is evidence that foreign workers are demanding higher wages, thus reducing the gap and those savings, in combination with transport cost, fuel, insurance, financing, and inventory are making it problematic that there is any cost advantage. Then there is the realization that while there have been perceived savings in manufacturing, there have been growing issues with quality and timeliness. And finally, with the loss of so many jobs and the amount of tax dollars vanishing from the economy there is possibility that the government will place a tax on imported goods across a whole range of products to both raise money and to protect the remaining industry from cheap labor.

We know that lean manufacturing does improve productivity. It reduces inventory and frees up working capital, reduces space required, produces less scrap, and still provides the needed quality, if not, in fact, improving it. And you get to keep your technology. As a strategy it has much to recommend it.

Summarizing Product Line Strategies

Product line strategies are a short-term strategy. One could almost say it is a tactic since there is some evidence it does not maximize effectiveness and profitability in the long run. However, there are certain product categories that serve over a longer life cycle and can almost be commodities. Some common items would include fasteners, nails, plumbing supplies, and on over to spices, condiments, and basics as in oatmeal, molasses, basic clothing, and so forth. These can rely on product line strategies for longer periods of time. The contrast is seen in the more advanced articles as with electronic devices, automobiles, fashionable clothing, and production tools and machinery.

The main strategies for this quad can be summarized in five areas: cost reduction, service improvements, incremental innovation, brand strengthening, and pricing.

Cost Reduction

The use of software, lean manufacturing, and other methods of cutting costs to allow improved pricing strategies. The activity will take into account supply chain reductions and perhaps even supplier price cuts. It may stimulate improved delivery and distribution methods and decreases in administrative costs through improved digital methods as with the Internet and reduction of paper work.

Service Improvement

A countermeasure to reducing prices is to increase value through improved services. Distributors of alloyed metals—stainless steel, copper plate, zinc sheets and so on—can offer cut-to-size and inventory services to offset cuts by competitors as an increased value proposition. Tailors may throw in extra adjustments, restaurants offer free additional coffee or desserts.

Incremental Innovation

Adjustments to packaging design can affect a "different" look to a product. Of course, unlike the Japanese who treasure the way a gift is packaged more so perhaps than the gift, customers look for real value in the end product. Some techniques make use of the package as the storage unit. Consumer goods producers add a little extra content to the package and small changes to product without increasing costs are used to add value.

Brand Strengthening

Companies will cobrand with others to improve product value. Starbucks and Nescafe recently signed a deal to enhance their brands. According to the *Puget Sound Business Journal* (July 19, 2007) the premium brand will "translate Starbucks coffeehouse flavors into delicious and distinct chocolate products," and officials at the Seattle coffee giant (NASDAQ: SBUX) said the chocolate will be sold "in a broad range of retail channels such as food, drug and mass merchandise outlets."

Price Reduction

It may be the case the firm has no choice but to lower prices, perhaps on specific product line items rather than the whole line. The question is: How deep should the cuts be? Obviously, the need is to stimulate sales and improve overall profit. Yet there is the always prevalent competitor who can and just may equally make the same cut or do a bit better and the war is on, so to speak. With B2B sales, a price cut to get the order may be managed with less regard for the competition, particularly in a large capital goods sale.

The final strategic move, however, is to innovate and rebuild the product to more sharply appeal to present and future customer needs. Companies cannot long stand still nor rest on the laurels of a success that grows older. They must be ever alert to new opportunities in meeting and exceeding customer expectations, the need to be more entrepreneurial than the competition.

CHAPTER 7

Brand Strategies

A brand for a company is like a reputation for a person. You earn reputation by trying to do hard things well.

—Jeff Bezos

Everybody knows what a brand is. We have brand name clothing, soft drinks, automobiles, airlines, and even political parties. The term originated as a method to differentiate one product from another when, during the industrialization period the production of consumer goods moved from small,

	Shrink to 1" x 1" or so
Low cost Hi product line	Hi value Hi innovation
Low cost Standard product	**X** Hi value Hi reputation

cottage, suppliers to mass produced plants. In those days the manufacturers would, literally, burn their name into the wooden barrels and containers they used to ship goods around the country. This served two purposes: one as to the contents and the other as identification as to the legitimate source for the product. Getting something *brand new* was quite a distinction, it meant it was not handmade, used, or a hand me down.

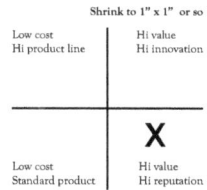

It was J.W. Thompson, a psychologist, who at the turn of the 20th century launched a major advertising agency and began to apply the comparatively new concepts of branding and trademark to advertising. In time companies soon adopted slogans, mascots, and jingles that appeared on radio and early television to identify their goods and services. From there on companies soon learned to build their brand's identity and relate it to personality such as youthfulness, fun, or luxury. It has become a practice we now know as *branding* where consumers buy the brand instead of the product. The trend continued to the 1980s and is now measured in terms of brand value and brand equity.

Your company must create and sustain a brand name for your product or organization, or both. The name you select should reflect what you do and convey all the genetics possible of the value your product will provide the customer. It needs to appeal for the most part to the cognitive, affective, and conative or experiential components of perception and decision processes. Cognitive information is the purely factual data, the logical aspects of what it will do for the customer. The affective dimensions include emotional elements, humor, affection, fear, and so on, that are called into play in solving the problem with the help of the brand. Then there is the more tangible experiential side of the brand image. Perhaps the customer has used it and the fact that it has worked left the clothing bright and clean with a pleasant aroma comes to mind, reinforcing the power and effect of Tide soap. The effect of word-of-mouth and digital "buzz" can express the same response. In the future, with the rising technologies of the Internet the ability to provide a feel for the product in a virtual setting will do the same thing.

The Brand Strategy Quad

Products and services in this quad are characterized by a perception of value for what usually is an established standard good. On one hand, it might be seen to be unique and important with a strong brand image that has either been modified through incremental innovation or it can be what might be considered a commodity that has had strong promotional support. Many household items—toiletries, cosmetics, and cleansers, for example—are slightly modified from time to time to keep the offering current while others, as with beer brands, rely on heavy advertising to give the impression of higher performance and value (Figure 7.1). We are often reminded of the "good time to come" if we drink a certain brand.

Then there are businesses and organizations (lawyers, engineers, NGOs) that retain the strength of their company's imagery or brand by doing well in what they know best; there is an element of trust in what is being promoted and perhaps emotion too. You are encouraged to turn to the services of one legal firm or another to make sure that your special case receives justice (and a large quantity of money) by using

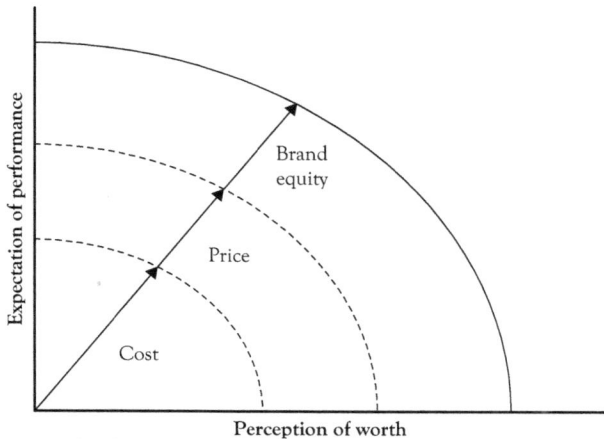

Figure 7.1 Brand value and performance—worth

their services. Of course, these enterprises have proven their worth and as long as they continue to do so the brand stays strong and value is continued. Also companies develop an overarching brand identification under which they launch their individual products. The Apple brand covers all its products and encourages a mix of brand strategies. For the PC the Mac is a branded product under the Apple name. On the other hand, the individual iPods, iPads, and iPhones are branded under the umbrella of the Apple name.

Of course, there is also the emotional investment people make in their favored brands as evident in Coca-Cola's attempt to introduce a new Coke a few years ago. After millions of dollars in market research to come up with a powerful and appealing taste experience, the company announced a "new Coke." The reaction was enormously negative. The brand had taken on an identity with the national self-image; it was a cultural icon of America! How dare someone change it? The uproar was so great the company had to reinstate the old Coke.

Your product in this quadrant can be moved into a strong market position as long as the expectation of performance remains high and the perception of value or quality is consistent with that expectation. The total perception of value or your brand equity must be matched with a commensurate expectation of performance to the buyer. In this position, your product or service can be sustained for some time with strong promotional strategies. Eventually, however, it drifts into the cost-price leadership sector where the brand is acknowledged and accepted, but there is not enough value to command a strong price position and you now need to apply cost-cutting strategies and process improvement tactics to maintain market share. Of course, your margins are not what they once were and it comes time to look at radical innovation to put you back into the innovation quad.

Strategy Overview

The value–utility quadrant is a temporary position, although for some brands or corporate reputations (image) it can last for some time. The purchase of a soft drink, Coca-Cola for example, requires little decision making. It is almost an impulse buy and so the strength of the brand image is what disposes the customer to make the purchase. A user product, such as Tide detergent, needs to meet varying conditions and so requires modifying changes from time to time combined with a strong promotional thrust to build and maintain its position. In both cases, when the strength of the image fades in the customer's mind so does the desire to make the purchase.

Each brand takes a differing position in the quadrant. Tide detergent continuously presents a new and improved image. It proclaims that it washes brighter and gentler because of its knowhow and technology. Thus, we see a drive to relocate into the innovation quadrant that justifies a higher price for the product (Figure 7.2). Many major brands present in this manner and the stronger the implication of innovation, the better the company is able to realize a higher price. In other words, the better the brand equity, the better your pricing strategy.

Coca-Cola has a strong brand image that assures acceptance and purchase from loyal customers. However, while the brand is satisfying and perhaps is a habitual purchase, it does not command a sense of value that allows a higher price than the competition. In fact, it often must balance its strategy with pricing issues as it competes with other cola drinks. Here we see the importance of innovation in strengthening the brand position.

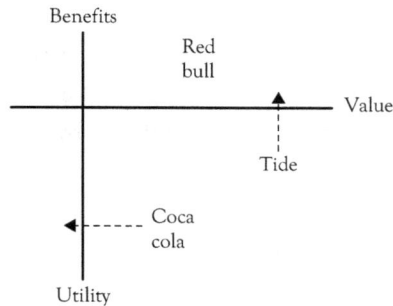

Figure 7.2 Brand location

It was likely this line of thinking that prompted Coca-Cola to come out with all new Coke in an effort to move into the innovation quad.

We see how the move to an innovation strategy has had an effect on the soda market with the entry of energy drinks from Red Bull and others that offer increased personal performance. The proposition of an energy drink, backed by a superb promotional campaign, has moved these new brands into the market and taken a position by offering something more than just "life" or thirst quenching. There is a new way of experiencing life using these products. However, it is really not a new phenomenon. Jolt Cola was introduced in 1985 with a marketing strategy centered on caffeine content to promote wakefulness. It was followed by others and in 1997 Red Bull charged its way into the market. By 2012 the energy drink market became a $37 billion market globally, with 36% of that in America. Its customer base comprises people between 13 and 35 years of age. They are mostly males, college or high school students, who use the product to stay awake for studying or for athletes who use them before games to gain energy. Much of its brand strength comes from their very strategic sponsorship campaign[1] that costs a fraction of what would be required to generate the same buzz.

The Need for a Brand Name

The brand is your company's identity whether it applies to your business name, products, or services. It goes beyond the logo on your print and

TV ads. It tells your customers, future and existing, who you are and what you stand for. A good brand will position your company over that of the competition and becomes your advantage in the marketplace, especially when it comes to setting your price levels. So by creating an active and dynamic brand presence, you differentiate yourself from your competition and encourage an equitable price too.

The brand defines who you are and introduces your company and product to all your future and current customers. The 1958 McGraw-Hill advertisement is a classic in the industry and makes a strong argument in support of advertising and good brand identification. It makes the challenging statements:

I don't know who you are.
I don't know your company.
I don't know your company's product.
I don't know what your company stands for.
I don't know your company's customers.
I don't know your company's record.
I don't know your company's reputation.
Now, what is it you want to sell me?

The brand image establishes credibility for you and your goods or services. It serves as a qualifying factor that introduces what you have to offer to your customer and those who would be your customer in the future. And it relies on continuous advertising and promotional support. William Wrigley, the chewing gum king, observed that advertising can be compared to powering the engines on an airplane; once they stop the airplane will fall and so too would your brand.

Brand Strategy

Marketers will develop an image as to a brand's purpose in appealing to and satisfying customer needs and one that is tied to value, market share, and profits. Quite often, the company assigns a brand manager to look after the brand where there may be a number of brands in the company product portfolio. They will target a brand position in the mental imagery of the customer's mind that will locate the benefits and value they expect the brand fulfill for the customer.

The primary thrust is to establish a brand position in the market-place. Positioning strategy is a very detailed and specific part of the marketing campaign since it provides the direction that is required to focus the entire company. Disney, for example, has the position of family fun entertainment, McDonalds is food and fun, while Apple is innovation.

Marketers strive to create a brand promise, or brand proposition, which is also known as the *brand statement*. The brand statement lists the benefits of using your company's products or services. For instance, a health food brand promise would present the energy, longevity, and good feeling, while an auto company would promise safety, reliability, and even social status in the new car model. Here are a few points that a brand promise should display:

- It should be grounded in the core values that are inherent in the brand.
- The drives and cues should be directed to a specific target market.
- There needs to be a strong emotional attachment that is positive and strong.
- It must be continuously reinforced and consistent within the mediums used.

Brand strategy is all inclusive of the product it represents. The same can be said of an organization that establishes a company image and brand or reputation identity. Brands follow a progression from introduction to awareness then acceptance and on to insistence. At first, it is important to gain an awareness of the product and its identity. Gillette invested heavily in giving out samples to make people aware of its shaving equipment. After some period, brand acceptance takes place as promised it delivers on its values and promise it reached a brand preference condition that assures a certain market position.

However, in the ever-changing climate of customer satisfaction, the emphasis continues to lock-in the customer and brand loyalty is the final objective, thus assuring repeat sales over the customer lifetime of usage. When all this is realized in whole or in part, we gain a distinction of having brand equity. This is defined the consequence of marketing efforts in creating a value perception beyond what we would have had without the brand development. Wikipedia tells us that brand equity is one of the factors that can increase the financial value of a brand to the brand owner, although not the only one. "Elements that can be included in the valuation of brand equity include (but not limited to): changing market share, profit margins, consumer recognition of logos and other visual elements, brand language associations made by consumers, consumers' perceptions of quality, and other relevant brand values."

The Latest Word on Branding

The need to establish a brand name or a good reputation for that matter is critically important to the firm that wants to survive and grow. The "miracle" life cycle of Apple, Coca-Cola, and Microsoft whose brand names are worth billions of dollars is their longevity. Table 7.1 shows the worth of the top ten brands in the world. The brands refer to the company and their products also carry the same brand identity. Apple, for example, has the Apple line of iPods, iPhones, iPads, and so on. You will note the products change almost every year, while the brand remains. An example of this importance is the fact that Proctor and Gamble's Tide brand has remained constant, but the product has changed incrementally over the years to accommodate changes in fabrics and mechanical washing machine technologies.

The top brand in 2012 was Apple estimated, at $185 billion, followed by Google at $114 billion, and IBM at $113 billion. The power of these brands is in their ability to evoke a rapid recognition in customers' minds and purchase. A brand removes most of the doubt one has and the risk in buying the item.

Table 7.1 Top global brands 2013

Rank	Company	Brand value billions USD
1	Apple	185.1
2	Google	113.7
3	IBM	112.5
4	McDonald's	90.3
5	Coca Cola	78.4
6	AT&T	75.5
7	Microsoft	69.8
8	Marlborough	69.4
9	Visa	56.1
10	G.E.	55.4

Source: Millward Brand[1]. http://www.millwardbrown.com/brandz/ Top_100_Global_Brands.aspx

Brand Divergence

But brands evolve. They do so as a form of evolution. In the recent book on the *Origin of Brands,*[2] Ries draw a leaf from Darwin in comparing brand evolution to that of Darwin's theory of two key components: evolution and divergence. Evolution was the adaption of species to the environment, which enabled a continued existence. This was referred to as survival of the fittest implying a more dramatic adjustment when in fact such was not the case. Divergence, on the other hand, is described as indiscriminate changes that produce new branches off of the ancestral tree, with the emergence of new species from the divergence of existing species.

The book describes the divergence as the driver toward a unique and effective strategy for effective branding. The rapid changes in the marketplace are creating numerous opportunities for companies to create new brands and to use these to gain position and improved bottom line figures. But to succeed you must create new categories first and then create a new brand in this category using a technique called category divergence. Ries tell us there are five remarkable strategies we can apply to move the brand

and the organization forward. The following observations are sourced from the book.

> Divide & conquer. *Every category tends to expand in many different directions, creating opportunities for narrowly focused brands. The typical American coffee shop that served everything has been upstaged by chains that focus on hamburgers (McDonald's), chicken (Kentucky Fried Chicken), pizza (Pizza Hut), donuts (Dunkin' Donuts), submarine sandwiches (Subway), roast beef (Arby's), ice cream (Baskin-Robbins), and many others.*
>
> Exploit divergence. *As time goes on, every category tends to branch off, creating many opportunities to build new brands. The soft-drink category branched off to produce a cinnamon-flavored drink (Dr Pepper), an all-natural drink (Snapple), a sports drink (Gatorade), an energy drink (Red Bull), and many others.*
>
> Survival of the firstest. *The first brand into the mind has an enormous advantage. Amazon, California Closets, Nike, PowerBar, Swatch, Starbucks, WD40, and many others. A small lead early in the game can become an insurmountable lead later on.*

Brands Don't Always Work

Brands aren't as powerful as they used to be.[3] Experience is now more important than brand name as the basis for a person's purchasing decision. The Internet allows people to share experiences about a company with millions of others. People now choose the products that give them the highest value, not just the best-known brands. Relying on a strong brand name is no longer enough. Consistent, predictable innovation is the answer. Each year, Tide researchers duplicate the mineral content of water from all parts of the United States and wash 50,000 loads of laundry to test Tide detergent's consistency and performance. When they find a problem they make adjustments to the brand's chemical composition.

On occasion companies with a strong brand will attempt to extend its effect to new products they want to put on the market. If the product is strongly aligned with an existing product or at least it is consistent with the genre of the existing brand line it can work very well. However, there have been some notable exceptions where firms have tried to overextend their coverage. For example, Harley Davidson made a bid to enter the perfume market and failed miserably. Apparently, the smell of exhaust fumes trumped the gentle aroma of cologne. On the other hand, the extension worked when they pushed their line chain of shops with a wide variety of branded merchandise: Harley Davidson T-shirts, socks, cigarette lighters, and ornaments.

The same experience took place when Sir Richard Branson extended the Virgin line into the cola arena. In the U.K. people wake up to Virgin Radio, put on Virgin clothes and make-up, drive a car purchased and financed through a Virgin bank. They may call a friend at a Virgin Active gym on a Virgin mobile phone or use the Virgin Internet service to shop or see what is on at a Virgin cinema. They may catch a Virgin train or plane, play a Virgin video game as they sip Virgin vodka at a Virgin hotel where they met someone and bought some Virgin condoms. But when they took on Coca-Cola with Virgin cola, it did not work.

Brand Rebranding

Over time, your brand will lose its luster. Despite ongoing promotional campaigns, the image begins to fade in the mind of customers where it can be challenged by another product that promises better performance. Some commodities, as with the cola drinks, have carved a cultural niche in the psyche of consumers and seemingly hold their position for a long time. But eventually, the product must be modified either with technology or improved service where it is seen to perform better than previously was the case.

The changing social, political, cultural, and technical fabric of society induces an expectation of better performance in goods and services. It is not likely those of us who shave each day with a Gillette product, for example, would be willing to return to the single blade of yesteryear. Customers are attracted to new ways and things that promise an improvement to life style and living. And your customer needs to feel your brand is changing too. Pepsi-Cola has changed its brand image 11 different times. While today the company brands its product with a performance promise that it will *"Refresh everything,"* not many can recall the promise Pepsi used before that assured customers *"It's the cola,"* or before that of *"The joy of Pepsi."* Here we see a brand recycle activity that modifies the expectation of service. Pepsico's management is committed to constant change. The company's CEO, Indra Nooyi, believes that "Every 5 or 7 years you've got to change out the approach to the brand, because you need a new boost of energy to think about the next iteration."

Al Reis[4] illustrates the importance of rebranding as a countermeasure to offset a brand failure. He brings into the discussion the experience of Tiger Woods whose brand appeal literally collapsed with the exposure of his affairs with ladies other than his wife. In a recent article he tells us there is only one rule: Go back to the Basics; the brand should stick to its original purpose. In Tiger Woods case it was by returning to golf and until his loss in 2012 to Brandt Snedeker for the Fed-Ex cup he won more PGA tournaments than any other golfer. Reis tells us there's a psychological reason why this works. It's because people can't retain two contradictory ideas in their minds, like "bad" person and "good" golfer. By emphasizing the good-golfer concept, the bad-person concept starts to fade away. The same thing holds for brands. We only have to reflect on the BP disaster of a few years ago and the fact that people now look on BP more favorably than they did before.

Summarization of Brand Strategies

Brands aren't as powerful as they used to be. Experience is now more important than brand name as the basis for a person's purchasing decision. The Internet allows people to share experiences about a company with millions of others. People now choose the products that give them the highest value, not just the best-known brands. Relying on a strong brand name is no longer enough. Consistent, predictable innovation is the answer. Tide soap has been chemically changed dozens of times to meet the changes in fabrics, washing media, and environmental issues. But the brand name keeps sales increasing and a lock on market position. The branding quad strategies can be summed up in the application of four key strategic moves: strengthening the value proposition, building on service reinforcement, pricing margin strategies, and innovation.

The Value Proposition

The confluence of the expectation a customer has of performance and her or his perception of value about your product is the meeting place where your brand reaches its value proposition. The degree to which your product or service meets and exceeds the expectations your customer has about your product is what commands a value perception and the value proposition itself. The considerable difficulty people had with trying to sign on to the U.S. Affordable Care (Obamacare) Act is a case in point. While many people supported the Act they became dissatisfied with the difficulties they experienced in trying to sign on to the program. This failure of IT technology colored the image people had of their expectation and lowered, at least temporarily, the value of the Act. Fortunately, the government worked out the glitches and the product or brand became accepted.

In communicating the expectation of performance, it is important that the cues presented in the message have integrity and accurately convey the representation of what the brand will do. Using effective customer research you can clearly identify the important attributes that customers accept and the type of emotion that is expressed by them when they think of the brand (Figure 7.3). The image of Tide detergent customers strongly turning down an offering of two of the leading competitive brands in return for one of a customer's Tide is a strong message that combines emotion and attribute strength.

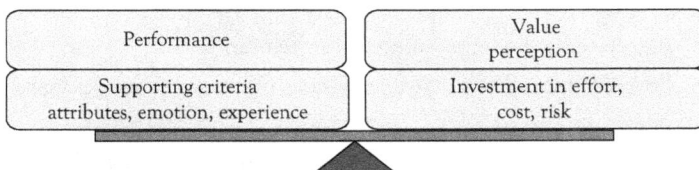

Figure 7.3 The value proposition

A second but equally important issue is balancing the perception of value with a customer's notion of cost including effort, risk, and monetary effect. Depending on the degree of involvement with the product or service, customers will invest some time in shopping around and travel for items they consider are important to them. Meanwhile, lesser items, commodity type products, for example, do not command the same desire.

Strengthening the value proposition means you will retain your position in the quad if not advance it toward a stronger brand equity and the ability to use improved pricing strategies.

Service Reinforcement

The credibility of your brand and contribution to the value proposition is also evident in how well the brand is supported in the service process. You enter a shop to pick up your favorite brand of single malt whiskey and the clerk is rude and brusque. You may brush that behavior aside but still and all you still wonder is why your favorite brand is placed in a shop that has bad service. Or you return a faulty kitchen appliance to your local hardware store and are treated as though you are attempting to pull a fast one on the company. Again you might forgive the bad service, but still will wonder how a reputable supplier can allow such poor assistance. Again the brand is threatened.

Maintenance of your position and strengthening its demand will occur with a strong service policy at all levels of the supply chain system. People have a tendency to recall only their last experience with an event or the conviction of esteemed friends or neighbors in the service that is associated with your brand. Consequently, there is a need to continually implement and even improve the service support for the brand. The following are but a few of the many ways you can easily increase brand value:

- Reiterate the benefits inherent in the brand
- Provide credibility for your attribute features and emotional ties to the product
- Reduce the effort to purchase the item in both clicks and mortar applications

- Improve customer interface communications wherever possible
- Reduce all perceptions of risk in acquiring the item
- Focus on the real target audience

Pricing Margin Strategies

Pricing is directly related to the value proposition. Ideally, the price could be set at the outer boundary of the brand equity curve (Figure 7.1) where performance expectations and value perception are a maximum. Of course, because all customers do not have exactly the same perceptions, it really behooves the marketer to scale back from that point to a place where most if not all will accept the listed price. Still and all there is room to maintain a higher price when possible. In fact, there is a compelling reason to do so. If we set a price too high, the chances are we will lose revenue, but of more importance is: If we engage a low price that is too low, we leave a lot of revenue on the table.

Table 7.2 offers an interesting discussion on the importance of judging where a price might be set, particularly if we have a strong brand value and position. An adjustment of only 1% has the effect of increasing the bottom line by 20%. If we can accept that our brand position is strong enough to justify as little as an incremental increase the benefit in the company's profit picture is very significant.

The example lends support for the discussion on blending pricing methods that occur when delivering a number of discounts to customers. By cutting price levels under one condition but increasing them due to

Table 7.2 Impact of a 1% price increase*

	Before	After	Net change
Revenues	$1,000,000	$1,010,000	1%
COGS	700,000	700,000	–
Gross margin	300,000	310,000	3.3%
SG&A	250,000	250,000	–
Net income	50,000	60,000	20%

Source: *See Harvard Site http://hbsp.harvard.edu/multimedia/flashtools/pricing/

other considerations such as using specialized distribution (convenience stores, for example), we can improve the bottom line. Equally we can justify an online price strategy that compares favorably with mass retail prices but also include additional income from the discount that would have normally gone to the distributor or retailer. Of course, the caveat is that we have a strong brand value proposition.

Innovation

The innovation quadrant is the profit zone for products and services. It certainly is the starting point for most and even as they experience the life cycle there is the need to make change in response to customer demand. But it also sets the objective for sustaining brand position and strength. There is a continuing need to renovate products and services in response to change in market conditions and more importantly to establish a strong competitive position. So it is with brand management. But despite the obvious need to innovate, few actually make the effort. In a recent Forrester study,[5] it was noted that only 11% of companies budget for innovation even though an overwhelming majority, 95% agree that innovation leads to better bottom line performance.

The response to a slow and low commitment to innovation is to dedicate an innovation budget that demands the development of brand improvement and new products. Coca-Cola follows a directed budget program where 70% of the marketing budget is for "now" product change, 20% is for "new" development, and 10% for "what's next" for the marketing program. They have mapped out their innovation future and follow it firmly.

CHAPTER 8

Cost-Price Leadership Quad

Here are three deadly sins, according to Drucker: (1) Worshiping high profit margins and "premium pricing"; (2) Mispricing a new product by charging "what the market will bear"; (3) Cost-driven pricing

Your company moves into the most competitive of quadrants when your products reach product life cycle (PLC) maturity and are on the way to decline. All products (and services too) arrive at a terminus where they are no longer in vogue, have fewer buyers, and then only at the lowest of prices. It is

Shrink to 1" x 1" or so	
Low cost Hi product line	Hi value Hi innovation
X Low cost Standard product	Hi value Hi reputation

unfortunate to see large companies apply the most basic and incorrect action to try and resurrect their corporations when they find themselves in this sector by cutting costs and laying off platoons of valued employees. Air Canada, once Canada's flagship airline, brought in an accountant to rebuild the company in 1996 when price levels and competition cut into company profits. Unfortunately, Robert Milton ignored the lessons from Jan Carlzon[1] who turned Scandinavian Airlines around a few years earlier by becoming customer-oriented. Instead Milton applied accounting procedure of cutting costs and services then turned to clever legerdemain with the company's cash reserves to award investors millions of dollars.[2] In the wake of this thick-headed tactic he left behind a demoralized company that is still struggling to stay aloft.

Products in this quad are of two characteristics; commodities that have (a) the support of brand identity and product line extension and (b) those running out on the product life cycle. Research in Motion (RIM or BlackBerry as it is now known) is a case in point of the latter condition (Figure 8.1). Once hailed as the showcase for the future of

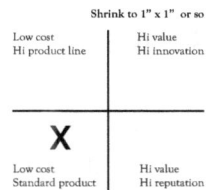

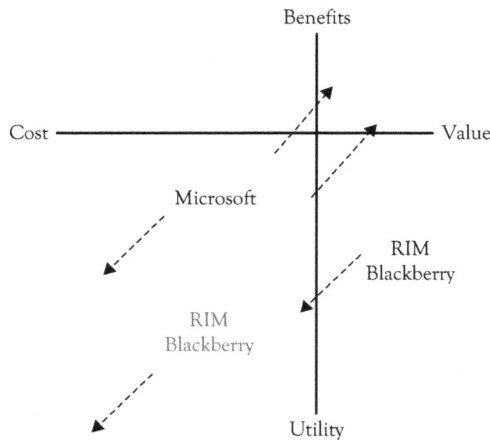

Figure 8.1 Cost-price leadership quad

smartphones to come, the company ignored the signals from competitors and the marketplace that user innovation was needed. They chose to continue doing things their way. Unfortunately, as with General Motors, the company's management stuck to what they had historically done best by improving the technology but not the user interface. Instead, Apple, already a leading proponent of customer response and cocreation, took the market by storm leaving the BlackBerry in the dust. In commenting on RIM's plight, Joe Castaldo[3] observed that, "Everyone—except maybe RIM (BlackBerry)—recognized competition would come to the smartphone market. Unfortunately, RIM reacted to Apple's iPhone and Google's Android operating system by ignoring them." While its reputation and brand name continued to carry it for a while eventually the memory was not enough and the company went into decline.

Microsoft, on the other hand, has a monopolistic position with what is essentially a commodity that has used innovation to force users to continually update the system. Unfortunately, the new advances are not meeting customer appreciation with many hoping a new substitute OS will come along or they are going back to the friendlier XP operating system. But more ominous, at least in terms of Microsoft, is the shift to more mobile data usage and less reliance on the standard desktop PC.

In scanning the future Jim Zemlin,[4] Executive Director of The Linux Foundation declares that, "Microsoft is stuck in the liminal space between the desktop-driven, cost per software license world they dominated and the era we are just now entering: a world driven by open source software and services."

Unless Microsoft is able to reposition their product toward the innovation quad, they can expect a decline in the software part of the business.

Why Products and Companies Decline

The PLC phenomenon has been known for years. New products and services are introduced, they flourish, and then they drop out of site. Here are a few of the more notable branded products that have recently left the commercial scene:

- Polaroid: This item led the world with instant photography but was overcome by the new digital technology
- Kodak: Followed the Polaroid path to extinction
- Wang: Once the world leader in mainframe computer technology was replaced by the PC
- Western Union: The telegraph company of great historical reputation now a memory replaced initially by the fax and cheap long-distance phone calls.

In most cases it is the introduction of new technologies that causes products to be replaced. And the trend continues. Even as the PC replaced the typewriter it now appears that the Cloud technology will be replacing some of the importance of the PC as we know it. Today an estimated 70% of PC capability can be handled with the mobile tablets and smartphones. Here are a few more products from a recent *Forbes* magazine article[5] that are either on the way out or have succumbed: encyclopedias; formal wear; map makers; brick and mortar movie rentals stores (like Blockbuster); hotel telephone systems; pay phones; personal computers (have you looked at the price of a simple desktop computer these days; fancy sneakers cost more); photo finishing; the postal service;

publishers (newspapers; magazines, books); and record stores. You can probably think of a number of products and brands that existed just a few years ago that no longer hold prominence or are in fact not readily available.

The point is that products and services are introduced and then over time they disappear. Today in some sectors of the economy that is happening almost annually. The introduction and decline of smartphones and droids takes less than a couple of years. No sooner does a product come on the market with a new feature than the company or competition introduces improved gadgetry and apps. In 2011, Apple Inc. brought out its new Apple iPhone 4S with a whole array of interesting applications. Yet their existing product the iPhone 4 was doing quite well. However, a closer examination shows that the iPhone 4 was starting to decline in percentage growth and so the company brought out the newer version to maintain their market position rather than wait for the sales volume to tumble too far. The strategy worked and Apple continued to dominate the market.

The Product Recycling Process

The cost-price leadership position is driven by price. There is very little in the way of real differentiation at this point. Companies in the sector must resort to merchandizing and branding efforts to induce the perception of value even as they continue to find new ways to reduce cost. Branded products are improved marginally from time to time so as to present to the consumer an *all new* characterization. They are *recycled*. McDonalds and other fast-food franchises rely on a combination of techniques including product changes, the use of incentives such as giveaway toys, and promotional campaigns to stimulate value perception.

On the other hand, management might simply let the product die off with the intention of introducing a brand new and innovative product or service. In this case, the strategy is to spend very little supporting the product but to harvest as much revenue as possible from it as it declines in the PLC.

The recycling process allows popular brands to attain highly extended life cycles (Figure 8.2). The Proctor & Gamble success with its array of

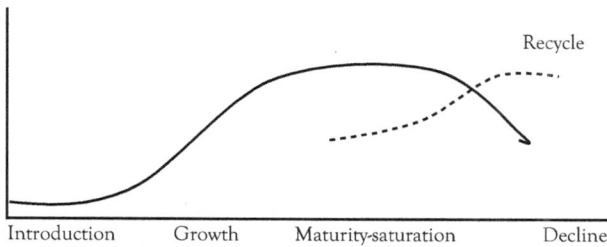

Figure 8.2 Product life cycle–recycle

consumer consumable goods is an outstanding example of life extension by improving the brand or mixing merchandising strategies with brand management to maintain and improve market share.

In some instances, a company may enjoy a monopolistic positioning because of patents, copyrights, and designs. In this case, where the product has a unique *secret* or copyright protection and, while, there is competition from substitute products, it is not so difficult to stay ahead in market share. Coca-Cola is an outstanding example of this position, but even so when Coke tried to be innovative with "new Coke" there was an iconic rebellion and they had to withdraw to the old position and embarked on a multiproduct line approach.

At the lower end of the spectrum, products and services in the cost-price field are essentially commodities and possibly subject to the concept of supply and demand. However, it is not a sustainable position and most companies strive to maximize price for profitability and ROI concerns through other means. It is really at the upper end of the quadrant that companies have the opportunity to modify products to appeal on the basis of value with combinations of brand effect, merchandizing, and even modest innovation or incremental innovation. Branded products like Tide detergent, for example, maintain and increase market share at good profit levels by constantly supporting the brand position and innovating the composition of the detergent.

Retailers of mass goods, Walmart among others, push the theme of *everyday low prices* as a strategy to move their low-priced consumer products. However, on the manufacturing supply side, the pressure is that of cost reduction to the extreme and major retailers search assidu-ously, sometimes in highly competitive fashion for the best possible price.

Some big store outlets have a strategy of price cutting on selected, high-turnover items but offset the losses with those SKUs by setting higher prices on less well moving merchandise. Consumers are not generally aware of this differential and assume that all products are cheaper at the store when in fact they are not.

A final technique is to export the mature and declining product or service to other markets, specifically export marketing. By continuing to apply economies of scale to mass produce the older maturity stage items and moving them to other countries, the manufacturer continued to gain in sales revenue without making any significant increase in investment. A few years ago, producers of medical equipment in the United States marketed their goods to lesser developed countries while introducing new innovations to their domestic market. It served to the advantage of the lesser developed countries (LDCs) with lower cost equipment they did not already have and provided a method for phasing out the old product for the company.

For smaller companies, the "pure price" competition is a challenging place to be. They do not have access to the lower cost inventories and the advantage of mass movement through the system that offers better economies of scale. Yet there are strategies that can be applied that will work well for them. The conceptual framework for a unique competitive strategy in the Beta price-cost field calls for an entrepreneurial skill. Companies will need to incorporate an ability to look for and recognize new opportunities. They will need to put in place service and *customer satisfaction* (CS) techniques, the engagement of *technology* and *product-niche* construction.

Role of Marketing in Cost-Price Leadership

Larger corporations typically struggle to avoid any competitive marketplace that is based on price only. This is the place that is closest to what economists might refer to as *perfect competition*; sensitive only to price where demand is only responsive to price. This is, of course, a fictional hypothesis and is based on a 100-year-old idea of satisfaction and price. At what *price* would you be *satisfied* with a product? Presumably, economists test for this range of satisfaction and price levels and come up with the classical demand curve. But people do not buy strictly on price, except in certain very narrow situations.

The study of human behavior and purchasing activity boils down to two variables in the purchase decision. The first is the expectation an individual has of product performance and the second is a perception of worth. In both cases, there are any number of marketing and social interactions that can move an individual's decision toward these two variables. It can take the form of prior exposure to information by way of advertising, word of mouth, and actual experience through trial or other activity. And it can be the offer of a discount on a store-wide sales promotion. The flow of information, experience, and exposures create a sense of value and an expectation level about a product, which can also be enhanced by a brand name. So we see that one person's perception will not necessarily be the same as another's valuation of the same item. Perception is in the eye of the beholder and it is certainly a truism in marketing. Price leadership subsumes all things are equal and in a general sense that might be so, but often the price is a qualifying dimension and not a determination for many consumer goods.

The cola market offers an interesting example of a standard product market. There are dozens of substitute colas available from supermarkets that produce their own generic brand of cola to smaller individual bottlers. North America has at least a dozen brands, along with Coke and Pepsi. These include Royal Crown Cola, Big Cola sold in Mexico, Jolt Cola of Rochester, New York, and Johnnie Ryan a regional cola bottled in Niagara Falls, New York, and Red Bull Cola available in the United States since 2008.

But it is the large Cola producers, Coke and Pepsi, who dominate the field. It has always been Coca-Cola Classic on top, with Pepsi coming in second. In recent years, Diet Coke has been in the number 3 spot behind Pepsi but has been eating into Pepsi's lead. In 2009, Pepsi sold 100,000 more cases than Diet Coke (936.4 million vs. 936.3 million) with an identical market share of 9.9%.

How Do Large Corporations Continue with Growth?

The cost-price leadership spot is usually held by larger companies that enjoy economies of scale in manufacturing that can include outsourcing. These are corporations that originally launched a new product and as a result of considerable success they have grown through the product life cycle, perhaps modifying the product and extending it to including a number of variations all supported by a strong brand image. We could look at Microsoft as a model and speculate as to its capacity to maintain market position. While there is some speculation that in the future such challenges as open source software development and the huge potential in Cloud technology may seriously challenge their success.

But that may not occur for a few years. Its current revenue is about $73.7 billion for 2012, up from $69.9 billion the year before. It is still dominant in both the PC operating system and Office suite markets (the latter with Microsoft Office). The company also produces a wide range of other software for desktops and servers, and is active in areas including Internet search (with Bing), the video game industry (with the Xbox), and so on. In June 2012, Microsoft announced that it would enter the PC vendor market for the first time, with the launch of the Microsoft Surface tablet computer. It also acquired Nokia as an extension to its mobile entry. Unfortunately, in both instances the company has not succeeded. As one blogger[6] has noted, the company "should have purchased Blackberry not Nokia. And, their first tablet shouldn't have focused on Office but the Xbox. Many of the iPad wielding parents were and some might still be console-goers. The Xbox brand would have given them some belief, be it real or nostalgia, that a Microsoft tablet would be good for them, i.e., their kids."

When we look at Microsoft's strategy, we see a mix of new product offerings to replace older software packages and their entry into other related industries, as with the gaming product line and Skype Communications. Still one can't wonder if these will be enough.

The Effect of Cutting Price

Larger firms have the ability to cut price in an effort to stimulate sales and stave off poor performance. BlackBerry's Playbook is a case in point. The product was introduced in North America in April 2011. But by the fall of that year, most of the 700,000 units sold were still sitting on the shelves of company vendor outlets. In November, the company decided to cut selling price dramatically and by the end of 2012 they had sold almost 2 million units.

But while the strategy worked, it cost the company $485 million in write-off to support the campaign,[7] and it is not a large win. The Playbook market share remains low at about 3% compared to Microsoft's 5%, Apple iPads at 61%, and Google Android at 30%. In its home market, however, RIM enjoys a 20% share,[8] which may be attributed to national loyalty.

The company's purpose was to support the product since it was looked on as a prelude to the BlackBerry10 that was released in 2013 with some success. The huge order by the U.S. DoD may just signal continuing success where the company has focused on what it does best—provides encrypted communications.

While the experience with the Playbook did to some extent maintain the company's status in the industry, it came at a very high cost. The lesson here is that cutting price is a poor strategy and really should not be pursued unless it is a part of a move to increase penetration and can be afforded by the company. It is a requirement for this kind of strategy to have deep pockets, which is to say the enterprise must have access to capital or be able to produce large economies of scale, which is less important than it once was. With technologies and highly improved systems, the ability to be extremely productive and to reduce costs no longer rests on mass volume.

Cost-Price Strategy and the Value Proposition

While the BlackBerry and Microsoft experiences are a bit disconcerting and certainly it is true that price cuts are a poor strategy, there are associative methods that do allow a long-term strategy, rather than a reactive strategy to increase revenues. The judicious application of (a) cost savings is one technique and the (b) creation of value or at least the perception of value enables the firm to succeed and profit. In the latter case, the company maintains its price offering but improves on its value proposition, thus taking business away from the competition. The rationale for this approach is found in earlier research that promotes the idea of a *value discipline*.

The Value Discipline

In 1993 Treacy and Wiersema[9] published a well-received paper that introduced a more holistic way of fighting competition in a very

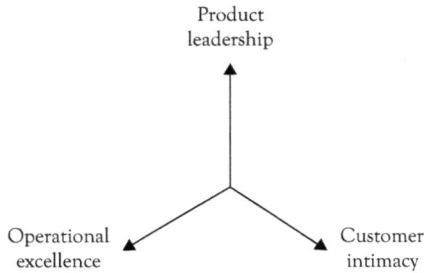

Figure 8.3 Treacy and Wiersema value-discipline model

competitive market. Their thesis set out a tridimensional approach to strategic management that opened the way for entrepreneurial behavior within the organization. They determined that three factors are necessary if the company wants to succeed in a price-sensitive marketplace: (a) product excellence, (b) operational excellence, and (c) customer intimacy (Figure 8.3). These value disciplines are intrinsic to this text where product excellence is the outcome from the quadrant of entrepreneurship and innovation while operational excellence is found in the entrepreneurial behavior of the organization in the execution or implementation of strategic performance.

Firms that plan on being competitive in the global marketplace need to be competent in all three elements, which means the incorporation of entrepreneurial behavior at all levels of the organization. First, there must be the sensitivity to customer requirements that exceeds their expectations. This means that the innovative company develops technology that precedes anything in use but is such that it can lead the user to better levels of satisfaction. The PC was not seen as a replacement for the typewriter but it was. Secondly, the company's products must be a part of the superior satisfaction delivery system; they must lead the industry as we see in Apple's products and finally the organization must deliver on all counts in meeting and exceeding customer expectations.

Cost Leadership

Michael Porter[10] identified five items that deliver value to customers of the cost-price leadership company. They are operations, inbound logistics, outbound logistics, marketing and sales, and service. But associated with the process of reducing the cost factor, Porter also stressed the need to add quality processes. The product or service must deliver and meet the expectations of the buyer. Cost leadership usually focuses on six key elements in the company's operations. Each of these can be used separately or combined to give the best advantage to the company:

1. *Operations*: Economies of scale in the operation can be realized from one of two sources; large runs of standardized products or the use of technology as with flex manufacturing in a lean operation (see Chapter 9). Smaller companies don't have the luxury of mass production. They must either innovate and move into the innovation or Alpha quadrant or develop new technologies in their operations that reduce costs and thus allow competitive pricing for products that are in the maturity and even decline stage of the PLC.

2. *Inbound logistics*: The company looks for ways to reduce inventory costs as exhibited in the auto industry. They can use just-in-time (JIT) methods first introduced by the Japanese for the auto industry, which also decreases inventory requirement since most of the inventory is on transport vehicles. They can reduce the cost of ordering using Internet LAN connections that link the supplier closely to the producer, thus reducing time and speeding up operations.

3. *Outbound logistics*: The emphasis is on reducing delivery costs to customers. This is accomplished by organizing bulk shipments or cooperating with other companies to bundle shipping goods to market.

4. *Marketing and sales*: Using an efficient sales force and automation methods, with cost-effective promotions and applying distribution systems to resourcefully deliver goods to the market.

5. *Service*: Providing customer relations management in less costly manner.

We find that companies in the cost-leadership sector are producing standardized products to a market that generally has similar characteristics whether they are in North America or other parts of the world.

Table 8.1 Differentiating features that lower buyer costs

An alternative to lowering the perceived price of a product is to incorporate features and attributes into the company's product/service package that: • Reduce the buyer's scrap and raw materials waste. • Lower the buyer's labour costs (less time, less training, lower skill requirements). • Cut the buyer's downtime or idle time. • Reduce the buyer's inventory costs. • Reduce the buyer's pollution control costs or waste disposal costs. • Reduce the buyer's procurement and order-processing costs	• Lower the buyer's maintenance and repair costs. Because of superior product reliability. • Lower the buyer's installation, delivery, or *financing* costs with 90-day *payment* • Reduce the buyer's need for other inputs such as energy, safety equipment, security personnel, raise the trade-in value of used models. • Lower the buyer's replacement or repair costs if the product unexpectedly fails later with longer warranty coverage. • Lower the buyer's need for technical personnel. With free technical support and assistance.

Source: Adapted from Michael E. Porter, Competitive Advantage (New York: Free Press, 1985).

There is little in the way of differentiation that makes them unique and they sell these at prices that are competitive with anyone else in the market. The main focus in the cost-price leadership strategy is the reduction of costs, which provides value to their customers. But as suggested in Porter's model, value can also be given in other ways and we will look at that in a moment.

Companies that wish to be successful by following a cost-leadership strategy must constantly work at lowering their costs (relative to competitors' costs). Table 8.1 summarizes the kinds of improvements that can be considered to offset low price competition.

Price-Value Leadership

The attraction of the price-value leadership strategy is that it takes a comparatively low investment to begin and maintain the position. In their discussion about creating value, Treacy and Weirsema offer you two ways to reduce costs while at the same time adding value to what you are offering to the customer. This common sense approach is refreshing and offers some very encouraging methods to develop strategies that will keep you ahead of the crowd. There are two avenues on which you can proceed: (a) operational and within the company and (b) by improving your service to the customer.

The case of the Air Brake Company (See Chapter 10, page 215) is a story about how the improvement in human capital saved the organization. When management was faced with a powerful need to increase revenue and productivity, they turned to the workforce and opened a floodgate of innovation and value creation. They had no funding to improve their capital equipment, but they could and did encourage the development of their human capital. At one time, companies relied heavily on the use of suggestion boxes spread around the plant that invited employees to come up with labor-saving ways to add value to the company product. For a time it worked. Today at best there is mixed feelings about its use.

The intention of the box is to stimulate employee participation and to encourage their contribution to the company's success, perhaps its survival. The Peters and Waterman's book *In Search of Excellence* presented the story of Tom Melohn and his company North American Tool and Die. Melohn turned the company into a multimillion dollar success, boosting sales from under $2 million to $20 million in a few years by encouraging employees to contribute to company improvement. Of course, most companies did not learn how to manage the suggestion box program and it soon became a nuisance, if not an embarrassment.

A survey of manufacturing companies found that American industries are able to stimulate a suggestion box response rate of less than one-half a suggestion per employee per year. In comparison, the Japanese collect nine suggestions per employee per year much to their credit. The problem is that companies are pretty casual about using the box. It becomes a hit-or-miss thing and results in employee disdain rather than stimulation. Also in most work situations, the box encourages ridicule where managers are asked to take a hike, or worse. Even in the case where managers do take the suggestions seriously, there is very little allowance for real employee involvement.

Operational Improvement

In Chapter 10, we talk about building a "people" organization. It calls for a four-step campaign that (a) hires and trains, (b) orients and stimulates, (c) communicates, and (d) innovates, rewards, and encourages. However, in the price-cost quadrant at least until the product is phased out (or the company ceases to exist), value is created by improving the internal performance of the organization. The objective is to eliminate waste, encourage efficiencies, and stimulate positive involvement of the company team. Here are the four methods you can apply:

1. Manage your team efficiently. It begins with hiring very competent people in the first place and ensuring they have the capacity to entrepreneurially organize their workplace. The objective is to have them perform in the most efficient way possible and at the lowest possible cost without jeopardizing their goals and responsibilities.
2. Increase the efficiency of all transactions within the company between people and departments and outside the company along the supply chain. The old maxim time is money is very much a truism today as it was in the last century.
3. Commitment to monitoring the systems by all participants in the company. There is a strong need to ensure rigorous quality and cost control, with measurement targeted at finding ways to reduce costs; and
4. Meeting and exceeding customer expectation, which is the obvious goal of a good customer relationship management program and you need to ensure the seamless application of the process between all members of the corporate team and the customer. Nor should this be constrained to immediate customers. In fact, it is an attitude that should prevail for the most part with all those who might one day be customers.

These developments form an important triad within the organization's internal system. They will provide operational excellence by improving on (a) the company's performance. They will contribute to the bottom line (b) by continuously reducing cost by having everyone analyze their work environment, including the material and resources that flow through the system. More importantly, they will ensure the continuation and hopefully (c) the ongoing improvement to quality products and service. Your company must work at all times to improve on this productive triad.

Customer Affiliation

Now the second focus is on the customer from whom all revenues flow. This campaign adds meaning to the process of customer relations management. Establishing a good customer relationship is a continuous and ongoing part of your strategy;. It begins with attracting customers to your business all the way through to and beyond working with them after they have purchases. Customers buy a product or service for two reasons: will it do the job and how much is it worth. If the product is simple and has a low personal involvement or is an impulse buy, the decision might easily be reduced to the price. Thus, the lowest price might do the job.

However, it is the company's purpose to ensure there is at least a minimal value attached to the item so that the product or service has an improved worth that will justify a slightly higher price than the competition or will ensure that the company's goods will be valued more so than the competition and the purchase will be concluded in its favor. Customer affiliation is characterized by aiming at one or a number of value-conscious customer niches and being obsessive about understanding the individual customers in detail. It is this position of excelling in customer attention and customer service that offsets the *price only* decision. The underlying philosophy of customer attraction is twofold:

- The company philosophy and business practices must completely embrace and encourage deep customer insight and breakthrough thinking about how to improve the customer's situation or business. Everyone in the organization must clearly understand that they are in business for the good of the customer. Here is a story that illustrates the point from Redditt.com.

  My mom is very worried about my grandfather, age 89. He's a navy officer of WWII who lives on his own in an apartment complex. He hardly keeps enough food for himself because he feels as though he can drive out whenever he's hungry (and live off of cereal and prune juice). The problem is that he got snowed in today. He told my mom that one day without food couldn't hurt, but my mom would not accept that. She ended up calling a bunch of places trying to find one that would deliver to him. She eventually ended up asking if Trader Joe's did delivery and they told her they could in this instance. She read out a big order and then proceeded to ask them how she should pay. They told there was no need to pay and said, 'Merry Christmas!' Trader Joe's doesn't do delivery, nor give food out for free normally. I'm glad to see people out in the world care about strangers and help out.

Here is the follow-up to the story:

They delivered the food within 30 minutes and further clarification from my mom reveals that when she was ordering food, they kept suggesting other items for him (he's on a low sodium diet). He ended up getting a few days' worth of food from them. In case people are wondering, it's the Trader Joe's in Wayne, PA. The funniest part is now my grandpa is trying to leave his apartment in the snow to thank them, but I think we've stopped him.

This is one episode, but it clearly shows the ingrained attitude of the manager at Trader Joe's. Clearly, his or her mission is customer satisfaction (CS) and high regard for their needs even without the promise of gaining attention from the effort. It is just part of doing business. Is there any doubt that Trader Joe's is quite popular and well patronized in Wayne, Pennsylvania?

- You need to provide all the services that are important to meeting and exceeding customer needs as and when required. This includes the services of the company as to information, warranty provisions, problem resolution, delivery times, product information, and any number of questions that customers generate by using your goods and services. It also applies to your outsourced agencies or contractors who take care of your company's servicing arrangements. This tells us that the whole organization and its affiliates are engaged in delivering services.

  The philosophy you have must be shared with your suppliers too. They must be part of the commitment to providing CS. Yet too often organizations overlook the obvious; that the customer is doing you a service in buying your goods or services. The value chain for guaranteeing customer service and performance must include all your suppliers and service providers.

Customer Service: Building the Future

There is no other way to succeed at failure more quickly than to give poor customer service. The Little House on the Lake was a newly renovated farm house on the shoreline of Lake Ontario with a striking view of the city of Toronto gleaming just across the water on the horizon. It was a great setting and it was located close to a busy four-lane highway joining Niagara Falls to the rest of the country, traveled by thousands of cars a day. The new owners had spared nothing to restore the ambience of the very large but very historic farmhouse including huge windows facing the Toronto skyline across the lake.

Unfortunately, they had overspent on the décor and so they skimped on the training of the serving staff and the quality of cooking. The resulting service was way below expectations and soon the venture lost its customer base. Word of mouth soon labeled the Little House as a terrible place for food and service but the view was to die for. In short order, it closed and the stigma was so great it took three years before new owners could build up the market and turn a profit.

Let's Define Customer Service

The reason your company is in business is to satisfy the needs of a customer. More so the success of your company relies on exceeding the expectations of your customer on a continuing basis and carrying that effort of exceptional satisfaction into the future. Your customer is your partner in the business and when the connection is soundly joined he or she relies on you as much as you rely on them.

Netflix is an illustration of how to and how not to build a business with CS. When first launched in 2001, it had the fastest and best streaming delivery and an equal CS platform. Customers were treated to quick-fire responses and easy connection service to its live streaming and by mail DVD delivery. Then in 2011 it announced an out-of-the-blue increase in prices and it spun off the DVD business into a separate business called Qwikster, which quickly failed. The shock quickly turned customers off and they lost hugely in customer subscriptions and revenue.

Quickly the company rebuilt its CS strategy and by 2013 had grown to over 24 million subscribers and rising. Here was a success story that could have been an even greater success story if they had consistently applied their CS approach. Instead, they ignored the customer with a unidimensional price hike, which in effect broke the bond of trust that had been established between the customer and the company.

So CS is a two-way link, a dyad between your company and your customer. It is a marriage and like any good marriage it requires constant nourishment and support on the part of both parties.

Customer Retention

All this leads to is the very real need to keep your existing customers and to build on their loyalty. In today's new economy, it will be tough to find new customers. In the last century, the marketplace grew very strongly as children matured into families and then became *boomers*. Today that dynamic has diminished and growth more often than not will come at the expense of someone else, hopefully your competitor losing his or her customers.

A customer retention program begins with a mutual agreement that the customer is important to the organization. It can be as simple as a thank you note or can expand to free products and services. Until recently, one of the more successful loyalty programs was the Aeroplan Program developed for Air Canada. Then the company in a drive to improve its balance sheet and satisfy investors spun off Aeroplan as a separate unit called AIMIA. Unlike the old Aeroplan the new corporation is seen as being more interested in delivering profit rather than CS and Air Canada is falling from grace as a desired carrier. In 2012 J.D. Power ranked WestJet as the ranking North American Airline over Air Canada, Southwest, and Alaska Air.

An interesting outline for a customer retention and loyalty building program is one that addresses seven key points.[11] These are deemed to add value to your customer's perception of value. They are as follows:

1. Use a simple point system.
2. Use a tier system to reward initial loyalty and encourage more purchases.

3. Charge an upfront fee for VIP benefits.

4. Structure nonmonetary programs around your customer's values.

5. Partner with another company to provide all-inclusive offers.

6. Make a game out of it.

7. Scratch the program entirely.[12]

The last point has appeal. It suggests that because there are so many loyalty programs around, they have lost their luster and do not deliver as effectively as they might. The suggestion is to build loyalty by providing first-time users with awesome benefits that will hook them, and to offer those benefits with every purchase. Sounds simple and perhaps that is the appeal.

Customer Service and Retention: The Future

Customer service is typically tied to the exchange between the customer and the company, which would include both your employees and members of your online channels. It is a key feature as customers seek out information or wish to resolve a problem or concern before, during, or after a purchase. In the days ahead, that is not likely to change as a prevailing need for maintaining customers and marketshare. However, as we move into the second decade of the 21st century, there are three trends that are going to some impact on how we develop our CS strategies.

First, social media is closing the gap between product support and keeping a strong brand identification. As we move into *social customer service,* we will be using the new technologies to provide customer service and support. People are using social media for communications and problem resolution as they share their experiences and are being informed of others who may have the same or similar issues. All of this is taking place in an open forum for all the world to see. Dave Carrol's broken Taylor guitar, which was posted on YouTube[13] in July 2009, is a case in point. As of February 2013 it has been seen by 12.8 million people who have been appraised of United Airline's mishandling of the artist's guitar. Perhaps the poor CS that United had up to this point may have contributed to its need to merge with American Airlines in 2013. Social customer service is offered publicly: The complaint and resolution (or lack of) are out there for the world to see. We are now very aware of the impact on brand sentiment and reputation that it has. A bad buzz about a product on social media can have a powerful and negative effect on a company's brand image. As a result, customer service is becoming an essential element to brand strategy.

Customer service *is becoming more proactive*. Traditionally, customers initiated contact with companies to request assistance. But proactive technologies are changing that. Proactive chat and click-to-call have been associated primarily with sales objectives, but there is growing interest among e-business leaders to employ proactive live help technologies to assist with customer service issues. This means proactive chat capabilities that have sat on the sales side of an organization are shifting onto the customer service side.

Mobile apps are expanding the scope of customer service. Mobile apps allow us to offer new functionality. We can now use our mobile devices to learn if an item is in stock, to deposit checks, and to get assembly instructions. This functionality is often a service or deflects a call for service.

This is fundamentally changing organizations' perceptions of customer service. Customer service was once viewed as an operational function, a cost center composed primarily of telephone reps. For the most part, marketing didn't want to own customer service. In my experience, we marketers just wanted customer service to work, to be the voice on the other end of the 1 to 800 numbers we put on brochures.

Summarizing Strategies in the Cost-Price Leadership Quadrant

The cost-price Beta quadrant is the most competitive place to be in the marketplace. For the most part, the products are in the closing side of the product life cycle and, even though there may have been modifications, some improvements, and reconfiguring in terms of size and packaging the product will ultimately be replaced by an innovation or new technology. The constant need to improve the value of the product or service soon runs out of options and the ultimate requirement is to replace the product entirely with a new and innovative product. The recycling of a brand, for example, as with Tide detergent is often based on real technological advances in chemistry and composition to improve the cleaning activity.

Yet there is merit in running out the product as long as possible to milk the maximum profit from the investment made in developing it. There are four strategic moves your company can make to extend the competitive life of your product and service in this quadrant: cost leadership, customer value leadership, service retention leadership, and brand or reputation improvement.

Cost Leadership

The improvement of your cost factors can go in one of the three directions. It can (a) take the form of direct cost to the product in better design for example; (b) it can manifest in reduced costs along the value chain, and (c) it can reduce costs through an improved manufacturing process with increased efficiencies and improved qualities.

Customer Value leadership

Equally important in strategic planning is the ability to increase customer sense of value in your goods or services. The mantra of the text is to increase value in the perception that customers have toward the company's offering by increasing the expectation of performance. Now, performance can be enhanced in any number of ways through services given to the customer along with the product. Perhaps, it can take the form of the warranty or augmented parts to the main product or brand itself. Hyundai has improved the perception of value in the 2013 Elantra with a seven-year bumper to bumper that prompted one e-zine to declare, "That the Hyundai Elantra GT offers more bang for the buck, with more standard features and a longer warranty goes without saying."

Service Retention leadership

Keeping customers is paramount in any strategic design.

We know markets are not growing as once they did. The presentation of a product or service is a reflection of the whole company. It must correlate to all the company provides in its goods and services. You cannot promise one thing and then deliver another. Netflix customers were shocked when the image they had of the company as a swift and reasonable supplier of entertainment suddenly demanded more without any advanced discussion or creation of a new understanding as to what they were going to provide. Many reacted by not buying and only returned when they were reassured and accepted the need for price increase. But Netflix had to rebuild its value proposition.

The process of engagement with the customer and the delivery of the product must always be consistent and positive as to what the customer expects and even more it should exceed what they expect. It is what keeps the customer coming back for more and so often the reason why, even when given a shock they return for more. Keeping customers with superior service must become the mantra of the cost-leader company and perhaps for most companies regardless of the strategy.

Brand and Reputation improvement

Finally, the brand and company image must be maintained and that means keeping it current in both context and content. The intrinsic product or service must be seen as improved even if only from a servicing position. The company's identification floats in a sea of competing offers. There are billions of websites and the brand position in the customers mind is greatly important in staying alive in the cost-price quadrant.

PART 3

How Will You Get There?

CHAPTER 9

Strategic Management in Four Quads and Resources

You've got to think about big things while you're doing small things, so that all the small things go in the right direction.

—Alvin Toffler

Many companies have more than one product line and so they find their products fit into two, three, or all four quads. It makes managing a bit more complex and close attention is needed to fix on specific outcomes. That is, a particular effort is required to apply a strategic approach to each product or product group separately. Apple Inc. has more than five lines starting with the Mac and on to variations of the iPad, iPhone, and such. Dealing with each of these in a strategic mode calls for a separation of the management approach. You simply cannot meld them together into one organized process and structure. It won't work, so the answer is: keep them apart. We need to departmentalize or divisionalize the product and service offering, each with its own strategic implemented plan. In fact, there is the advantage of maintaining an entrepreneurial style in each of the separate product areas. Over the years, companies have tried to develop a more effective marketing–management thrust by using brand managers to act as product champions within a combined centralized structure. It worked reasonably well, but certainly is not as effective as if it were more creatively directed with an entrepreneurial drive in focused operations. But it must also be coordinated with the overall strategy for the organization too.

Shrink to 1" x 1" or so

Low cost Hi product line **X**	Hi value Hi innovation **X**
X Low cost Standard product	**X** Hi value Hi reputation

How we apply our resources to strategic plans depends on how important the expected outcome is. The higher priority targets will obviously get the better allocation of funding, manpower, and effort. In the examination that follows, we will look for the link between entrepreneurial application, competitive response, and implementation in the quads.

The Four Quads

If your company fills all four quads, it needs a strategy to keep the activities separate and distinct. Al Ries[1] tells us that GM was in trouble at least a decade before their insolvency in 2008 and bankruptcy in 2009. He noted they were into anything and everything on wheels and they applied the use of an "umbrella brand" to cover all products. It was their argument that the GM logo (and its very effective dealership network) would move each of the company's diverse models from trucks to sports cars in response to anything the competition might throw at them. It did not work. Their hundreds of model variations on 22 platforms were simply too much. "Imagine a medical practice saying to itself: 'We are known as terrific brains surgeons, so let's get into the heart, liver, lung, and limb business.' It never happens in medicine, but it does in business and only when it's too late does a company notice they have become precariously unfocused."

If you wish to pursue a multifocal strategy you need to keep each product separate so managers in each business unit can exercise a consistent, directed strategy and tend to the knitting as it were. Figure 9.1 clearly shows a different expectation from customers in each quadrant. Each has a unique perception as to cost or value: utility or benefits. The innovator customer will not relate to a cost-price strategy except perhaps to wonder what has been cut out of the product to make it cheaper. Customers who embrace a branded product may or may not accept a full product line array as long as their particular brand is fulfilling its mandate; otherwise, there may be a tendency to start looking around at other more focused competitive brands. There will always be the individual who buys a product at the cheapest price. But to remind the reader, it is the marketing job to build value into the product, to alert the buyer to the worth of what is

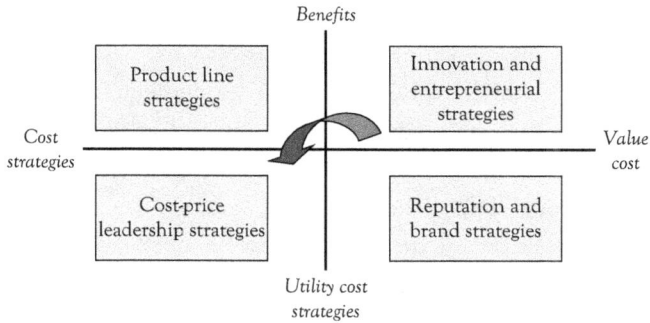

Figure 9.1 Four quads of business strategy

being offered, and for that in a multiproduct strategy setting you need to assign managers who do just that.

The Entrepreneurial Product Manager

The idea of engaging a brand manager to handle a brand began way back in 1931 when Neil McElroy, a young graduate from Harvard, worked with Proctor & Gamble on an advertising campaign for Camay soap. He was a little frustrated that there were a number of brands within the company all competing for resources, and, so, he wrote a now-famous memo arguing that more focus should be given to Camay, and by extension to other P&G brands as well.[2] "In addition to having a person in charge of each brand, there should be a substantial team of people devoted to thinking about every aspect of marketing it. This dedicated group should attend to one brand and it alone." In effect he signalled the need to have a more entrepreneurial and dedicated engagement in the marketing of a product.

What do brand managers do? The position calls for a very generalized and entrepreneurial managing style. They are responsible for *product development* where they initiate research to assess the needs of customers. They work with research and development (R&D) and the customer to create the features and perceptual benefits the customer wants. They interpret data about all aspects of a potential product— its color, texture, smell, and packaging—in order to make the product as appealing as possible. In B2B product development, the product managers who lead the marketing charge to assess what customers want so they come up with the specifications for production. They then take on the *promotion* of the product to create a brand image that hopefully is positive and prompts a strong perception of value and brand equity. Finally, they worry about the bottom line.

If a brand is successful, the brand manager might be encouraged to go into brand extension, which is the process of building on the success of a pre-existing brand. They might come up with a new flavor of granola bar or a user-friendly bottle of ketchup. These extensions serve two objectives: they can generate sales in a new market (Frosted Cheerios) going after customers who want a sweetened cereal, and they can help invigorate a sluggish brand. Additional product innovations can give a new image to an old brand—all-new Tide, for example. These usually take the form of incremental innovations. This area is the source for product extensions into the Product Line Quad. The strategy is to create variations that fill out the line, capture more shelf space, and grab market share; or at least keep the momentum going for a bit longer in the product life cycle (PLC) downshifting into the cost-price quad. In some cases, companies are able to maintain the "managed" sector of the Merchandise-Brand Quad for what appears to be an indefinite time, again as with Tide soap. When all else fails the manager might come up with a new, perhaps radical innovation like Steve Jobs's great successes.

The brand or product manager is intimately involved with the brand and is best able to initiate and guide the development of the strategy for it. The brand managers determine the expected sales volumes and forecasts for the brand. The effort includes all the details from market research, packaging design, advertising theme to sales force management. He or she implements the strategy in the communications programs that follow, which convey the desired value perceptions to customers. They are involved in the financial aspects of the brand and its performance. They help set the price, select the media, work with manufacturing, and perhaps even the suppliers. In effect, the brand manager is the entrepreneurial manager for that brand and takes full responsibility for its success.

Quad Strategies Over the Product Life Cycle

The performance of products within the four quads generally follows the staging over the life cycle of a product (Table 9.1). Products begin as innovations, created by entrepreneurial managers or individuals. They proceed through growth, assuming acceptance by customers and in time they become *old* in the marketplace, superseded by technology and innovation, or they become old-hat. We just get tired of things; a tendency to believe the grass is greener over the fence and when we see someone with a new device we may become anxious about it and start to think about getting one too. But we still need to deal with the idea about why things go through a life cycle. Products are not living things so why do they have

Table 9.1 Product life cycle strategies

Stage or quad	Introduction *innovation quad*	Growth ◄—►	Maturity-saturation *product line and brand quads*	Decline *cost-price leadership quad*
Customer	Early adopters	Early majority	Late adopters	Laggards
Market size	Tight niche	Expanding	Mass market	Shrinking
Product	Innovation	Standardize	Product line extension	Kill off, incremental change
Promotion	Selective, primary demand	Persuasive	Battle of brands	Reminding
Sales	Slow, select	Volume growth	Peaking	Decreasing
Competition	None/Substitutes	Few	Many	Moderate
CRM requirements	Build awareness	Build customer satisfaction	Loyalty	Fragmented
Strategy	Focused niche	Targeted	Retention	High retention
Price	High, value proposition	Selected reduction	Competitive push benefits	Low, price point
Innovation	High, perhaps radical	Adoption	Incremental	None

life cycles? The reason is that society accepts products at different rates, but they all go through somewhat the same stages of societal acceptance and ultimately rejection.

When you develop your strategy, a key position is to assess where it sits in the eye of the customer. If you are in a growth stage it is easy to stay focused on satisfying customers while you build a brand image for the product, as a new item in the marketplace. Demand is good and will grow for some time to come, although in today's market that might be a few months or it could be a few years. Electronics have a shorter time frame than heavy machinery, for example, and likely need adjustments over a shorter time span.

As the product or service begins to sink into the decline stage, the options are pretty clear. You can (a) let it ride down the curve and milk the profit for as long as you can without supporting the product or (b) modify the product with incremental innovation through packaging and size modification. This allows you more spread on the supermarket shelves and hopefully a larger share of the sales for that item a you rely on your brand image to support the product line extension. Of course, this calls for an increased investment in brand advertising to your customer base. On the other hand, you can (c) look for new markets to extend coverage perhaps by entering the international markets. Many small firms are very active in global marketing, assisted by their associations and networks and the access provided by the Internet.

At some point your product is redundant and has reached the decline point of no return. In many situations, this can signal the demise of the company as well. What is needed is to be ready with an alternate plan: a new product or a radical innovation that will reinvent the company's market position. The astute marketing manager or general manager has his or her eye on the pulse of the customer and is aware of what new products or radical product changes are needed to keep the company in a strong position. Taking a leaf from Apple's market approach the idea of cocreation—working intimately with customers in creating new product applications—is a growing positive strategy.

The Company and Its Resources

The theme of the book is that the entrepreneurial implementation of strategy is key to success. Mitchell Osak[3] reminds us that the company's strategy must be created within the realities of the organization if we are to successfully implement our plans. What are the capabilities, the competencies, and resources of the organization in the context of what is to be achieved? "All too often issues such as skill gaps, conflicting priorities, and weak management are ignored during strategy formulation. As a result, execution risk increases as 'implementors' cope with under-investment, inadequate resource allocation, and poor congruence between corporate capabilities and the new strategy."

Your organization will need to be more readily in sync with the marketplace. It will need to be more agile, more able to adjust, and flex the organization and its resources to opportunities as they arise. Even so, resource allocation will be a challenge since the process will need to set aside the old method of allocating resources to build on the status quo. Instead, employees will determine what resources are needed. SAS Institute[4] is unique in the software industry not only for its development of new software to handle massive amounts of data but also for its customer relations methods and employee treatment. SAS employees are treated with respect and are trusted to carry out their work, including the use of resources as and when required. They are given the freedom, the flexibility, and the resources to do the job. In a *60 Minutes* interview with Morley Safer in 2002, CEO Goodnight said that "95% of my assets drive out the front gate every evening. It's my job to bring them back."

Five Resource Categories

A company's resources are the assets, tangible and intangible, that help the firm do business. For the most part, this aspect of strategic planning takes into account the use of human capital, physical assets, intangible resources, financial resources, and all those possessions the business uses to make a profit. Managing the enterprise calls for astute husbandry of those resources. Too often, the allocation of resources is a piecemeal process where a certain number of units are disposed to a department or division: a certain number of vehicles or people or dollars or tons of material. This accounting approach to allocating resources can be a problem since departments may lay claim to these resources even if they are not being used.

For our purposes, we identify five areas that define the sources from which managers can extract their supply of talent and support. We get a better grasp of the use of our resources if we group them into actionable areas. Companies often misallocate their resources when there isn't a match between the strategic priorities and arrangement of resources throughout the company.[5] The five sections are as follows:

1. Customer-oriented activities—resources that create customer value through innovation and knowledge
2. Technology know-how and intellectual property
3. Productivity and process improvements—resources that improve efficiencies, productivity and operations know-how, supply chain management (SCM), and enterprise resource planning (ERP)
4. Competency and management know-how—resources that develop internal knowledge, competencies, and know-how, and
5. Financial resources—financial resources and profit maximization through measurement, feedback, and control of funds.

Customer-Directed Activities

The first line of resource development is to those actions that attract, engage, and retain customers. The customer is the reason we are in business. He or she, at least figuratively, is a partner in our enterprise and just about everything we do is directed toward meeting and exceeding their expectations. So what resources do we need to make that happen? How do we organize our resources most effectively? Your enterprise will be able to achieve differentiation of your offering through innovation and also through the satisfaction customers will appreciate in the use of your product.

Firstly, there is need for the development of a solid customer relations management (CRM) strategy that will initiate and sustain the flow of orders. But the nurture of that CRM thrust requires trained employees who will become skilled in communications and people sensitivity. The first resource is then for the sales force and its support contingent that the company will marshal into the business arena. Poorly trained personnel can only harm a company's image and relationship.

There is another banner that needs waving in the discussion of resources directed toward the customer and that is the involvement of the whole organization. It has become almost critical that employees throughout the company are aware of and positively motivated about the need to keep the customer happy. Customers as well as employees are communication lines that deliver important information to management that enable stronger relationships and performance. But employees need to know and understand the important role they play in both serving and in keeping customers. Customer satisfaction has become the mantra of organizations today because keeping a customer is less costly than going out and finding new customers. It does not take much from a disinterested employee to turn off a customer when he or she is trying to get service from their supplier: your company.

Recently Delta, one of the more poorly rated carriers in the system, decided to rebuild and improve their operations. According to the *Wall Street Journal*,[6] "among major airlines Delta finished with the highest rate of customer complaints filed with the Department of Transportation in the first nine months of 2010, and was second-to-last in on-time arrivals and baggage handling through November. Delta also had the highest rate of cancelled flights among major carriers, according to FlightStats. com." In the last few years the company has enjoyed a strong turnaround. Management became customer-oriented and learned how to respond to complaints and establish good empathy with their customers—part of a $2 billion turnaround program. Just think where they would have been had they made that investment in their frontline employees a few years earlier.

People, particularly the frontline people who deal with customers, are the principal resources that should be directed to a company's strategy. But a truly effective organization aligns its employees from bottom to top with the customer. Indeed, the mission statement, which should be emblazoned on the consciousness of everyone in the organization, including its publics, should begin with the declaration that the enterprise's primary business is the satisfaction of the customer. Secondly, the company must orient and train its people to be receptive to and at the service of the customer.

Technology and Innovation

We know that product life cycles are getting shorter. The emerging nations, China in particular, will exert enormous pressure on companies in North America to improve and be nimble in customer relationships as well as the creation of new and innovative products. Meeting this challenge will call for much effort and the employment of innovation as a constant philosophy. But the business of innovation is not universally accepted by corporations according the Harvard Business School online forum.[7] One participant observed that "Nearly all current performance management models are stacked against innovation." What is evident is that management in contemporary organizations is unable to spark the move toward innovative thinking and strategic growth. Innovation is tied to the attitude of managers and they seem unlikely to be the ones who will stimulate innovation in the corporation. They are risk avoiders and are not paid to "stick out their necks." What is required is a new style of leadership that is the theme of the book—an entrepreneurial management style.

At the same time, the movement calls for the inclusion of almost everyone in the organization to participate in the creation of innovation and improvement. It cannot be left to senior management since the propensity is to reduce risk if not avoid it. The organization needs to work along two avenues. The first is to constantly improve the processes within the company: the production process, the administrative process, and the external sales and purchasing processes. These are important parts of the value chain. The second is to be alert to opportunities within the changing marketplace, to be responsive with an ever-effective CRM program that will keep the company ahead of customer needs. But also, it must constantly measure how well it is performing and how to keep on top of customer satisfaction and loyalty. Innovation is a company-wide responsibility.[8] "The success of an organization's idea management program is at the mercy of its supporters—the employees. The innovation team and top management must effectively communicate their goals to employees so they understand what's expected of them and feel confident that their ideas will be taken seriously." Innovation needs to be a systemic component of the organization. Everyone must participate. Companies also need to be transparent. Communications within the organization must be open and clear so that everyone knows what is to be done and what contributions they make will be important.

Incremental Innovation and Radical Innovation

The identification of two forms of innovation has been around since the 1980s starting with a number of engineering publications, moving over to Michael Porter in 1986 who talked about *continuous and discontinuous* technological innovation while others ranged from incremental versus breakthrough and conservative versus radical innovations.[9] These two definitions are vested in two dimensions within the enterprise. The first definition occurs within the context of the company and accounts for knowledge and skills inherent to the firm. Thus, we see that incremental innovation is built within that context and adds to the competency of the firm. On the other hand, radical innovation calls for an entirely new knowledge and resource base, which usually offsets, perhaps even destroys, the current competency level, perhaps rendering it obsolete.

The second dimension, which is outside the organization, relates innovation to technological changes and what its impact will be on the market and the company's competitiveness. Obviously, incremental innovation will involve modest technological changes with little need to change existing products. But radical innovation will instead involve large technological advancements, which will challenge all existing products and render them noncompetitive and obsolete. As we can see, the pressure here challenges the incumbent management to no end. With incremental innovation there is no real threat to the status quo. But radical innovation, will call for the need to change their knowledge background. It calls for a different mindset, perhaps an entrepreneurial mindset. Strategically, they have less of an incentive to invest in the innovation since it will cannibalize the company's existing product line. One can picture the confusion in the managerial ranks of companies like Remington, producers of typewriters and computers who could not make the leap into the new information age to say nothing of the Kodak film company in a digital age.

Innovation Strategies

Innovation can be illustrated in a comparative table[10] that sets out the different features of the two innovation descriptors (Table 9.2). Companies favoring their operations in the existing markets will be more disposed to making cosmetic changes, hoping their customers will be satisfied with the offering of presumed innovation. The example of adding racing stripes to a standard automobile with the expectation this will render it as a "sport" model. Companies will also push into new markets with slightly modified features, hoping to extend the product life cycle, which would include efforts to develop export markets where customers may be seeing the product for the first time.

However, when the firm comes up with a new tech product, one of a radical form, the potential for profit becomes significant, particularly if the item breaks into the early adopter segment. The Apple iPod was in some respects both an incremental and a radical innovation. It was essentially an extension of the MP3 technology first introduced in Korea in the late 1990s. In 2001 the first iPod was released into the market. It had a 5-GB hard drive with a $400 price tag and by 2007, Apple had sold 100 million iPods. To this date it is still the most popular MP3 player brand in the world.

Research and Development

The onus is on management to adopt a culture that incorporates the innovation factor. An entrepreneurial organization is constantly alert to opportunities that evolve from customers, competition, and the business

Table 9.2 Innovation strategies

	Innovation	
	Incremental	**Radical**
Existing markets	Competitive, cost reductions	High risk competitive strategy
New markets	Low risk, many competitors	High risk high profits

Source: Hutch Carpenter, The Four Quadrants of Innovation.

environment. The primary source of product innovation is, of course, the customer. Magna International is about as entrepreneurial a large organization as you will find. This multiplant, multibillion dollar company uses its R&D departments to improve products, which they take to their customers and propose the innovations and technological advances to enhance the customer's competitive advantage; they help their buyers be more competitive! The company has a Corporate Constitution that requires all divisions to spend no less than 7% of pretax profits on R&D. It is at least partially responsible for the great success in the 200 plants worldwide.

Studies[11] in the application of R&D find that access to knowledge or a company's knowledge stock is the most important determinant of innovation and that R&D intensity has a positive impact on innovation. In fact, the innovation rate is the main determinant of the growth rate of output. R&D creates new or improved technologies that provide a company with a competitive advantage. It is a risky business and much R&D fails to achieve solid financial results. It is only the few successful innovations that finance the whole effort. But without it there is the assurance that it will only be question of time as to when, not if, the company will fail. It is a resource that needs to be developed so it may then contribute to the company's growth and success.

Productivity and Process Improvements

The efficiency of an organization is reflected in its output and its productivity. It enables the firm to improve at all levels of the value chain and maintain competitive position. Innovation in product development is very important to business operations. Productivity and process improvements are internal and relate to reducing costs, thus contributing to profit margins. The degree of improvement is a condition of where the enterprise sits in the four quadrants of the strategy field. It becomes almost vital in the cost-leadership quad where price leadership is the principal market differentiation. If the company is unable to meet and perhaps exceed the lower price position of its competitors, it ultimately faces economic loss and failure. He who has the deepest pockets and the deepest cuts will win the day!

People and Productivity

Your company will succeed or not on the strength of your team but on the caliber of people you have hired and employed to manage the affairs of the enterprise. They are the lifeblood and creative juices of the organization. Laurette Koellner,[12] Senior Vice President of Boeing Company, declared that, "Our people are our greatest strength and our competitive advantage." In her address to the conference on employee involvement (EI), she cited eight principles the company uses that have made them one of the leading companies in the United States that people would like to work for. EI comes from

- a workplace where we focus on common goals;
- the expectation of every employee that part of the job is to improve processes;
- empowerment for employees and teams within well-understood boundaries;
- an environment that embraces learning and change and that models breakthrough thinking and continuous improvement;
- information and communication systems that support team-based decision making;
- fair compensation, reward, and recognition systems that support team behavior and results;
- a positive work environment where employees feel listened to and engaged;
- a quality of work life that provides personal and professional satisfaction, pride, and mutual respect.

There is reason to be more accommodating and encouraging about company employees. It makes good sense to stimulate EI. Studies show that companies with higher levels of EI are financially better off. More importantly when employees are part of the company, they become more involved and more entrepreneurial in outlook. It is the basis for encouraging dynamic behavior in the company.

There is another more compelling reason, which is that good employees are becoming harder to find. A recent McKinsey report[13] shows there is a disconnect between the caliber of the existing labor force and what is needed today. "The Western economies have built a workforce optimized for mid-20th-century national industries, yet the jobs now being created are for 21st-century global ones—we need knowledge workers, not factory workers. And there just aren't enough of the former, anywhere. Companies across the globe consistently cite talent as their top constraint to growth." Obviously there is going to be an enormous need to either upgrade employees or remove them if untrainable and hire young people with the hope of training them to handle the requirements for a more sophisticated workforce.

Improved Methods and Technologies

The four topics that more producers and manufacturers are turning to for improvements in productivity and improvement to customer relations are flex manufacturing, agile manufacturing, lean manufacturing, and the full application of SCM. Some of these ideas have been around for generations. In fact, much of the content for these improvements have been stimulated by Edwards Deming, an American consultant hired by the Japanese auto industry to improve its output and global sales. Deming[14] told the Japanese managers that if they followed his recommendations "they would capture markets the world over within five years." In fact, it began happening within 4 years!

Lean manufacturing considers the entire company as a system, from source of supply (SCM) to process systems and the final customer. It strives to provide value, to eliminate waste, incorporate quality planning and control, just-in-time (JIT), supplier integration, automation, team working, empowerment, behavior, total productive maintenance (TPM), delivery frequency, selling techniques, new product introduction, and customer satisfaction. Lean manufacturing is a management philosophy derived mostly from the Toyota Production System (TPS).

Agile manufacturing is a term applied to an organization that has created the processes, tools, and training to enable it to respond quickly to customer needs and market changes while still controlling costs and quality. It includes the manufacturing support technology that allows the marketers, the designers, and the production personnel to share a common database of parts and products, to share data on production capacities and problems, particularly where small initial problems may have larger effects.

Flex manufacturing is a flexible manufacturing system (FMS) in which there is some amount of flexibility that allows the system to react in the case of changes, whether predicted or unpredicted. This flexibility is generally considered to fall into two categories. The first category, *machine flexibility*, covers the system's ability to be changed to produce new product types, and ability to change the order of operations executed on a part. The second category is called *routing flexibility*, which consists of the ability to use multiple machines to perform the same operation on a part, as well as the system's ability to absorb large-scale changes, such as in volume, capacity, or capability.

Process Improvements

In addition to the foregoing manufacturing aids, how do you maintain flexibility and manage change in the dynamic of strategic implementation? The ability of the organization to meet and deal with variable conditions is the mark of an entrepreneurial organization. Anything less may disport inefficiencies in resource applications and reduce the company's effectiveness.

Information technology (IT) software is now a large part of systems improvements and assisting management to better organize and direct the workplace. It has created a host of managerial tools and processes to guide and assist management to help organize and direct resource distribution in strategic planning and the implementation. Two examples of the newer technologies that companies use are business process management (BPM) and optimization of systems protocols (OSP):

> *Business process management:* One of the most important is BPM. Wikipedia tells us that BPM is a holistic management approach focused on aligning all aspects of an organization with the wants and needs of clients. It promotes business effectiveness and efficiency while striving for innovation, flexibility, and integration with technology. BPM attempts to improve processes continuously. It is a *process optimization process.* BPM helps organizations to gain higher customer satisfaction, product quality, delivery speed, and time-to-market speed.[15]

Enterprise resource planning: ERP is an important programming aid for small and large businesses. At one time, it was principally used by larger firms but SAS and others have developed smaller packages that can greatly assist in resource management including

- customer relationship management;
- business intelligence;
- core financials, analysis, and reporting;
- planning and budgeting;
- human resources administration;
- manufacturing: supply chain management;
- sales force automation.

Competency and Management Know-How

A company's major resource is measured by the number of knowledgeable people in the organization. The lesson in all this is that good people are an investment. It is not capital alone that assures success but rather it is the effort of knowledgeable, motivated people in the company who make things happen. One of the greatest stories in recent times is Microsoft and how Bill Gates assembled a team[16] of knowledgeable people who built the company. It was a collection of individuals who brought to the company the early awareness of what the Internet would become and collectively they each made a major contribution to Microsoft's huge success. Success is measured not by the brilliance of a new concept or technology, but by the creativity of individuals who know how to interpret and apply the innovation to what the marketplace and the world needs.

The literature tells us a company's core competence is usually expressed as a set of skills or the shared experience from which the organization develops an exceptional methodology or procedure. Core competence does not include physical assets but rather is a corporate capability in some activity. It's something you can do better than the competition.

Financial Resources

The balance sheet and the income statements are very important as to records of past performance. They tell us of the worth of our enterprise but they are not resources. Our financial strength is displayed in the money we have in the bank, so to speak and how much we might borrow should we need to do so. These are our financial resources. Our cash resources depend on how rapidly we can access it when required. Actual cash in the bank is the most available and liquid to us. Other forms would be cash available from short- and long-term investments that would have to be liquefied, accounts receivable from customers, which could be used as collateral for debt lending or factoring as well as the sale of certain assets.

Management of Financial Resources

Managing a company's financial resources is a planning activity that has as its goal the assurance of cash flow when it is needed. It's an administrative process that dwells on identifying and dealing with risk. The primary effort is on the analysis and assessment of an organization's performance, usually at the end of some activity. Even as customers are an asset to the organization so are the financial institutions that would serve your enterprise. Banks, credit unions, factor companies, merchant banks, even your suppliers who extend credit to you are part of your company's financial asset reserve. That is not to say that these are all the same in providing capital or taking on some of the risk of supporting or underwriting your venture. There are differences between these and the astute manager knows how to work with each resource to enable his or her strategic plans.

There is a tendency to give more importance to the financial side of management output where money is looked on as the key resource that a company has. The Wall Street and fund managers who run the financial markets, including bankers and venture capitalists tend to dwell on the money side of things; they are always stressing the management of funds and the leveraging of accounts as main markers of a company's performance and net worth. But in fact these very public issues are really the consequences of something else, the *management* of company resources and the effectiveness of that management in the orchestration of all resources in the enterprise.

The demand for quarterly performance by public corporations, for example, is a misplaced measure. One astute observer[17] declares, "When quarterly earnings conference calls come around, I yearn for insight beyond the heaps of financial data. Thanks to elaborate accounting techniques, even shaky public companies can dress up numbers as walls crumble." On the other hand, a study of e-companies[18] shows that paying attention to performance as determined by the stock market has very little impact on a company's success or failure; less than 9% showed it as a factor. Thus, it is not important that executives should worry about stock performance in managing their companies unless, of course, they are guided by pecuniary interests such as stock options and the value of their own holdings.

It is more important to supervise the use and allocation of resources as they are dispensed to the company's operation about the financial position. Entrepreneurs look on cash or wealth as a measuring stick, rather than to worry a scorecard that shows how well the venture has performed. Money is nothing until it is put to work in an effective way. But the focus needs to be on the performance and not just the consequence of the performance. It is the managerial mandate to use resources including money to do the company's business.

The Innovation and Growth Quad

This acceptance of new technologies by societies is identified as the diffusion of innovations first articulated by Rogers.[19] As society begins to adopt and accept an innovation, the new product grows, eventually reaching maturity. When there is a better alternative to the product or when public preference changes, the product will enter a decline, possibly ending with its demise.

The diffusion-of-innovations concept organizes society according to the speed with which individual members adopt a new product. It classifies people into the five categories of innovators, early adopters, early majority, late majority, and laggards. There is no exact time that a product takes to move through its life cycle. As a rule, consumer products have shorter life cycles than business products. The availability of mass communication devices such as television and the Internet informs consumers faster and shortens life cycles. Also, technological change tends to shorten product life cycles as new product innovation replaces existing products.

But business in the 21st century is even more forceful about innovation. Here's an observation[20] that presses all the buttons of urgency in getting innovative. "A marine geologist would have no problem grasping one of the main mechanisms of the IT industry: after new technology is introduced, it sinks, often quite quickly, to the bottom of the IT ocean and becomes part of its sediment—commodities that are well understood, easily copied, and hence not very profitable. This is why IT firms are always trying to move *up the stack*, reducing their dependence on hardware and pushing up into software and services, where margins are higher."

The Innovation Quad demands constant attention to moving up the stack. High-tech products and services are the dominant industries that need to prevail in keeping ahead. The more standard products need to rely not so much on technology but service innovations need to retain a competitive position. In both cases, the use of resources is a key factor.

Product Line and Brand Quads

There is a strong bond between three elements of the brand management[21] proposition: performance, advertising, and price. When we consider the performance of a brand, or a product for that matter, we perceive it in terms of quality and the ability to satisfy our expectations. In considering the advertising issue, we look on the effort more in terms of emotion and meaning. Does the advertisement appeal to our sense about what the brand or product should represent? However, the price is a summation of the previous two elements where we perceive the results of the trade-off or gradient from pure cost to value. If there is a high value attached to the brand, then the cost to us has no real import because we look on the item as being beyond price. Hallward tells us that, "Price is not as important as value. A premium priced-brand can be successful, provided that it maintains a performance or equity gap with cheaper alternatives. Attitudinal equity can often be built by advertising. Advertising has the power to differentiate the brand via emotions and imagery."

Obviously, we want to maintain our brand position for as long as we can without the investment of more R&D and innovation until necessary. But it does mean resources need to be applied toward advertising and the maintenance of brand equity. Further more we can't push the price upward or maintain too small a gap between lower priced brands and our brand. Doing so might encourage a growing perception of competitive brands as having equal value to ours and the loss of any brand position advantage we may have had.

The Cost-Price Leadership Quad

One of the great entrepreneurial stories to emerge in the latter part of the 20th century was hatched over drinks by flamboyant CEO of Southwest Airlines, Herb Kelleher, who saw a strategic window of opportunity, exploited a target niche, and grew from a four-plane airline into a 141-plane fleet and took on the big flyers at the same time. In 2010, Southwest made $459 million in profit and emerged from the worst decade in aviation history without furloughs or degradation of the customer experience. The company carved a niche in a cost-price market quadrant using a powerfully unique strategy of cost reduction, excellent service, and an entrepreneurially driven employee base.

The company used smaller airports that not only cost less per flight but were also less congested. They mostly used standardized aircraft, Boeing 737s, that were easily maintained but more importantly could be turned around in a matter of minutes, which added to flight efficiency. There were three factors that played heavily in Southwest's success in the highly competitive cost-price leadership quad: operating cost reduction, employee empowerment, and well-managed use of resources.

- Operating cost reduction: Use of Boeing 737s only, thus reducing maintenance costs as much as 70% by some accounts. Elimination of seat assignments, baggage transfers, meals, and free drinks.
- Employee empowerment: Negotiated flexible work rules, leaner crews, thus assuring no layoffs when times were tougher, a fun workplace, and ownership.
- Managed resources: Growth was pursued consistent with available resources, allowing a commitment to launch a new destination with 10 to 12 flights a day, rather than just one or two, a strategy of concentrating on a few areas, thus conserving resources.

Southwest was able to build a highly effective competitive advantage by offering lower prices, better service, and superior quality. They targeted a very identifiable niche market of air travellers who looked for transportation value based on service, price, and personable quality service from dedicated people. They operate in a price-sensitive environment, now helped by brand allegiances. Here is an example of moving toward a more value-respected position and improving profit through volume. The important consideration, however, is found in the fact that there is no competitive advantage more powerful than a committed, enthusiastic workforce—a Southwest hallmark.

Some or all of the quad strategies come into play at this position. Table 9.3 illustrates the various strategic moves you might consider across the quadrant fields. Each quad column moves the strategy into a different realm of value creation and defence. The most complex is in balancing brand and product line strategies even as you wonder about the final move into cost-price leadership or decline.

Entrepreneurial Flexibility

Entrepreneurial flexibility in the planning and implementation of company strategy is the ability of an organization to bring about changes in allocation of resources within the plan that can enable a response to shifts and challenges in the business environment. It applies to the four resource categories. In the case of customer-directed resources, entrepreneurial flexibility empowers an organization to be more innovative and responsive to customers. It also can apply to the external environment where company changes in policies and procedures can be made quickly and proactively in response to or in anticipation of changes from these uncontrollable variables.

Flexibility is manifested in the productivity and process improvements with the application of production equipment and its layout that would permit multiple and customized output on the same production lines with reduced cost due to changeovers. In all this there is the ongoing concern for balancing the allocation of resources among different activities that have the potential to change as time goes by. For example, if a company had set its budget for the sales department prior to a downturn

Table 9.3 Strategy selection guide for competing

Stage of PLC	Introduction Innovation quad	Growth brand and product line quad	Maturity and saturation product line and brand quad	Saturation to decline cost-price leadership quad
Product or service	New into the market	Has caught on and is gaining in sales. One or two competitors	An established product or service; Number of competitors fighting for market share	Older known product with many competitors and extensive offshore supply
Competitive strategy	Primary demand stimulation stressing value through innovation.	Promotion to establish brand equity. Initiate CRM	Heavy promotion and move to cost reduction	Harvest as move to innovation to recycle product
Product	Enhance product value for adoption leader.	Quality emphasis	Line extension	New product development
Positioning	Meanwhile find a niche(s) or new markets that do not yet relate to the new product. Cater to this target with all support possible	Strive to hold market share against innovative competitor	Battle of brands strategy Strong CRM	Brand retention and position
Promotion	Emphasize the advantages of your older product. Reminding users of solid previous success	Strong promotional thrust, all media	Initiate social media with conventional promotion	Social media and channel support
Pricing	Will need to offer extras or bonuses, rebates and incentives	Strong price—value strategy	Initiate pricing advantage through discounting	Meet competition but engage value proposition
Resource management	Customer-directed action	Stress on technology and Innovation	Development of incremental innovation	Productivity and process improvements.

in the economy, should they increase their sales activities or decrease them? The conventional approach might be to cut cost and have sales personnel increase their efforts.

But perhaps the astute strategy would be to increase the sales force and its activities. Of course, this would reduce the pool of funds available for other activities, which would require either cuts elsewhere or increasing the funds resource perhaps through loans or other financial means. When in 2005, Ford Motor Company realized there was a crunch about to take place in the economy, they borrowed heavily to ride out the trough; unlike GM and Chrysler, they did not need to seek out governmental assistance. The strategy worked and by 2010, the company earned net income of $6.6 billion, its best results since 2000, and over that year the company was able to reduce its debt position by $14.5 billion.[22]

The tradeoff between resource allocations is usually prompted by shifts in the environment, whether it might be a demand shift or a threat from a new entrant. It can be in the customer-oriented area in the operations side where productivity is critical. The normal approach is to produce a standard product at low cost–high volume to meet customer needs but using a flex manufacturing process with small batch output or switching back and forth between product types.

CHAPTER 10

Putting the Entrepreneur Into the Strategy

The People in Your Organization

When one treats people with benevolence, justice, and righteousness,
and reposes confidence in them, the army will be united in mind and
all will be happy to serve their leaders'.

—Sun Tzu

Entrepreneurship is not only important to an economy but also serves to satisfy social and psychological factors in society. The actions and processes an individual follows in creating a new endeavor, in fulfilling a dream, are a very human and behavioristic activity. In a free society, individuals are able to play out their ambitions and to grow in character and personality. The entrepreneurial organization endows its people, from the CEO to the shipping clerk, with an entrepreneurial attitude. It is the vital way of thinking that excites and infuses the organization. It is the antithesis of management in a common company that does not care for its people or believes they are ciphers who can be replaced if they fail to perform as directed. In a revealing article for CBS News, Jeff Haden points to eight reasons[1] people in an organization don't care. He cites the lack of freedom on the job, the lack of goals, and no sense of mission as key issues. The appendix at the end of the chapter has the listing. Look them over.

How does your organization compare? How many of these points does management convey to employees? The suggestion is that even if only one of these is evident in your company, it is one too many. By enrolling people as entrepreneurial agents in the organization, management can offset each of the foregoing deterrents to good behavior and productivity.

Each of Jeff Haden's observations is a characteristic that stifles human initiative and satisfaction on the job. We know that key people in the future are going to be well educated and quite intelligent. They will not work in the old, stifling environment with its lack of open communication, freedom, and self-expression. They will demand an equal status in the organization, the kind of engagement that will allow them to express their individuality and contribution, of being entrepreneurial.

So What Works?

A recent study[2] finds that entrepreneurial managers become entrepreneurial when they come to see themselves as being entrepreneurial; a condition that occurs when they are given resources and the capacity to make their own decisions. "Preliminary findings reveal that managers' subjective interpretations of their sociopolitical support and access to resources significantly stimulate entrepreneurial behavior."

Another study confirms that corporate entrepreneurship (CE) can be manifest when there is the scope to behave in that manner.[3] "Managers can, through deliberate actions, affect the level of CE within a given organization. .... What is more, the findings help narrow the specific activities that are important to the facilitation of CE where leaders are likely to get the most return by expressing their management support, providing organizational members some discretion and autonomy, and rewarding and reinforcing innovative, proactive, and prudent risk taking behaviors." In effect, managers can stimulate entrepreneurial action thus releasing individuals in the organization to become more involved in delivering a strong competitive position for the company.

Here's what a brilliant CEO[4] did with one of the outstanding software companies in America, HCL Technologies, the $6 billion IT services giant. He defied conventional wisdom by putting his employees first, not the customer. He created an organizational culture of employee trust by opening up and making transparent all communication and information within the company. In effect, he inverted the organizational hierarchy by making the management and the enabling functions accountable to the employee in the customer value zone. What he did was to unlock the potential of the employees by fostering an entrepreneurial mindset, he decentralized the decision making, and transferred the ownership of *change* to the employee in the workplace or value zone from which goods and services flowed to the customer. As noted in a recent HBR article,[5] the company takes pride in its philosophy of "Employee First," which empowers its 62,000 employees to create real value for their customers.

Innovation, Commercialization, and Entrepreneurs

There is a bonus to having entrepreneurial people in the organization. They are innovative. They look for opportunities or at least are on the lookout for opportunities to be innovative on the job. The act of commercializing a new product, concept, or service is the entrepreneurial act. The entrepreneur sees a new opportunity for a new technology and makes it happen or a creative manager sees a new market or a new need with existing customers for a product and makes it happen. It is the business of applying innovation to the market place that really defines what the entrepreneur does. Peter Drucker saw this as the primary function in an organization. "Because the purpose of business is to create a customer, the business enterprise has two—and only two—basic functions: marketing and innovation. Marketing and innovation produce results; all the rest are costs. Marketing is the distinguishing, unique function of the business."[6]

Here we see the issue that sets one organization apart from any other. The company that is alive and growing is one that continuously maintains an innovation-marketing management style. We see Apple's continuing success through the creation and introduction of new products. Even before that, after having pioneered the PC, the company had to reinvent itself. It had to decide whether it was going to remain in the same playing field as IBM and Asian producers or do something different. Instead, the company opted to specialize and serve a niche market in publishing and the graphics industry. Even though it lost in terms of sales volume, it gained in profits and value. Microsoft has pursued a strategy of improving its product almost annually. But even as it continues to expand its creative offerings it is aware that newer technologies threaten its global position and so it must redouble its creative efforts.

This is the primary entrepreneurial secret of commerce; you are not in the business of providing goods and services to the marketplace. You are in the business of serving the marketplace with your goods and services. You exist at the behest of your customer. She or he is your cue and it is they who determine your business. And there is a dyad here, a second issue that compels your company to be competitive and that is the constant need for innovation and new technologies. Your company must continuously engage in a process that embraces market and customer sensitivity and organizational innovation and renewal.

The 3M Company is a 100-year-old enterprise that spends twice the national average on innovation; it budgets an annual 6% to 7% of sales for R&D. The company, a dynamically creative, entrepreneurial company[7] with first quarter sales in 2010 exceeding $6 billion, produces 55,000 products that range from dental implants to the universally famous Post-It® Notes. It builds a strategy around emphasizing new products and technologies and constantly promotes a 15% *bootlegging* policy whereby established technical employees are urged to spend 15% of their time on projects of their own choosing. Thirty years after the invention of the ubiquitous Post-It® Notes, the company's investors are reaping the rewards of a culture of innovation at 3M.

Drawing from this success, Google has incepted a motto they call the *Google way* that allows its engineers to spend 20% of their time working on something company-related that interests them personally.

Well, that is the world of business giants, but what about the lesser players in the economy? Do SMEs feel the need to innovate and be entrepreneurial? Recent studies confirm that even as larger companies are more sensitive and do accommodate to change more quickly SMEs in fact do actively pursue innovation.[8] They are increasingly adapting to open innovation practices, although with a bit of a difference. Larger companies adapt more quickly with more structure and an administrative approach in applying innovation. They also have a different motivation where they are more interested in pursuing market-related objectives such as meeting customer demands or keeping up with competitors. However, in both cases, large and small, they bump into the same barrier: the organization and its cultural differences. Each firm over time or beginning with its founder acquires an operating philosophy that reflects its culture.

If it is an open culture, it encourages openness and participation. If it is a closed culture, it reflects a secretive style, particularly when cooperating with other partners.

The application of innovation in SMEs is very real and is a global phenomenon. A forum[9] on the topic determined that innovation is shifting from a closed and controlled environment of the corporate laboratories toward more open model that is based on cooperation between various different parties. *Knowledge connection* and *knowledge brokering* are becoming just as important to innovation as *knowledge discovery*. Knowledge and new technologies are no longer found in major corporations. SMEs, suppliers, consultants, and universities play an important role in networks and innovation clusters and are being recognized as driving forces in the innovation process.

We can observe here that the term *open* innovation is receiving more attention and limelight. Open innovation implies using external sources of information and knowledge to evolve innovative products, procedures, and processes. This would include support from suppliers, customers, government, universities, and such to prompt a company's approach to innovation. It contrasts with closed innovation where the company seeks total control over its unique knowledge, perhaps in the form of patents and copyrights.

Companies, large and small, can take one of three approaches to using innovation in their strategies. They can use it to their own purpose within the company and its business or they can license it to others. There are examples where smaller companies have let out the intellectual property (IP), to others on a geographic basis or within certain product groupings, thus exercising more control. Or the company can set up a new organization to exploit the new technology or innovation.

Finally, even the large and dynamic companies are not always ahead of the mob. Microsoft, the world leader in software, has its problems. In a review of performance in 2009, the board was pleased with its CEO, Steve Ballmer, for increasing sales 7% to a record $62.5 billion and for cutting costs and pushing along Cloud computing and gaming efforts. "But a discussion of Ballmer's pay in the company's annual proxy filing also referred to the need for the company to pursue innovations to take advantage of new form factors."[10] Microsoft's Kin, a feature phone aimed at teenagers, flopped in 2009 and was dropped less than three months after launch with poor sales. Its Windows mobile phone software has been losing share sharply over the last few years to Apple's iPhone and they missed entry into the iPad world. Of course, Ballmer need not worry too much since he owns about 4.5% of the company, worth about $10 billion. Nevertheless, the comment shows even larger firms need to run hard in keeping up with innovations or they can lose their position in the industry. Still and all, Microsoft still retains much of its entrepreneurial culture and will likely prevail for some time to come.

The Organization and Entrepreneurship

Managers and academics have long known that structure follows strategy. Once you have set in place a strategy for the company you then build or modify the organization to carry out the objectives. Yet larger organizations are often incapable of being innovative even though they have the ability to set up an organizational structure to carry out innovative actions. The result is that a lot of the innovation in the economy comes from smaller firms. The United States Department of Commerce notes that smaller companies account for half of all employment but remarkably they produce most of the radical or market-changing innovation and half of the incremental or product-adjusted innovation. Smaller firms are assuredly more creative. Perhaps we can find a clue where William Baumol makes the point that "the giant oligopolies provide the overwhelming preponderance of R&D expenditures, but in general those outlays are carefully directed to projects with minimal risk, which are therefore apt to yield non-negligible improvements, but improvements that typically are only incremental."[11] In other words, large companies are risk averse. They choose to move along well-paved roads rather than bumpier ones but perhaps smaller roads are more lucrative, at least in the beginning.

Larger companies suffer the attitude or culture of an adaptive style, an administrative approach rather than attempting to create new conditions. They prefer the notion of maximizing profit in contrast to setting objectives and striving to achieve them. Large organizations worry about failing when it comes to innovation. But smaller firms are like the old bumblebee anecdote, which says, "The laws of aerodynamics prove that the bumblebee is incapable of flight, since it does not have the capacity in terms of wing size or beat per second to achieve flight. However the bumblebee does not know this and it flies anyway!" Administrators, bound by the rules of precedence and of procedures, steeped in past successes, do not have nor are they encouraged to have the ability to see new opportunities and vistas. They only see the history of their position and what was good enough in the past as being good enough for the firm now.

Drucker[12] reveals the condition so clearly. A business is an organic system that exists not for its own sake but for the purpose of fulfilling societal need. So a company is judged by the purpose its serves. Managers are appendages to or within the organization. They cannot exist outside the organization. So the firm or enterprise defines the manager. But what happens, particularly in larger organizations, is that managers start to see themselves and their methods as being important and the company and its purpose as being secondary. "Management divorced from the institution it serves is not management," states Drucker. "What people mean by bureaucracy, and rightly condemn, is a management that has come to misconceive itself as an end and the institution as a means. This is the degenerative disease to which managements are prone, and especially those managements that do not stand under the discipline of the market test. To prevent this disease, to arrest it, and, if possible, to cure it must be a first purpose of any effective manager." To which might be added that innovation may be very hard if not impossible to encourage in the bureaucratic firm.

Making the Transition

Now that you are planning your strategy, the next and most important step is to build an entrepreneurial organization that will execute the plan. The one theme we hear throughout these economic slow growth times is the need for innovation and entrepreneurship. Innovation means bringing new products and services to the market and also improving on the processes that provide goods and services. But the actor in all this is the creative person who seizes on the innovation and makes it come into being as a commercial success or as a means of increasing productivity. In carrying out this vital activity, entrepreneurs also create jobs. The Kauffman organization[13] makes the following point. "With virtually all the net new jobs growth in the United States over the last 25 years coming from entrepreneurial companies, we need more entrepreneurs—entrepreneurs like those who founded Pfizer, Yahoo, Intel, DuPont, eBay, and Proctor & Gamble." So entrepreneurs are both needed and important to the company and to the economy.

Another spin-off in the need to have entrepreneurial people is that if the firm is sensitive to keeping these creative individuals they will remain with the organization and help it grow. It is often the case that employees see new opportunities and submit their ideas to company officials only to be turned down. This, of course, prompts their leaving to start their own new ventures.

But the important consideration is to let people be more entrepreneurial within the firm in the sense of controlling their own workplace. The freedom to be in charge of one's own space invites not only more creativity but also a personal commitment to the organization which enables that behavior. That does not mean encouraging everyone in the organization to be free spirits, so to speak, since many will not willingly accept that responsibility. Some employees are very happy with a secure job and an accommodating management who accept and recognize their contribution. They do not need the obligations of doing much more than a good, perhaps professional job. Their satisfaction comes from other things they do outside the job, their family, hobbies, and recreational pursuits. But for key people, particularly those who embrace more responsibility, there is the likelihood of encouraging entrepreneurial behavior. In this chapter, we talk about the process that moves a company from being managed by standard operating procedures (SOP)[14] to one that is dynamic and able to negotiate the roiling waters of the new economy.

But here's an additional point to consider. When employees are involved, when they are stakeholders in the company, the company performs much better. Research[15] into how employee-owned businesses performed before and during the recession found they create more jobs and recruit better employees than conventional firms. They are more profitable, more stable over business cycles, and are lower risks than others. The point is that there is something very tangible about employee involvement that goes to the bottom line.

Defining Entrepreneurial Action

Entrepreneurial managers are those who display characteristics of corporate entrepreneurship,[16] which is the process of recognizing an opportunity, applying resources to it, and creating something of value within the bounds of an established organization. It takes place away from the entrenched policies of senior management or a parent company. It is about being an entrepreneur but doing so within a structured environment. Harvard[17] acknowledges the need for a new entrepreneurial model with the observation that three strategic imperatives should play out in the manager's role. These are that the behavior should (i) spur innovation, (ii) build commitment, and (iii) adapt to change. In the first instance, the role of exciting or at least setting an environment for "creative tension" is important. It permits new thinking to encroach on old problems and has prompted a number of firms, like 3M Corp and Google—for example, to encourage the use of "bootleg time" of 15% to 20% for certain key personnel, allowing them scope to dream up new concepts or solutions. This is a reasonable expectation since most of the new ideas for innovations and inventions occur in a person's workplace. People in the company are closely aware of the manner in which products affect their customers and perhaps intuitively "see" new ways or radical changes that can be made that might positively improve customer satisfaction. Given there is an allowable, if not a nurturing, environment in which to offer an improvement, they will come forward. In the past, companies used a suggestion box for new inputs. Unfortunately, some managers either used the concepts for their own purposes or discarded them altogether. Unfortunate too was the idea of separation between the higher levels and the lower levels in the use of a box, rather than allowing face-to-face dialogue, which may have enabled more clarification and acceptance of ideas submitted.

Entrepreneurial action harkens to Kirzner's[18] view of the entrepreneur as being ever alert to opportunities. Entrepreneurial people can be developed or grown in an entrepreneurial incubator that is provided by the company she or he works in. The workplace is familiar ground and is a place where they seek a competitive opportunity to grow and achieve personal goals, which are hopefully consonant with company goals. Obviously, motivation is a key element in fostering entrepreneurial behavior.

Given an individual is motivated on the job then she or he will be receptive to impulses that inspire entrepreneurial happenings.

Harvard's Joe Hadzima tells us we "need employees[19] who regularly demonstrate entrepreneurial characteristics and work habits. Management of entrepreneurial companies must work diligently to recognize, identify, and attract this type of employee during the recruitment process to assure a steady stream of the people with the right stuff to fuel growth of the venture." Though he was referring to new technology companies, the idea is surely important to most companies that look to grow and improve their chances for survival. So it is important that organizations hire people who will respond to the concept of entrepreneurism and to develop those already in the company to have the right stuff being especially careful to weed out those who interfere with the process.

How can we recognize those who will take on the entrepreneurial role? Hadzima lists a number of characteristics that boil down to five key markers. Managers should look for people who:

1. Are willing to take reasonable chances when given the opportunity to do so, to make something new happen in the workplace. It can be a new process, the introduction of a product improvement, or a new way of doing things.
2. Are goal-directed, result-oriented. They have a vision of what is to be done and direct their actions to the targeted outcome. They are persistent in pursuing their goal and are willing to press their arguments with senior people to go there.
3. Take the initiative in what they have created or wish to accomplish with energy and drive. These are not laid back people. They have high levels of enthusiasm and energy and are committed to the organization, its goals, and overall success.
4. Willing to take on responsibility and are growth-oriented. These are people who can take on more senior positions in the company provided, of course, there is a commensurate recognition of their work and suitable credit for what they are able to accomplish.
5. Are team players, part of the group. They know the need for everyone to pull together so the organization can succeed and not just individuals in the firm. They recognize the need for everyone to take

a stake in what they hope to accomplish and are willing to share the accolades and recognition for a job well done.

Implementing the Implementation Process

The purpose to all this is to develop an employee-centered methodology that will help us implement strategies more effectively. When we do that we release the opportunity for creative and entrepreneurial action by all the company people in the customer supply chain: sales, administrative, operations, and support personnel throughout the organization. The entrepreneurial strategy management (ESM) model tells us to begin our strategic planning by embracing that concept.

The first step (Figure 10.1) is to determine your primary customer. We must examine our customers in some detail so we can really get a handle on their needs and aspirations. While we're at it, we need to figure out what their potential needs might be in the next three years or so. After considering the environment, new technologies, and competitors, what are the product or service features and value propositions we need to build into our offering that will better serve our market? We know that given a choice, the customer will choose the company that gives 100% effort to their satisfaction. Nothing less will do. This step is critical since it is the point of departure for the entire strategic plan. The determination as to customers requires serious thinking as to who is the primary customer. There can be no equivocation about trying to blend all your customers

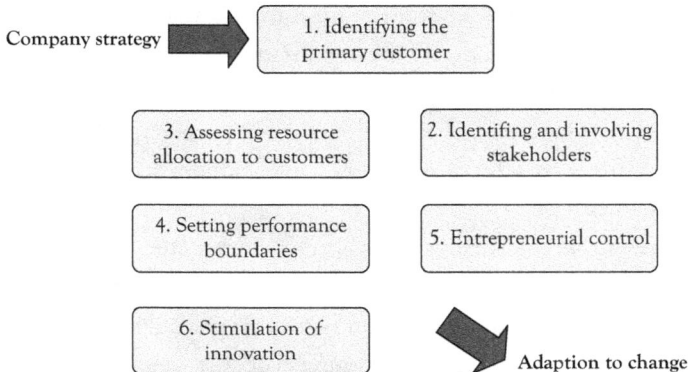

Figure 10.1 Implementing the implementation while creating strategy

into a single image. There needs to be a very clear profile as to the company's primary customer and purpose. As we take up this task, we begin to incorporate the components that are typically displayed in the conventional strategy procedure. First by coming to understand our customer we begin to understand a vital part of our mission and purpose. It is, as Drucker tells us, to *create a customer* and we can do that by engaging her or him in a customer relationship.

Secondly, we set out the goals and objectives we wish to accomplish. We take these down to our people in the organization with the intention of extracting their perspective as to what strategy will work most effectively in accomplishing our goals. The challenge is to engage all key players in the company from managers to supervisors, knowledge workers, and throughout the operation. From this point on our planning methodology incorporates execution and strategy development together like the caduceus, the medical symbol with intertwined snakes. And by the way, in ancient times, the caduceus actually referred to the associations of business and commerce and not medicine.

The second step is to identify people who will deliver on our strategic efforts. Who will fulfill the mission? Who will accomplish the goals and objectives? What will be their contribution to the company's success? We need to prioritize our employees, shareholders, and others as to our core values our objectives and to encourage their commitment to those values and fulfillment of the strategy. This step is a critical part of the model. It is within this action we begin to create an entrepreneurial organization. We begin to ask individuals to take on the role of creative managers and executives of the corporate strategy from the highest level to the lowest. In effect, we wish to moderate the organization to an organic state where all members of the body know how to behave in carrying out the mission of the body, where even if they do not know implicitly they can communicate freely to acquire the needed information that will help them complete their task.

Everyone in the organization is now represented in the planning activity. The discussion at all levels can address the objectives to be considered and be a part of the decision as to what goals should be achieved.

The third step aligns the resources of the organization to the customer-people blend. All the assets, (tangible and intangible) brands, personnel, financials, plants, equipment, IP, management know-how, values, and the customer franchise need to be allocated or pooled to be drawn on as strategy is developed and implementation is assigned. It is not so much that resources are tagged for each particular strategic move. In fact this is not always a good move since it holds the promise of bureaucratic allotment and the potential for turf warfare over assets. Instead, the resources that may be drawn down as needed or they may be assigned on a point-by-point basis as the business proceeds. Obviously, people within departments are not subject to reassignment, except as may be urgently required in a crisis, but funding and technologies can be shifted to meet needs brought on by change.

This is also the time when the classical SWOT analysis can be called on to assess the strengths and weaknesses of the company's resources and how they may play in dealing with the opportunities and threats facing the company or as they crop up during operations. The planning section will have set out the objectives and goals for the organization and determined which of those resources in hand will be used and what new resources need be mustered to accomplish those goals. A downturn in the economy will stimulate a need to increase the selling and CRM effort, which in turn may call on extra funding that will come from some other department.

The fourth step accounts for the limits that will define the boundaries for individual action. These are spelled out in the form of a role prescription. This feature posts the objectives and responsibilities for the key positions in the company position-objectives-responsibility (POR). It does not detail how the job is to be carried out. Individuals are tagged with the role they are expected to fulfill in terms of the specific goals and responsibilities they must discharge in meeting or exceeding their objectives. The intention of the POR is to make each individual a manager, an entrepreneurial manager of her or his work area.

The strategies are actually carried out through the POR instrument. Typically, objectives are set out by departments who may then create specific programs to accomplish the goals. The manager of these departments then assigns various responsibilities to individuals and supervises them as to performance and outcome. The manager also controls the resources the department will need to carry out the job. However, in the ESM model, the manager releases some or all responsibilities in the details to individuals in the team or department. It is this activity that encourages the entrepreneurial spirit to the organization.

The fifth step moves the process to an organic perspective where individuals are enabled to monitor their actions within the entrepreneurial set. The POR not only sets the limits but also spells out the network within and from which the individual can obtain information and vary his or her actions albeit consistent with the overall objectives of the department and company. If the company is to be creative, it must also allow for the individual creativity of people in it which is encouraged by allowing people to adjust their work flow to more effectively complete their task and objectives.

An examination of the role of a professional salesperson gives us an excellent picture of the entrepreneurial potential of individuals in the company. Sales people use company resources: automobiles, samples, money, technology, know-how, and time as they see fit in the execution of their responsibilities. These individuals consume resources, manage their work environment, and accept their responsibilities in terms of CRM and growth as they accomplish their individual objectives.

The sixth step is an expected result from having created an entrepreneurial environment in the organization. It encourages people to be innovative and creative in their jobs. It lends itself to creating value chains within the system where individuals are encouraged to use technology when and where applicable to facilitate their operations. Hitt et al. point out that innovation is the foundation of business creativity and is critical for all firms, large and small, to compete effectively in the 21st century. Smaller firms are most productive when it comes to innovation. They produce most of the radical innovation and half the incremental innovation in the economy even though it is the larger firms who spend more than 80% of the R&D in developed nations.[20] The statistic clearly shows there is a powerful need for large firms to encourage entrepreneurial management.

The ESM model calls for the full commitment of management and employees to the entrepreneurial strategic mode. It calls for the company, as a primary objective, to deliver value to the customer at the intake side and continuously to retain existing customers. It opens the organization to develop and sustain an entrepreneurial culture; one that is continuously looking for opportunities to improve but also to use innovation in creating opportunities both within the company, to build value chains, and externally, to deliver unique products and services to customers. The model also encourages continuous response to the environment and to performance criteria so that critical responses can be made quickly and effectively. Finally, the model encourages participation in the rewards of effective entrepreneurial activity by all employees in the company.

The Corporate Entrepreneur—the Corpreneur

Jack Welch, the iconic former General Electric CEO, wanted to leave GE early in his career. He was not happy with the way the organization was being directed nor did he feel his contributions were sufficiently acknowledged. But it was his mentor, Reuben Gutoff, who talked him out of it and he stayed. It can be argued that Welch was very entrepreneurial and was able to bring creative changes into the corporation through his leadership and style that encouraged individual autonomy, if not independence, in his executives. There have been many corporate entrepreneurs over the last few decades who have championed corporate causes and made significant contributions to their companies, for which, one might add, they have been handsomely rewarded.

Consulting companies[21] now specialize in corporate entrepreneurship programs. McKinsey Company has developed a series of tests and a program for developing corporate entrepreneurs, and books[22] are being published to encourage entrepreneurial growth in companies. The economic crisis has alerted industry and governments to the need for creativity and innovation within corporations if there is to be significant improvement in the economy.

We can profile the corporate entrepreneur, the corpreneur as some have coined the term, as a dynamic individual who manifests the foregoing profile of the entrepreneur within the permissive confines of the organization, permissive in that management encourages individuals to be creative, seeking opportunities to achieve titular independence, acknowledged for their achievement, and yet permitted to take some risk as they and their colleagues create something of value for customers, the company, and society at large.

Strategic Entrepreneurial Management

If we compare two well-known companies in terms of growth and innovativeness, we see a remarkable difference. Sears began in 1891. It grew to 864 stores by 1980 and on to 1,293 full stores by 2010. It generated over $44 billion in retail sales in 2009. On the other hand, Walmart started in 1962 had only 600 stores in 1980 and today is the world's largest retailer with $400 billion in sales revenue through 8,400 stores. Presumably, Sears has had competent managers and as much opportunity as Walmart, yet they are one-tenth the size and scope of Walmart. Obviously one answer is leadership. But that begs more questions. What kind of leadership? Why were they able to grow so fast? Was the difference in merchandise or in advertising? We are told that Sears may not make it past 2014; that it will fall from the scene unless it dumps K-Mart.

Michael Hitt[23] tells us there is a new competitive environment out there—one filled with threats to companies that continue to do business in the same way they did in the past and opportunities too, for those who are willing to "form competitive advantages through innovations that create new industries and markets." What this implies is the capacity to establish a dominant influence in the company that stimulates the development of entrepreneurial strategies. The difference between Sears and Wal-Mart is in the attitude toward innovation and expansion. Wal-Mart founder, Sam Walton, had built within the organization a culture of entrepreneurial thinking that carried over in the creation and implementation of business strategies for the firm. He encouraged risk taking. He encouraged his people to be different and in response to successful growth he shared the profits with his associates. Above all he spoke out for the customer when he observed, "There is only one boss. The customer. And he can fire everybody in the company from the chairman on down, simply by spending his money somewhere else." He was truly an entrepreneurial leader. Your ability to innovate and bring about change will be tied to your attitude and response as an entrepreneurial manager.

There is an entrepreneurial revolution taking place in the world.[24] Lesser developed countries are leapfrogging into economic growth powered by emerging domestic entrepreneurs. Iceland, Rwanda, Chile, and Israel have proven to be fertile grounds for entrepreneurship.[25] In the United States, according to the Department of Commerce, "The entrepreneurial revolution has totally transformed both our sense of the scale of economics and methods of transactions. Consider the youngest and most visible manifestation of entrepreneurial start-ups, electronic commerce. According to the U.S. Department of Commerce, between 1995 and 1999 e-commerce was less than 1% of the U.S. economy but accounted for 35% of the GNP. At the heart of the revolution is the entrepreneurial propensity to be innovative where small entrepreneurial firms have been responsible for half of all innovation and 95% of all radical innovation in the United States."[26] This translates into 24 times as many innovations per R&D dollar compared to those spent by firms with more than 10,000 employees.

And the revolution is taking place in existing enterprises too. Companies need to apply all the entrepreneurial skills they can muster if they are to compete and succeed in the global community. They must take on entrepreneurial strategic planning and actions in finding new products, new markets, and competitive space if they are to create new wealth. In effect, according to Ireland et al.[27] they must find new ways that will "disrupt an industry's existing competitive rules."

As an entrepreneur, Steve Jobs was able to see opportunities in the marketplace. He was chided by the industry when in 2001 he announced the launch of iTunes. The digital music industry was in disarray as Napster and other free music download sites came under copyright infringement charges and were shut down. But Jobs had a strategy in which iTunes was but an introductory stage. After racking up more than a million downloads in just a few short months, it quickly became clear that iTunes was every bit as revolutionary as Apple hoped and the music copier was merely the opening shot of a campaign that would redefine the company. In October 2001, Steve Jobs revealed "an oddly named, undeniably sexy hand-held device. Built exclusively to leverage the popularity of Apple's music app, iPod came bundled with a brand-new version of iTunes that allowed it to seamlessly integrate with the songs and playlists stored on our Macs."[28]

Who Is a Strategic Entrepreneurial Manager?

The entrepreneur is defined as an individual who is motivated by four key drivers: desire for independence of action, need to achieve with an internal locus of control, and willingness to take a risk. The entrepreneurial manager sees opportunities and drives hard to exploit or commercialize them. Lee Iacocca, former Ford Vice President and known as the man who saved Chrysler in 1979 to 1980, had a vision of a new sports car targeted at the young generation of boomers moving into the workplace. In 1964, he produced the Mustang as a fulfillment of that vision with original sales forecasts projected at about 100,000 units for the first year. This mark was surpassed in three months from rollout. Another 318,000 would be sold during the model year (a record) and in its first 18 months, more than one million Mustangs were built.[29] What is not so well known is that a good part of the success was in fact attributable to the older executive types who saw in the car a return to their adolescence and so, donning cloth caps and a long scarf they bought the toy of their dreams and drove off into the sunset.

The issue today is in the difference between the trained manager— one who has grown professionally in a structured corporation or has obtained a business degree (the "A" type manager) and the entrepreneurial ("E" type) manager. E-managers do not fit the conventional corporate mold. They are endowed with a drive to be creatively different but within the structure of an organization. Their desire for independence is struck more in the context of an internal self-recognition of difference, hence independence through their work—an acknowledgment that to all intents and purposes they can do what they want (but consistent with corporate goals). An examination of Table 10.1 quickly establishes there is a strong behavioral difference between two classes of managers.

The Entrepreneurial E-Manager

Here then are the two challenges you face in developing entrepreneurial strategies. The first is to be an entrepreneurial E-type manager, one who will initiate change in the product line by seeing opportunities that exist or arise in the marketplace and exploiting them to the company's benefit. And you develop the ability in others in the organization to be entrepreneurial. Jack Welch, former iconic Chairman and CEO of General Electric Corporation, in his early years, saw the company as a relentless bureaucracy and he struggled for 40 years to build a more entrepreneurial

Table 10.1 Comparison of managerial types

Professional "A" type manager	Entrpreneurial "E" type manager
Tends to be a concrete thinker	Tends to be an intuitive thinker
Some initiative	Takes initiative
Income and status dependency	Performance dependency
Little innovation	Seeks change
Risk averse	Risk taking
External, some internal locus	Internal locus of control
Controlled, ordered lifestyle	Innovative lifestyle
Controlled workplace	Varied workplace
Motivated by status and income	Motivated by achievement
Doing things right	Doing the right thing

Source: Entrepreneurship: Process and Management, Ken R. Blawatt

organization, one that balanced the need for effective administration against the needs for efficient production and market agility.

So, secondly there is an urgent need to change the organization or at least modify it to be totally responsive to entrepreneurial strategies. Many companies make the attempt to become more entrepreneurial but are unable to do so because they cannot overcome the major obstacle—the prevailing corporate culture. Managers in a company are often a reflection of the company culture. The professional A-type manager takes on a risk-averse, conservative, status-quo, and controlled job environment because that is what is expected of him. In turn, he is given recognition, status, and commensurate income for doing things right. To implement entrepreneurial strategies that style cannot prevail.

Strategic entrepreneurship applies to both opportunity-seeking and advantage-seeking behaviors of which innovation is a main point of the strategic entrepreneurial initiative and can take place at any place throughout the company. On the one hand, you can engage an opportunity-driven mindset where management sets out to achieve and maintain a product or process that establishes a competitive advantage for the firm. In some cases the innovation can take the form of an incremental or radical change from the firms' past market and business behavior, its products, markets, distribution, or business models (an internal transformation). And, on the other hand, innovation can represent fundamental change where the company itself is dramatically differentiated from the rest of competition. In this case, it exhibits the entrepreneurial dynamic of transition relative to the environment and competition; it breaks with convention.

To summarize, the entrepreneurial E-type manager is a dynamic, customer-oriented manager who seeks his independence within the organization by controlling the business environment, changing it, and improving it internally and externally to accomplish growth and profitability, in which expectantly he shares. In this regard, the entrepreneurial manager is characterized as being

- a visionary who sees opportunities and develops clear goals for the organization;
- willing to push the at the boundaries, to develop markets, and create new products;
- a calculating risk-taker, applying corporate resources;
- motivated to achieve desired outcomes, thus affirming an independent status within the company;
- persistent, but patient and determined to succeed through cooperation with others; and
- a professional manager and a strong communicator.

Maintaining the status quo is no longer tenable. We have but to recall the words of Captain Edward J. Smith who said, "I cannot imagine any condition which would cause a ship to founder. I cannot conceive of any vital disaster happening to this vessel. Modern ship building has gone beyond that." On April 15, 1912, the Captain Smith's ship the HMS *Titanic* sank in the early morning darkness after having struck an iceberg two and half hours prior. Tragically, over 1,500 people perished. The *Titanic* was on its maiden voyage and considered nearly unsinkable by the owners and many of the officers and crew on board.

Developing Entrepreneurial Strategies

In the 1964 movie *Zorba the Greek* starring Anthony Quinn, the hero is asked about his lack of fear to taking risk. He responds by declaring that, "Life is trouble. Only death is not. To be alive is to undo your belt and look for trouble." In another scene, Zorba (Quinn) announces that, "A man needs a little madness... or else he never dares cut the rope and be free." The movie profoundly evokes an entrepreneurial flavor that literally forces the viewer to think about freedom, independence, and entrepreneurship. The strategic manager looks for trouble and dares to cut the rope.

Figure 10.1 sets out the entrepreneurial approach that is needed to set in motion innovative strategies. The urgency to apply corporate entrepreneurship has arisen from a number of issues that have grown in importance[30] given the stimulation global competition has brought about in terms of:

(a) the need for changes to systems, innovations in products and processes, and improvements in management, particularly in strategic planning;

(b) the inability of many organizations to change, to overcome weaknesses, particularly in addressing corporate culture; and

(c) the growing number of innovative-minded employees who are willing to abandon their bureaucratic organizations.

Jack Welch almost left the General Electric organization. He was so disgusted with the bureaucracy and slow-witted thinking in the company; he had sought out and been offered a job with another company. Fortunately for GE he was talked out of the move by a senior executive who challenged Welch to change the organization and make it more entrepreneurial. And he did. An entrepreneurial orientation has two characteristics. The first is that managers are themselves entrepreneurial; they develop a propensity to see an opportunity and have a passion, a strong commitment to exploit it. One must have passion perhaps born of a need to achieve the goals that are set out and to serve the customers who they see as part of an opportunity. The second dimension is that of orienting the company itself, changing the culture if necessary in the creation of the company's strategy. The firm usually has a culture and some performance criteria. However, with most SMEs, there is not likely to be a strongly entrenched culture or behavioral norms; thus these can be changed more readily to the entrepreneurial orientation than with the larger, more bureaucratic organizations.

Finally, there is a caveat in all this. It is a conundrum given to us by Peter Drucker from his text *Innovation and Entrepreneurship* where he claims that, "Planning as the term is commonly understood is actually incompatible with an entrepreneurial society and economy... innovation, almost by definition, has to be decentralized, ad hoc, autonomous, specific and microeconomic."[31] The observation clearly signals danger in planning where the plans themselves become the dictums that are carved in stone, as it were, and are followed slavishly or as is more often the case not acted on at all. Winston Churchill is credited as stating that "Plans are of little importance, but planning is essential." Plans must be carried out.

Here then is the entrepreneurial imperative. Plans must be creatively developed, but then they must be implemented in an entrepreneurial fashion, which is to say that in the field and in the marketplace they change or become obsolete and must be amended and even altered. Thus, plans become not the road to follow but rather a horse to ride from which position any entrepreneurial maneuver can be made.

Wayne McRann and his brother were two entrepreneurial workers who finally quit their jobs working in the shipping department of a large western mining company. They came to the conclusion that there was need for a shipping services company and since they were familiar with the business they created a business plan, raised money, and started their new enterprise that provided shipping services to the region. But alas, they found there were many more qualified competitors than they had planned for and it soon became clear they would not likely succeed. However, in calling on the market, Wayne became aware of a need for store retailing fixtures. Very quickly, the brothers changed their operation to one of producing wire displays, stands, and tables and established a successful company. They abandoned the original plan and adjusted their operations to a new opportunity.

Making Employees Into Entrepreneurial Employees

If it is the intention to cast managers into an entrepreneurial mold, we must also ask their team members, the employees to take on a more creative role too. Some years ago, I conducted a survey of suppliers to the Ontario automotive manufacturing sector.[32] The study was drawn from a population of over 900 companies and its purpose was to develop strategies that would assist the government of Ontario to help its automotive sector improve and compete with offshore producers. One of the key areas of interest was the productivity of companies, in particular Canadian-owned companies and their ability to survive in a global market. In all the companies studied, one firm stood out head and shoulders above all others. Its productivity was almost double that of the average. It was an American subsidiary that produced air brake systems for heavy trucks, and its story was an extreme example of employee entrepreneurship.

It seems the company was about to be closed and its 200 employees were facing permanent layoff. However, head office decided to allow Canadian managers of the company: the general manager, the production manager, the sales manager, and comptroller a free hand in trying to turn the company around. Within the first year, they stopped the bleeding from the bottom line. In the second year, they generated a small profit and by the fourth year the company was achieving fantastic productivity while generating enormous profits. How did they do it? The average age of machinery in the plant was over 40 years old. Some dated back to the First World War. It certainly was not due to capital equipment. What management did was they referred the problem back to the employees. On a department by department basis, they asked employees how they would improve on their work output. Using limited funds and a lot of know-how and the freedom to be creative in the workplace, they rebuilt the manufacturing process, turning it into a lean, agile production unit—an amazing tale of success.

The example demonstrates what can happen when you encourage entrepreneurship within a workplace setting. There were three strategic parameters at work in this example. First, the men were *motivated* to keep their jobs. Secondly, they were given a clear set *overall objective*; improve productivity so the company could survive and make a profit. Thirdly, they were *empowered* to undertake and implement their own objectives within their own territory so to speak and using limited resources. Had they also been *rewarded* for their efforts after resurrecting the company, it is probable the company would have continued in a leadership position in the industry.

The Entrepreneurial Process

The workplace of 50 years ago is gone. The humble workers who dutifully toiled at their tasks and accepted whatever wage was given are long gone. In her or his place is an all-together different being: the knowledge worker, the Internet savvy employee, the educated, and perhaps bored individual who needs an income to live. But many are also looking for a livelihood to which they can commit themselves and perhaps do some good in the world. Punching a clock and tightening a nut for eight hours a day does not cut it. Nor does sitting at a desk and shuffling papers or making computer entries.

Fortunately, the more enlightened organizations are leading the way in creating a meaningful workplace, a place of self-fulfillment. Encouraging the development of an entrepreneurial organization does that. It begins by including the team in the creation of strategy and that leads to the successful execution of strategy.

The Management Innovation eXchange[33] makes the point that an entrepreneurial organization is better. "We believe that it is possible to instill in employees 'a culture to innovate' by equipping them with the following: awareness, opportunity, ownership and recognition." These are the elements of workplace entrepreneurship. It begins by giving the objectives and goals from senior management to the company team—the unit supervisors and employees (Figure 10.2). These members develop their views as to the elements of the strategy they would engage and how these might be accomplished from their perspective including a listing of the resources required.

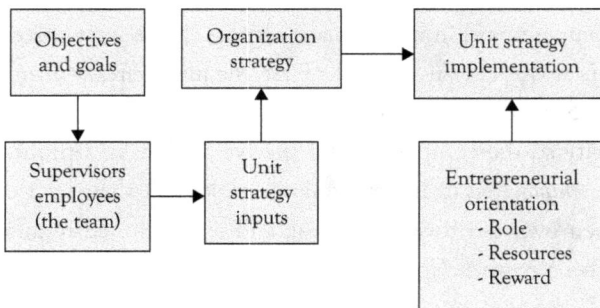

Figure 10.2 The entrepreneurial process

In turn, management compiles an aggregated strategic report that reflects the overall direction for the organization. Perhaps the process might go back and forth, one or two more times to hone the unit strategies and synchronize them with the main strategic body. The organization strategy is then given back to the units along with a breakout of their specific strategic role for implementation.

The control feature is proscribed by the overall objectives. The resource issue is dealt with from an entrepreneurial prospective where the individual used his ingenuity and innovation to compensate for lack of resources.

A recent article in the *Harvard Business Review* tells us about the innovative and entrepreneurial approach Proctor & Gamble has used to bring them into leadership in the consumer marketplace. "Back in 2000 the prospects for Procter & Gamble's Tide, the biggest brand in the company's fabric and household care division, seemed limited. The laundry detergent had been around for more than 50 years and still dominated its core markets, but it was no longer growing fast enough to support P&G's needs. A decade later Tide's revenues have nearly doubled, helping push annual division revenues from $12 billion to almost $24 billion. The brand is surging in emerging markets, and its iconic bull's eye logo is turning up on an array of new products and even new businesses, from instant clothes fresheners to neighborhood dry cleaners."

What P&G[34] does to sustain its unique leadership position as an innovator and entrepreneurial organization is to continuously imbue their management and project team members with an entrepreneurial mindset. It is a mindset that fosters disruptive growth. It incorporates entrepreneurs and entrepreneurial thinking in the project groups, creating new products.

The purpose for creating entrepreneurial employees is to engage them in the process. According to Watson Wyatt,[35] "Companies cannot develop effective teams and working relationships unless everyone involved clearly understands the connections between their jobs and objectives… Workers and their companies excel when they know why their jobs matter and they understand what's in it for them."

The ESM methodology engages people in the organization early in the planning process and then involves them in the execution.

The process further requires transparency in all dealing with people in the organization. In addition to involving them in the planning and execution of strategy, it requires open communication with employees about all matters that affect them, sharing of financial information, and other information important to the operation of the enterprise with employees.

The Payoff

When we build an organic, entrepreneurial organization, we build a creative, responsive, and productive enterprise that meets the most rigid of criteria for sustainability. We are contributing to what John Mackey and Rav Sisodia write about in their new book[36] on *Conscious Capitalism* where, based on some of today's best-known companies, they illustrate how "these two forces can—and do—work most powerfully to create value for all stakeholders: including customers, employees, suppliers, investors." We also learn that in doing so we improve the bottom line considerably. Earlier studies of entrepreneurial organizations[37] show that "Today's best companies *get it*. From Costco® to Commerce Bank, Wegmans to Whole Foods®: they're becoming the ultimate value creators." They're generating *every* form of value that matters: *emotional, experiential, social, and financial.* And they're doing it for *all* their stakeholders. Not because it's politically correct: *because it's the only path to long-term competitive advantage.*

This study of entrepreneurial firms found that they returned 1,026% for investors over a 10-year period ending in June 2006 as compared to 122% for the S&P 500, a very competitive 8:1 ratio. When examined over a five-year periods, the ratio was even higher with a 128% return compared to the S&P 500 of 13%.

When we build an entrepreneurial company, we build a greatly effective organization where everyone succeeds: a win-win condition. When employees are part of a team that works productively and creatively, and they are commensurately rewarded for their efforts, they not only assure corporate success, but also establish an almost unassailable competitive position.

Appendix

Eight Reasons Your Employees Don't Care

1. **No freedom.** Following procedures are important, but not slavishly. People need autonomy because it breeds engagement, satisfaction, and innovation. Decide which process battles are worth fighting; otherwise, let employees have the freedom to work the way they work best.

2. **We need targets.** Goals are fun. (I've never met anyone who wasn't at least a little bit competitive.) Targets create a sense of purpose and add meaning to even the most repetitive tasks. Without a goal to shoot for, work is just work.

3. **No sense of mission.** We all like to feel a part of something bigger. Striving to be worthy of words like "best," "largest," "fastest," or "highest quality" provides a sense of purpose. Let employees know what you want the business to achieve; how can they care about your dreams if they don't know your dreams?

4. **No clear expectations.** While every job should include decision-making latitude, every job also has basic expectations regarding the way certain situations should be handled. Criticize an employee for providing a refund today even though last week refunds were standard procedure and you've lost the employee. (How can I do a good job when I don't know what doing a good job means?) When standards change, always communicate those changes first—then stick with them. And when you don't, explain why this particular situation is different.

5. **No input.** Everyone wants to be smart. How do I show I'm smart? By offering suggestions and ideas. (Otherwise, no matter how hard I work I just feel like a robot.)

6. **No connection.** The company provides the paycheck, but employees work for people.... Employees want to be seen as people, not numbers. Numbers don't care. People care—especially when you care about them first.

7. **No consistency.** Most employees can deal with a boss who is demanding and quick to criticize as long as she treats every employee

the same way. The key to maintaining consistency is to communicate; the more employees understand why a decision was made, the less likely they are to assume favoritism or unfair treatment.

8. **No future.** Every job should have the potential to lead to something better, either within or outside the company. Take the time to develop employees for jobs they hope to fill—even if those positions are outside your company. They will care about your business because they know you care about them.

Source: Haden, J. (2011).

Notes

Preface

1. Pfeffer and Sutton (1999).
2. Sisodia, Wolfe, and Sheth (2007).

Chapter 1

1. Sassoon (2007, January).
2. *Ford Motor Company* (2009, January).
3. Reis (1997).
4. Kaplan and Norton (2001, June).
5. Charan and Colvin (1999, June).
6. Rumelt (2011, June).
7. Thompson, Strickland III, and Gamble (2005), p. 33.
8. Thompson, Strickland III, and Gamble (2005), p. 9.
9. Mankins and Steele (2006, February).
10. Fujimoto (2010, March). John has been senior advisor for Dr. James Womack's Lean Enterprise Institute since its inception in 1997. John Shook was director of University of Michigan's Japan Technology Management Program, and taught in the university's Department of Industrial and Operations Engineering from 1994 to 2000.
11. Kaplan and Norton (2001).
12. Rumelt (2011).
13. Refers to an old movie starring Ronald Reagan as Knute Rockne who was the coach of the U.S. Notre Dame team in the 1920s and George Gipp was his star player. The story goes that Gipp fell ill and when dying he asked Rockne to promise that, when things were going badly for the team, he should inspire them by asking them to "win one for The Gipper."
14. Neilson, Martin, and Powers (2008, June).
15. Cloke and Goldsmith (2002).
16. Christensen (1997).
17. Hamel (2007).
18. Gochman (2002).
19. Orrell (2010).
20. Knowledge@Wharton (2003, April).
21. Rouse and Miller (2010).

22. Gunther McGrath (2000), p. 1.
23. Hartley (1995), p. 60.
24. Burgelman (1983, December).
25. Sunter (2010).
26. Sarasvathy and Venkataraman (2000).
27. Ireland, Hitt, Camp, and Sexton (2001, February), pp. 49–63.
28. Ireland, Hitt, Camp, and Sexton, (2001, February).
29. Sahai (n.d.).
30. Hines (1998), pp. 1–5.

Chapter 2

1. Edmunds Auto Observer (2007).
2. In 1943, General Motors asked Drucker to study its management practices. His colleagues advised him not to accept the offer because studying corporate management would destroy his academic reputation. Drucker did accept and spent 18 months researching and writing the 1945 book, *Concept of the Corporation.*

   Drucker interviewed executives and workers, visited plants, and attended board meetings. While the book focused on General Motors, Drucker went on to discuss the industrial corporation as a social institution and economic policy in the postwar era. He introduced previously unknown concepts such as cooperation between labor and management, decentralization of management, and viewing workers as resources rather than costs.

   Drucker claimed that an industrial society allows people to achieve their dreams of personal achievement and equality of opportunity. He referred to decentralization as "a system of local self-government," in which central management tells division managers what to do, but not how to do it. The young executives are given the freedom to make decisions—and mistakes—and learn from the experience.

   Top leaders at General Motors disliked the book and discouraged their executives from reading it. Many other American executives criticized *Concept* as a challenge to management authority. One exception was Henry Ford II. When he took over Ford Motor Company from his aging father after World War II, he used Drucker's ideas to restructure the company.

   The Japanese also embraced Drucker's advice. Japan's emergence as a major economic power following World War II has, in part, resulted from the implementation of Drucker's ideas.
3. Orrell (2010).
4. Beinhocker (2006).
5. Smith (1776).

6. Krugman (2009).
7. Sherden (1997). He researched the records of economic market forecasters. The following is a summary of his findings:
   - Economists can't predict the turning points in the economy. Of 48 predictions made by economists, 46 missed the turning points.
   - Economists' forecasting skill is about as good as guessing. Even the Federal Reserve, the Council of Economic Advisers, and the Congressional Budget Office had forecasting records that were worse than pure chance.
   - No economic forecasters consistently lead the pack in forecasting accuracy.
   - No economic ideologies produce consistently superior economic forecasts.
   - Increased sophistication provides no improvement in economic forecasting accuracy.
   - Consensus forecasts offer little improvement.
8. During his keynote speech at the MacWorld Expo in San Francisco today, Apple cofounder and CEO Steve Jobs quoted Hockey Great Wayne Gretzky after unveiling the Apple TV and iPhone, January 9, 2007.
9. Hansen (2000).
10. Blawatt (2008).
11. Blawatt (2013).
12. Blawatt (2009).
13. The term is the union of market forces and economics. It represents a social scientific approach to economics as set out in the Blawatt papers.
14. Rogers (1976).
15. Baumol (2003).
16. Blawatt (2013)
17. Utterback (1993).
18. Fullan (2006).
19. Raps (2004, June), pp. 48–53.

Chapter 3

1. Buss (2009, August).
2. Sirkin, Zinser, Hohner, and Rose (2012 March).
3. Blawatt (2008, June).
4. Langdon (2003, May).
5. Foster and Kaplan (2001), p. 14.
6. Toffler (1971).
7. Capital Match Point (n.d.).

8. http://www.bloomberg.com/video/-the-brink-episode-1-the-makers-4-22-6TzWD6QNRHO6-ztdC8Hk4Q.html

9. Corbin (2002, May).

10. Kurzweil and Meyer (2003, May).

11. Tyson (1996, June).

12. The Conference Board, Economic Outlook (2012).

13. Englis and Solomon (1997), p. 61–63.

14. Kelly (2003).

15. http://www.internetworldstats.com/stats.htm

16. The Budde Group (2009).

17. Mock (2005, August).

18. Kaplan and Haenlein (2010), p. 53.

19. Marketing Profs (2012, January).

20. Jorgenson, Ho, and Samuels (2010, November).

21. TRU Group (2003, January).

22. The Intuit, Future of Small Business Series June (2007, June).

23. Manufacturers' Handbook (2002).

24. Brynjolfsson, Renshaw, and Marshall van Alstyne (1997, January).

25. Gunasekaran (2008).

26. Computer Sciences Corporation (2012).

27. Maslow (1943).

28. Corbin (2002, May).

29. Marlin Company (2008, May).

30. McKenzie (2007, January).

31. Harris (2006).

32. Perrin Tower (1992, April).

33. Cooper (2007, May).

34. Brooks (2011, November).

Chapter 4

1. Drucker's second book, *The Practice of Management*, was written in 1954 as a follow-up to his studies of GM. In the early 1940s, General Motors invited Drucker to study its inner workings. That experience led to his 1946 management book *Concept of the Corporation*. For many years GM ignored nearly every recommendation in the book even though its own executives had commissioned it. This seminal study introduced the concept of decentralization as a principle of organization, in contrast to the practice of command and control in business. Drucker reported that he was told any manager found with a copy would be fired. The ideas in this book,

however, launched the field of management and essentially created the field of consulting.

2. Drucker (2008, April).

3. Billionaire Guy Laliberte rockets to space from Kazakhstan. The founder of "Cirque du Soleil" paid $35 million to be the world's seventh space tourist. September 30, 2009.

4. French, LaBerge, and Paul Magill (2011, July).

5. CRM (UK) Ltd (2002).

6. LaMalfa and Kyle (2010).

7. Blawatt (2008, June).

8. Jensen (1987).

9. Denning (2013).

10. Reis (1995), pp. 279.

11. Kha and Le (2000, June).

12. A carbon tax is an environmental tax that is levied on the carbon content of fuels, usually expressed in dollars per ton of CO_2 produced. Carbon credits are those values arbitrarily assigned to noncarbon systems such as solar power and these can be sold to companies that pollute.

13. Phillips (2006), p. 212.

14. Maddalena (2010).

15. ©KRB Associates.

Chapter 5

1. OECD (2000).

2. Kanter (2010, October).

3. *Forbes* List of Innovative Companies (2013).

4. Ante (2012, January).

5. Cohen (2000).

6. Kurzweil (2006).

7. Rogers (1995).

8. Kogan (2006, September).

9. OECD (2009).

10. Sherwood (2001).

11. Burke (2011).

12. *Bloomberg Business Week* (2006, April).

13. Nix (2006, Decmeber).

14. Idea Connection Ltd. (n.d.).

15. http://www.ideaconnection.com/innovations.html

16. Carpenter (2009, December).

Chapter 6

1. Investopedia (2013).
2. MacDonald (2009, April).
3. Sabuhoro and Yvan Gervais (2004, May).
4. Cohen and Klepper (1996, May), pp. 232–243.
5. Aiman-Smith (2001, May).
6. Hill and Jones (2008), p. 464.
7. YouSigma (2008).
8. Bovay (2008, May).
9. Ries and Trout (2000, December).
10. Peppers and Rogers (1993, December).
11. Folino (2009, November).
12. Internet Technologies (n.d.).
13. Nash and Nash (2005).
14. Jutra and Westenhoefer (2010).

Chapter 7

1. Aaker (2012, December).
2. Reis and Ries (2004).
3. Kogan (2006, September).
4. Al Reis is the author of several books, including *22 Immutable Laws of Branding, The Origin of Brands, War in the Boardroom,* and *Positioning: The Battle for Your Mind.*
5. DuMars (2013, August).

Chapter 8

1. Carlzon (1989, February).
2. DeCloet (2009, May). "After Air Canada came out of CCAA (An Act to facilitate compromises and arrangements between companies and their creditors) Milton achieved what very few in the airline business ever have: He made billions of dollars for investors in the space of just four years. But the record is anything but one-sided. Some people, particularly the union leaders who represent the airline's 26,000 employees, argue that he did so purely by taking out cash and the most valuable ancillary parts of the operation, namely the Aeroplan loyalty program and Jazz Air, the regional airline that feeds passengers from the hinterland to hubs like Toronto. In this recession, unlike the last one, Air Canada must lean on one business—the notoriously unstable one of selling national and international travel. In the critics' version of events, the airline would not be anywhere near CCAA if Milton hadn't left it so naked. 'He was not following a strategy that would

guarantee the long-term success of the company,' says Leslie Dias, head of a Canadian Auto Workers local that represents some 7,000 customer service agents, mechanics, and others at Air Canada and Jazz." He was looking for quick gains to fill his own pockets and the investors' pockets.

3. Castaldo (2012, January).
4. Dean (2012, October).
5. Brown (2012, May).
6. http://www.jayweintraub.com/2013/09/microsofts-surface-lack-of-success-explained-in-one-word-kids.html
7. Marlow (2011, December).
8. SRG (2012, July).
9. Treacy and Wiersema (1993, January–February).
10. Porter (1998).
11. Kendall (2012, April).
12. http://blog.hubspot.com/blog/tabid/6307/bid/31990/7-Customer-Loyalty-Programs-That-Actually-Add-Value.aspx#ixzz2LHAATg48
13. Carrol (2009, July).

Chapter 9

1. Ries (1996).
2. McCraw (2000).
3. Osak (2010, December).
4. *Encyclopedia of Business* (2013).
5. Cascella (2002, November).
6. McCartney (2011, February).
7. Heskett (2007, November).
8. Scholz (2011, June).
9. Abernathy and Clark (1984), pp. 3–22.
10. Carpenter (2009, December).
11. Ulku (2005, May).
12. Koellner (2002).
13. Bisson (2010, June).
14. Austenfeld (2013).
15. Underdahl (2011).
16. Ichbiah, Knepper, and Wedell (1993).
17. Mintz (2011, April).
18. Korgaonkar and O'Leary (2006).
19. Rogers (2003).
20. Schumpeter Business and Management (2011).
21. Hallward (2005).
22. Pride, Hughes, and Kapoor (n.d.), p. 568.

Chapter 10

1. Haden (2011, September).
2. Mair (2002, June).
3. Team AIM High (2011, May).
4. Nayar (2010, June).
5. *HCL Technologies: Client success story* (2012). Harvard Business School Publishing.
6. Drucker (1985).
7. Daley (2010, October).
8. Vrande, de Jong, Vanhaverbeke, and Rochemont (2009, June–July), pp. 423–437.
9. Mochizuki and Jacobs (2005, February).
10. Rigby (2010, October).
11. Baumol (2005).
12. Drucker (1985); Baumol (2005); Chapter 7.
13. Shane (2009, August).
14. Standard Operating Procedures.
15. Lampel, Bhalla, and Jha (2010, January).
16. Zimmerman (2010).
17. Simons (2010, May).
18. Kirzner (1999, November), pp. 5–17.
19. Hadzima (2005).
20. Ireland, Hitt, Camp, and Sexton (2001).
21. Foley (2011, November).
22. Wolcott and Lippitz (2010).
23. Hitt, Ireland, Camp, and Sexton (2002).
24. Priestley (2013, March).
25. Isenberg (2010, June).
26. Timmons, Spinelli, and Zacharakis (2004).
27. Ireland, Hitt, Camp, and Sexton (2001).
28. Simon (2009, November).
29. Kelly (2004), p. 367.
30. Kuratko et al (1990), pp. 49–58.
31. Drucker (1985).
32. Blawatt (1985, June).
33. Team AIM High and MIX (2011, March).
34. Brown and Anthony (2010, June).
35. Greenberg and Lucid (2004).
36. Mackey and Sisodia (2013, January).
37. Sisodia, Wolfe, and Sheth (2007, February).

References

Aaker, D. (2012). *How red bull creates brand buzz.* Retrieved December 21, 2012, from HBR Blog: http://blogs.hbr.org/2012/12/how-red-bull-creates-brand-buzz/

Abernathy, W., & Clark, K. B. (1984). Innovation: Mapping the winds of creative destruction. *Research Policy 14*(1), 3–22.

Aiman-Smith, L. (2001, May). Product champions: Truths, myths and management. *Research-Technology Management 44*(3).

Ante, S. E. (2012, January 7). Avoiding innovation's terrible toll. *Wall Street Journal.*

Austenfeld, Jr., Robert B., & Edwards, W. (2013). *Deming: The story of a truly remarkable person.* Retrieved from International Quality Federation www.iqfnet.org

Baumol, W. J. (2003). *The free-market innovation machine, analyzing the growth Miracle of capitalism.* Princeton, NJ: Princeton University Press.

Baumol, W. J. (2005). *Small firms: Why market driven innovation can't get along without them.* Office of Advocacy, SBA.

Beinhocker, E. (2006, June 1). *The origin of wealth.* Boston, MA: Harvard Business School Press.

Bisson, P., Stephenson, E., & Viguerie, S. P. (2010, June). The productivity imperative. *The McKinsely Quarterly.*

Blawatt, K. (1985, June). *Study of suppliers to the automotive industry in Ontario, for the Ontario Centre for Automotive Parts Technology.* St. Catharines, Ontario, Canada.

Blawatt, K. (2008, June). *A market force model of economic behaviour: Defining entrepreneurship and enterprise decline.* Proceedings of the International Academy of Business and Economics, Stockholm, Sweden.

Blawatt, K. (2009, March). *Testing the market forces macroeconomic model: Establishing the importance of entrepreneurship in smaller economies.* SALISES Tenth Annual Conference, Cave Hill Campus, Barbados.

Blawatt, K. (2013, January). *Reality based economics: Casting off mythology.* World University Forum, Vancouver, Canada.

Bovay K. (2008, May). *When to use a product line pricing strategy.* Retrieved from http://EzineArticles.com/1341523

Brooks, M. (2011). *Light pulled out of empty space.* Retrieved November 18, 2011, from New Scientists: http://www.newscientist.com/

Brown, B., & Anthony, S. D. (2010, June). How P&G tripled its innovation success rate: Inside the company's new-growth factory. *HBR.*

Brown, P. (2012, May). Why everyone will have to become an entrepreneur. *Forbes Magazine Entrepreneurs.*

Brynjolfsson, E., Renshaw, A. A., & van Alstyne, M. (1997). *The matrix of change: A tool for business process reengineering.* MIT Sloan School of Management.

The Budde Group. (2009). Retrieved from https://www.budde.com.au/ Research/2009-Global-Digital-Economy-E-Commerce-M-Commerce -Trends-Statistics.html?r=51

Burgelman, R. A. (1983). Corporate entrepreneurship and corporate strategy: Insights from a process study. *Management Science 29.*

Burke, J. (2010). *The knowledge web.* New York, NY: Simon & Schuster.

Buss, D. (2009, August). Rethinking manufacturing strategy. *Chief Executive Magazine.*

Capital Match Point (n.d.). Retrieved from www.Capitalmatchpoint.com; http://www.bloomberg.com/video/-the-brink-episode-1-the-makers-4-22 -6TzWD6QNRHO6-ztdC8Hk4Q.html

Carlzon, J. (1989). *Moments of truth.* New York, NY: HarperBusiness, Reprint edition February 15, 1989.

Carpenter, H. (2009). *The four quadrants of innovation: Disruptive vs incremental.* Retrieved December 1, 2009, from http://www.cloudave.com/1129/the -four-quadrants-of-innovation-disruptive-vs-incremental/

Carrol, D. (2009). *United breaks guitars.* Retrieved July, 2009, from http://www .youtube.com/watch?v=5YGc4zOqozo

Cascella, V. (2002). *Effective strategic planning, quality progress.* Retrieved November 2002, from www.asq.org

Castaldo, J. (2012, January). How management has failed at RIM. *Canadian Business.*

Charan, R., & Colvin, B. (1999, June 21). Why CEOs Fail. *Fortune.*

Christensen, C. M. (1997). *The innovator's dilemma: When new technologies cause great firms to fail.* Boston, MA: Harvard Business School Press.

Cloke, K., & Goldsmith, J. (2002). *The end of management and the rise of organizational democracy.* San Francisco, CA: Jossey Bass.

Cohen, L. Y. (2000). *Top 10 reasons why we need innovation.* Chemical Innovation, American Chemical Society. Retrieved from www.amcreativityassoc.org

Cohen, W. M., & Klepper, S. (1996, May). Firm size and the nature of innovation within industries: The case of process and product R&D. *The Review of Economics and Statistics 78*(2), 232–243

Computer Sciences Corporation, *3D Printing and the Future of Manufacturing,* CSC Leading Edge Forum, Technology Program Fall 2012.

The Conference Board. (2012). *Economic outlook.* Retrieved from http://www .conference-board.org/data/globaloutlook.cfm

Cooper, R. B. (2007, May). Doing it right: Winning with new products. *Journal of Product Innovation Management,* Ivey School of Business.

Corbin, C. (2002, May 31). *Big picture view of the 21st century, Conference on library Stewardship for the 21st century.* Sacramento, California.

CRM (UK) Ltd (2002).

Daley, W. (2010, October 4). 3M first-quarter profit, 2010 forecast beat. *Business Week.*

Dean, S. (2012). *A new era of operating system competition dawns.* Retrieved October 26, 2012, from Ostatic http://ostatic.com/blog/a-new-era-of-operating-system-competition-dawns?utm_source=feedburner&utm_medium=feed&utm_campaign=Feed%3A+ostatic+%28OStatic%29

DeCloet, D. (2009, May). Air Canada disaster, *The Globe and Mail.*

Denning, S. (2013). How modern economics is built on "The world's dumbest idea." Retrieved from http://www.forbes.com/sites/stevedenning/2013/07/22/how-modern-economics-is-built-on-the-worlds-dumbest-idea/

Drucker, P. F. (1985). *Innovation and entrepreneurship.* New York, NY: Harper & Row Publishers.

Drucker, P. F. (1985). *Management: Tasks, responsibilities, practices.* New York, NY: Harper Business, Division of Harper Collins Publisher.

Drucker, P. F. (2008, April 22). *Management* (Rev. ed.). New York, NY: HarperBusiness.

DuMars, B. (2013, August). *Most brands aren't budgeting for innovation: Why marketing leaders must rethink their culture.* Retrieved August 07, 2013, from Ad Age http://adage.com/article/cmo-strategy/brands-budgeting-innovation/243533/

Edmunds Auto Observer. (2007, July 6). *June sales: GM hits all-time low market share.*

Encyclopedia of Business. (2013). *Jim goodnight 1943–Biography* (2nd ed.). Retrieved from http://www.referenceforbusiness.com/biography/F-L/Goodnight-Jim-1943.html

Englis, B. G., & Solomon, M. R. (1997). Special session summary I am not therefore, I am: The role of avoidance products in shaping consumer behavior. In M. Brucks & D. J. MacInnis (eds.), *Advances in consumer research* (Vol. 24) (pp. 61–63). Provo, UT : Association for Consumer Research.

Foley, S. (2011). *Professional corporate entrepreneur, corporate entrepreneurship.* Retrieved November, 2011, from http://www.corporate-entrepreneurs.com/ceprofile.html

Folino, L. (2009, November 3). There's no substitute for great customer service. *Inc.*

Forbes List of Innovative Companies. (2013). Retrieved from http://www.forbes.com/special-features/innovative-companies.html

Ford Motor Company. (2009). *Ford motor company—Their own stimulus package, no bailout money needed.* Retrieved January 26, 2009, from http://whatsthestoryjerry.wordpress.com/2009/01/26/ford-motor-company-their-own-stimulus-package-no-bailout-money-needed

Foster, R., & Kaplan, S. (2001). *Creative destruction* (p. 14).

French, T., LaBerge, L., & Magill, P. (2011, July). We're all marketers now. *McKinsey Quarterly*.

Fujimoto, T. (2010, March 9). Interview: Manufacturing management research center. In J. Shook (ed.), *Toyota troubles: Fighting the demons of complexity*. Tokyo, Japan: University of Tokyo.

Fullan, M. (2006). *Turnaround leadership*. San Francisco, CA: Jossey Bass, a Wiley Imprint.

Gochman, I. (n.d.). *Watson Wyatt 2002 Study*. Retrieved from http://www.watsonwyatt.com/render.asp?catid=1&id=10390

Greenberg, R., & Lucid, L. (2004). *Four principles of performance leadership: Beyond performance management*. New York, NY: Watson Wyatt Worldwide, Contents © 2004 WorldatWork.

Gunasekaran, A. (2008). *Agile manufacturing: The 21st century competitive strategy*. Amsterdam, Netherlands: Elsevier.

Haden, J. (2011). *8 reasons your employees don't care, CBS money watch*. Retrieved September 6, 2011, from CBSNEWS.COM

Hadzima, J. (2005). Seven characteristics of highly effective entrepreneurial employees. *Boston Business Journal*.

Hallward, J. (2005, February). *Understanding brand value; a review of price, performance, equity, and category dynamics*. Paris, France: Whitepaper, Ipsos-ASI.

Hamel, G. (2007, October). *The future of management*. New York, NY: Harvard Business School Press.

Hansen, T. (2000). *Consumer decision-making: A research note*. Unpublished paper, Frederiksberg, Denmark.

Harris, R. (2006). *The new paradigm of business and emerging strategies for leadership and organizational change*. American Association of Retired People.

Hartley, R. F. (1995). *Marketing mistakes* (6th ed.). Hoboken, NJ: Wiley & Sons, p. 60.

Heskett, J. (2007, November 30). What is management's role in innovation? *HBS Working Knowledge*.

Hill, C. W. L., & Jones, G. R. (2008). *Strategic management: An integrated approach* (8th ed.). Boston, MA: Houghton-Mifflin Company, p. 464.

Hines, J. (1998). Evolutionary management: Five rules for organizational improvement. *Systems Thinker 9*(6), 1–5.

Hitt, M. A., Ireland, R. D., Camp, S. M., Sexton, D. L. (2001). *Strategic entrepreneurship: Integrating entrepreneurial and strategic management perspectives*. Retrieved from www.blackwellpublishing.com/pdf/HittSE001

Ichbiah, D., Knepper, S. L., & Wedell, C. (1993). *The making of Microsoft: How Bill Gates and his team created the world's most successful software company*. Mainz, Germany: Prima Publications.

Idea Connection Ltd. (n.d.). Retrieved from Idea Connection: http://www
.ideaconnection.com/team.html

Investopedia Dictionary. (2013). *Product line definition.* Retrieved from http://
www.investopedia.com/terms/p/product-line.asp

The Intuit. (2007, June). *Future of small business series Sr-1037b.* Retrieved June
2007, from http://www.iftf.org/our-work/global-landscape/work/future-of
-small-business/

Ireland, R. D., Hitt, M. A., Camp, S. M., & Sexton, D. L. (Guest eds.) (2001,
February). Special issue: Creating wealth in organizations. *Academy of
Management Executive 15*(1), 49–63.

Isenberg, J. (2010, June 20). The big idea: How to start an entrepreneurial
revolution. *HBR.*

Jensen, K. B. (1987, Autumn). Field test of a strategic market planning model
for privately held small/medium businesses. *Journal of Small Business and
Entrepreneurship.*

Jorgenson, D. W., Ho, M., & Samuels, J. (2010). Information technology and
U.S. productivity growth: Evidence from a prototype industry production
account. In M. Mas, & R. Stehrer (eds.), *Industrial productivity in Europe:
Growth and Crisis. Cheltenham Glos,* United Kingdom: Edward Elgar Pub

Jutra, C., & Westenhoefer, Z. Jr. (2010). *Think your organization is too small for
ERP? Think again.* Retrieved from www.aberdeengroup.com

Kanter, R. M. (2010, October). *SuperCorp: How Vanguard companies create
innovation, profits, growth, and social good.* Pine Street, London: Profile Books.

Kaplan, A. M., & Haenlein, M. (2010). Users of the world, unite! The challenges
and opportunities of Social Media. *Business Horizons,* p. 53.

Kaplan, R. S., & Norton, D. P. (2001). *The strategy-focused organization: How
balanced scorecard companies thrive in the new business environment.* New York,
NY: Harvard Business Press.

Kaplan, R. S., & Norton, D. P. (2001, May/June). Building a strategy-focused
organization. *Ivey Business Journal.*

Kelly, F. J. (2004). *American cars, 1960–1972: Every model, year by year.* McFarland
& Company, p. 367.

Kelly, K. (2003). *New rules for the new economy, 10 radical strategies for a connected
world.* Retrieved from http://www.internetworldstats.com/stats.htm

Kha, L. (2000, June). *Critical success factors for business to consumer E-business:
lessons from Amazon and Dell.* Master's Thesis, Sloan School of Management
at M.I.T.

Kirzner, I. M. (1999). Creativity and/or alertness: A reconsideration of the
Schumpeterian entrepreneur. *Review of Austrian Economics 11,* 5–17.

Knowledge@wharton (2003, April). *What makes Southwest Airlines fly.* Retrieved
April 2003, from http://knowledge.wharton.upenn.edu/article/what-makes
-southwest-airlines-fly/

Koellner, L. (2002). *The importance of people.* Retrieved from http://www.boeing .com/news/speeches/2002/koellner_020730.html

Kogan, S. (2006, September). *CEOs need to embrace innovation.* Retrieved September 2006, from Industry Week http://www.Industryweek.com

Korgaonkar, P., & O'Leary, B. (2006). Management, market, and financial factors separating winners and losers in e-business. *Journal of Computer-Mediated Communication 11*(4), article 12.

Krugman, P. (2009, September 6). How did economists get it so wrong? *New York Times.*

Kuratko et al. (1990). Developing an intrapreneurial assessment instrument for effective corporate entrepreneurial environment. *Strategic Management Journal 11*, 49–58.

Kurzweil, R. (2006). *The singularity is near: When humans transcend biology.* London, United Kingdom: Penguin.

Kurzweil, R., & Meyer, C. (2003, May 1). *Understanding the accelerating rate of change* (originally published in Perspectives on Business Innovation). Retrieved May 1, 2003, from KurzweilAI.net

LaMalfa, K. (2010). *The top 9 ways to increase your customer loyalty.* Soputh Jordan, UT: Allegiance Inc.

Lampel, J., Bhalla, A., & Jha, P. (2010, January). *Growth: Do employee-owned businesses deliver sustainable performance?* Cass Business School, sponsored by The John Lewis Partnership.

MacDonald, B. (2009). *Management lessons to be learned from the failure of General Motors.* Retrieved April 6, 2009, from http://bobmaconbusiness.com/?p=230

Mackey, J., & Sisodia, R. (2013, January). *Conscious capitalism: Liberating the heroic spirit of business.* Boston, MA: Harvard Business Review Press.

Maddalena, L. (2010). *The art of execution—12 strategies for building a culture of getting things done.* Retrieved from ezinearticles.com

Mair, J. (2002, June). *Entrepreneurial behaviour in a large traditional firm; Exploring key drivers* Research Paper No. 466, Research Division IESE, University of Navarro.

Mankins, M., & Steele, R. (2006, February). The problem with strategic planning. *HRM Magazine.*

Marketing Profs. (2012). *Integrating social media still challenges marketers.* Retrieved January 17, 2012, from www.marketingprofs.com/topic/all/ research-summaries

Marlin Company. (2008). *14th Annual poll, Attitudes in the American workforce.* Retrieved May 2008, from www.the marlincompany.com

Maslow, A. (1943). A theory of human motivation. *Psychological Review 50*, 370–396.

Marlow, I. (2011, December). RIM finds new ways to disappoint investors. *The Globe and Mail.*

McCartaney, S. (2011, February). Delta sends its 11,000 agents to charm school. *WSJ Digital Network*.

McCraw, T. K. (2000). *American business, 1920–2000: How it worked – P&G: Changing the face of consumer marketing*. Wheeling, IL: Harlan Davidson.

McGrath, R. G., & MacMillan, I. C. (2000). *The entrepreneurial mindset: Strategies for continuously creating opportunity in an age of uncertainty*. Boston, MA: Harvard Business School Press, p.1.

McKenzie, H. (2007, January 18). *The growing gap project*. Canadian Centre for Policy Alternatives.

Mintz, S. L. (2011, April). 7 verbal clues that an earnings call is BS, Bnet. *The CBS Interactive Business Network*.

Mochizuki, H., & Jacobs, E. (2005, February). *R&D and Innovation in SMEs, A joint Japan – EU seminar Tokyo*. Royal Netherlands Embassy—Tokyo, Office of Science and Technology.

Mock, D. (2005). Perspective: *Envisioning a wireless future*. Retrieved August 15, 2005, from cnet.co

Morris, L. (2003, May). *Business model warfare*. An Innovations Lab White paper.

Nash, S., & Nash, D. (2005). *6 steps from customer service*. Retrieved from http://www.teamtechnology.co.uk/customerservice.html

Nayar, V. (2010, June). *Employees first, customers second: turning conventional management upside down*. Harvard Business Press Books.

Neilson, G. L., Martin, K. L., and Powers, E. (2008, June), The secrets to successful strategy execution. *HBR Magazine*.

Nix, O. (2006, December). Lessons learned: Open innovation. *RTI Tech 3*(5). Retrieved December 2006, from www.rti.org/technology

OECD. (2000, September). *Science, technology and innovation in the new economy*. OECD Policy Brief.

OECD. (2009). *Innovation in firms; A microeconomic perspective*. Retrieved from http://www.keepeek.com/Digital-Asset-Management/oecd/science-and-technology/innovation-in-firms_9789264056213-en

Orrell, D. (2010). *Economyths: Ten ways economics gets it wrong*. New York, NY: John Wiley.

Osak, M. (2010, December). Strategy: The best plans will fail without resources, time, expertise. *Financial Post*.

Peiguss, K. (2012). *7 customer loyalty programs that actually add value*. Retrieved April 3, 2012, from HubSpot http://blog.hubspot.com/blog/tabid/6307/bid/31990/7-Customer-Loyalty-Programs-That-Actually-Add-Value.aspx; Read more: http://blog.hubspot.com/blog/tabid/6307/bid/31990/7-Customer-Loyalty-Programs-That-Actually-Add-Value.aspx#ixzz2LH8w8z3n

Peppers, D., & Rogers, M. (1993). *The one-to-one future: Building relationships one customer at a time.* New York, NY: DoubleDay.

Perrin, T. (1992, April). Priorities for competitive advantage (IBM Study). *HR Magazine.*

Pfeffer. J., & Sutton, R. I. (1999). Knowing what to do is not enough: Turning knowledge into action. *California Management Review 42*(1), 83–108.

Phillips, J. (2000). *Investing in your company's human capital.* New York, NY: AMACOM, p. 212.

Porter, M. E. (1998). *Competitive strategy: Techniques for analyzing industries and competitors.* New York, NY: The Free Press.

Pride, W. M., Hughes, R. J., & Kapoor, J. R. (n.d.). *Business* (11th ed.). Stamford, CT: South Western Cengage Learning, p. 568.

Priestley, D. (2013, March). *Entrepreneur revolution: How to develop your entrepreneurial mindset and start a business that works.* London, United Kingdom: Capstone Publishing Ltd.

Raps, A. (2004, June). Implementing strategy. *Strategic Finance,* 48–53.

Reis, A. (1995). *Focus.* New York, NY: Harper Business, Division of Harper Collins Publishers, p. 279.

Reis, A. (1997). *Focus: The future of your company depends on it.* New York, NY: Harper Collins Publisher.

Reis, A., & Ries, L. (2004). *The origin of brands: Discover the natural laws of product innovation and business survival.* New York, NY: Harper Collins Publishers.

ReVelle, J. B. (2002). *Manufacturers' handbook of best practices: An innovation, productivity and quality focus.* CRC Press. Retrieved from www.crcpress.com

Ries, A., & Trout, J. (2000, December). *Positioning: The battle for your mind* (1st ed.). New York, NY: McGraw-Hill.

Ries, J. (1996). *Focus: The future of your company depends on it.* New York, NY: Harper Business, Division of Harper Collins Publishers.

Rigby, B. (2010, October). Microsoft CEO Bonus Curbed for Kin, Tablet Failures, *Reuters News.*

Rogers, E. M. (1995). *Diffusion of innovations* (4th ed.). New York, NY: Free Press.

Rogers, E. M. (2003). *Diffusion of innovations* (5th ed.). New York, NY: Simon and Schuster.

Rouse, R. R., & Miller, L. A. (2010). *Creating value from HR: The new credentialed manufacturing workforce.* Research Institute, University of Phoenix.

Rumelt, R. (2011). *Good strategy/bad strategy: The difference and why it matters.* New York, NY: Crown Publishing.

Rumelt, R. (2011, June). The perils of bad strategy. *McKinsey Quarterly.*

Sabuhoro, J. B., & Gervais, Y. (2004, May). *Factors determining the success or failure of Canadian establishments on foreign markets: A Survival Analysis*

Approach 11F0019MIE No. 220, Business and Trade Statistics Field Statistics Canada.

Sahai, A. K. (n.d.). *Learning from evolution: A study of Acer's corporate strategy.* Working paper, System Design and Management, Sloan School of Management, Massachusetts Institute of Technology, Cambridge, MA.

Sarasvathy, S. D., & Venkataraman, S. (2000, December). Strategy and entrepreneurship: Outlines of an untold story. In Hitt et al (eds.), *Strategic management handbook.*

Sassoon, S. (2007). *Shock! fashion designer knockoffs,* Designer, copy victims banned from knockoff shop. Retrieved January 30, 2007, from www .secondlifeherald.com

Scholz, E. (2011). *How to communicate the value of idea management.* Retrieved June 20, 2011, from Innovation Management http://www.innovationmanagement. se/2011/06/20/how-to-communicate-the-value-of-idea-management/

Schumpeter Business and Management. (2011, August 19) Hewlett-Packard's Overhaul: Seismic shift in Silicon Valley. *The Economist.*

Shane, S. (2009, August). *That's why we need more entrepreneurs, Kaufmann Foundation.* Retrieved August 2009, from Growthology Blog http:// www.growthology.org/growthology/2009/07/thats-why-we-need-more-entrepreneurs.html

Sherden, W. (1997). *The fortune sellers: The big business of buying and selling predictions.* New York, NY: Wiley.

Sherwood, D. (2001). *Smart things to know about, innovation and creativity.* Oxford, UK: Capstone Publishers.

Simon, M. (2009). *The complete iTunes history.* Retrieved November 9, 2009, from http://www.maclife.com

Simons, B. (2010, May 20). *Seven strategy questions: A simple approach for better execution, faculty research symposium.* Working Knowledge, Harvard Business School.

Sirkin, H. L., Zinser, M., Hohner, D., & Rose, J. (2012, March 12). *U.S. manufacturing nears the tipping point.* BCG Perspectives, Boston Consulting Group.

Sisodia, R.S., Wolfe, D. B., & Sheth, J. N. (2007, January–February). *Firms of endearment: How world-class companies profit from passion and purpose.* Princeton, NJ: Prentice Hall.

Smith, S. (1776). *Inquiry into the nature and causes of the wealth of nations.*

SRG. (2012). Smaller, cheaper tablets take bite out of apple's market share. Retrieved July 15, 2012, from http://www.srgnet.com/index.php/2012/07/ 15/apple-market-share/

Sunter, C. (2010). *Toward a culture of entrepreneurship, News24.* Retrieved from http://www.news24.com/Columnists/ClemSunter/Toward-a-culture-of -entrepreneurship-20101007

Team AIM High, MIX. (2011). *Entrepreneur employee–How to innovate in corporations*. MBA 2011 at Asian Institute of Management. Retrieved March 20, 2011, from http://www.managementexchange.com/hack/entrepreneur-employee-way-innovate-corporations

The world's most innovative companies (2006, April 24). Special report—Innovation, *Bloomberg Business Week*.

Thompson, A. A., Strickland III, A. J., & Gamble, J. E. (2005). *Crafting and executing strategy*. New York, NY: McGraw Hill Irwin, p. 9, 33.

Timmons, J. A., Spinelli, S., Zacharakis, A. (2004). *How to raise capital: Techniques and strategies for financing and valuing your small business*. New York, NY: McGraw Hill.

Toffler, A. (1971, January 1). *Future shock*. New York, NY: Bantam Books.

Treacy, M., & Wiersema, F. (1993, January/February). Customer intimacy and other value disciplines. *Harvard Business Review*.

TRU Group White Paper (2005). *The Canadian economy is strategically threatened!* Retrieved January 15, 2005, from http://trugroup.com/canadian-competitiveness

Tyson, K. W. (1996). *Competition in the 21st century*. Baco Raton, FL: CRC Press.

Ulku, H. (2005, May). *R&D, Innovation and growth: Evidence from four manufacturing sectors in OECD Countries* (Paper No. 12). Institute for Development Policy and Management, University of Manchester.

Underdahl, B. (2011). *Business process management for dummies*. New York, NY: IBM Limited Edition, Wiley Publishing, Inc.

Utterback, J. M., & Suarez, F. (1993). Innovation, competition, and industry structure. *Research Policy 22*(1), 1–21.

Van de Vrande, V., de Jong, J. P. J., Vanhaverbeke, W., & de Rochemont, M. (2009, June–July). Open innovation in SMEs: Trends, motives and management challenges. *Technovation 29*(6–7), 423–437.

Watis.com (n.d.). *Internet Technologies*. Retrieved from http://whatis.techtarget.com/definitionsCategory/0,289915,sid9_tax1670,00.html

Wolcott, R. C., & Lippitz, M. J. (2010). *Grow from within: Mastering corporate entrepreneurship and innovation*. New York, NY: McGraw Hill.

YouSigma (2008). *Little remedies product line strategy*. Retrieved from http://www.yousigma.com

Zimmerman, J. (2010). *Corporate entrepreneurship at GE and Intel*. EABR & ETLC Conference Proceedings Dublin, Ireland.

Index

OTHER TITLES IN THE STRATEGIC MANAGEMENT COLLECTION

William Q. Judge, Old Dominion University, Editor

Announcing the Business Expert Press Digital Library

*Concise E-books Business Students Need
for Classroom and Research*

This book can also be purchased in an e-book collection by your library as
- a one-time purchase,
- that is owned forever,
- allows for simultaneous readers,
- has no restrictions on printing, and
- can be downloaded as PDFs from within the library community.

Our digital library collections are a great solution to beat the rising cost of textbooks. E-books can be loaded into their course management systems or onto students' e-book readers.

The **Business Expert Press** digital libraries are very affordable, with no obligation to buy in future years. For more information, please visit **www.businessexpertpress.com/librarians**. To set up a trial in the United States, please email **sales@businessexpertpress.com**.

www.ingramcontent.com/pod-product-compliance
Lightning Source LLC
Chambersburg PA
CBHW070549200326
41519CB00012B/2164